WHEN VICTORY IS NOT
AN OPTION

When Victory Is Not an Option

Islamist Movements in Arab Politics

Nathan J. Brown

CORNELL UNIVERSITY PRESS   ITHACA AND LONDON

First published 2012 by Cornell University Press
First printing, Cornell Paperbacks, 2012

Printed in the United States of America

Library of Congress Cataloging-in-Publication Data

Brown, Nathan J.
   When victory is not an option : Islamist movements in Arab politics /
Nathan J. Brown.
      p. cm.
   Includes bibliographical references and index.
   ISBN 978-0-8014-5036-5 (cloth : alk. paper) — ISBN 978-0-8014-7772-0
(pbk. : alk. paper)
   1. Islam and politics—Arab countries.   2. Arab countries—Politics
and government—1945–   3. Political parties—Arab countries.   4. Islamic
fundamentalism—Arab countries.   I. Title.
   DS39.B76 2012
   320.5'57—dc23   2011037090

Cornell University Press strives to use environmentally responsible suppliers and materials to the fullest extent possible in the publishing of its books. Such materials include vegetable-based, low-VOC inks and acid-free papers that are recycled, totally chlorine-free, or partly composed of nonwood fibers. For further information, visit our website at www.cornellpress.cornell.edu.

Cloth printing   10 9 8 7 6 5 4 3 2 1
Paperback printing   10 9 8 7 6 5 4 3 2 1

To Alexandra, Lillian, Aviva, and Elizabeth

Contents

Preface

Much of what has been written about Islamist movements in Arab politics in recent years has been motivated by immediate policy questions (should Western governments "engage" them?) and fears about their intentions (are they threatening internationally or totalitarian internally?). Such questions are motivated by real events: the Egyptian Muslim Brotherhood's electoral performance in 2005; Hamas's victory in 2006; and the Egyptian and Tunisian revolutions of 2011. Readers looking for answers to these questions should probably not turn to this book.

Rather than prescribe policy, probe hearts and minds, reassure, or condemn, I seek to understand how Islamist movements operate in Arab politics. Or, more precisely, I try to probe how operating in politics shapes them. In the process, however, I hope to lead the reader to better understandings of the movements and the political systems in which they operate.

Why have I devoted several years to study Islamist movements? It is not because I support or oppose them. I should state that I do not find Islamist movements particularly frightening. I have been struck in my conversations and readings with how much Islamist movements seem to be motivated by a strong sense of the public good: in a part of the world where political cynicism is deeply (and probably justifiably) engrained, Islamists often stand out for their willingness to put principles above person. But I do not endorse those principles. There are large aspects of their programs I would not want to see implemented in any place where I have lived or studied. While I have met many Islamists who show admirable personal qualities and high social ideals, I share neither their religion nor their views on the proper relationship of religion to political life; in conversations with Islamists from various countries, I have discovered that I differ with them on a whole range of policy issues. But I also believe that healthy political systems (and I would not describe any extant Arab political system as sufficiently healthy in this sense) should be able to absorb challenges from, and harness the positive energies of, such movements. Such healthier systems would probably be able to steer these movements in directions that would be productive for their societies. The Arab revolutions of 2011 may offer some possibilities for politics to evolve in such directions, but even exploring those possibilities demands that we first probe what Islamist movements have become and how they have evolved.

My interest is much less to evaluate the movements in normative terms and much more to understand them and the systems in which they operate. In undertaking this effort, I have received an enormous amount of help. I should mention first of all the movements themselves; most leaders and activists responded quite openly to my requests for meetings, material, and information. Indeed, Islamist leaders have been easy to contact and their debates have proved to be one of the most accessible topics I have studied in the Arab world. I was invited to campaign rallies in Kuwait, meetings with top party officials in Jordan, and numerous homes, offices, and other institutions.

I was also aided by a considerable body of writings that came before me: work by scholars, reports by study centers, and writings by activists. I focus on four movements in particular (in Egypt, Jordan, Palestine, and Kuwait) and had to overcome the temptation to lead the reader on a protracted tour of the debates that each movement has engendered. Had I done so, this book would be more footnote than text. Instead, those interested in past writings on the movements will find in Chapters 4 and 5 that the discussion of each of the four movements starts with a single (but long) footnote discussing these various sources and mentioning the names of my interviewees.

I have also been given an enormous amount of help and guidance from colleagues. Some was quite sustained: I began my interest in this topic in collaboration with a close personal friend, Amr Hamzawy, and I continue to work with him. Other help was far briefer but still quite valuable: Lisa Blaydes, for instance, made a stray remark to me about the idea of commitment that planted the seed for a part of the argument in this book, though she told me later that she did not remember what she said. I have similarly benefited deeply from the thoughtful comments, help, guidance, and stray remarks of Judy Brown, Tom Carothers, Michele Dunne, Scott Field, Muhammad al-Ghanim, Skip Gnehm, Michael Herb, Julie Chernov Hwang, Amaney Jamal, Mustapha El-Khalfi, Miriam Kuenkler, Clark Lombardi, Ellen Lust, Michael McFaul, Marina Ottaway, David Patel, Bruce Rutherford, Emad Eldin Shahin, Kristen Stilt, Mary Ann Tetreault, and Stacey Yadav.

I also owe a considerable debt to a group of colleagues who have done significant research themselves on Islamist movements in the Arab world. Some of them have worked far more intensively on the topic than I could even hope to. Not a single one treated me as a competitor; they shared contacts, comments, and thoughts of various kinds and have made this a much better book as a result. Indeed, I have never worked on a topic for which there has been such a strong sense of scholarly community. In this regard, I acknowledge Janine Clark, Shadi Hamid, Marc Lynch, Tarek Masoud, Quinn Mecham, Josh Stacher, Jillian Schwedler, Samer Shehata, and Carrie Wickham. The footnotes do not reflect how much I have learned from them.

In each of the countries where I conducted research, I found a group of scholars and political observers ready to swap impressions and facilitate contacts. For their help, I thank Nabil Abd al-Fattah, Muhammad Abu Ruman, Khalil al-Anani, Deborah Jones, Vlad Pran, Oraib Rantawi, Adel Omar Sharif, Amr al-Shobaki, Lindsey Stephenson, and Husam Tamam.

Dina Bishara has worked with me on various phases of the project and deserves special thanks for that help. But she is hardly alone: Abdulaziz Algharabally, Maha Batran, Sabine Boots, Russell Burns, Jano Charbel, Mohamed Fahmy, Jessica Guiney, Natasha Hall, Rona Hitlin-Mason, Melinda Michaels, Majdal Nijem, Aws Al-Shaheen, Jordan Steckler, Dillon Tatum, Khaled Waleed, Katie Zimmerman, and Diane Zovighian have all provided valuable assistance of many different kinds.

I owe thanks as well to those who sat through and contributed to discussions in a number of settings where I presented various parts of this work—at workshops at George Washington University (including two that brought together leading scholars of Islamist movements) and at seminars at Princeton University, Stanford University, Harvard University, FRIDE (Fundación para las Relaciones Internacionales y el Diálogo Exterior), the Woodrow Wilson Center, the University of California at Berkeley, and the College of William and Mary. Students in a graduate seminar at George Washington University gave me some suggestions for final revisions. My biggest debt of gratitude in this regard is to colleagues who attended a day-long workshop on an earlier draft of this book. My argument is much cleaner, clearer, and better informed as a result of the intensive discussions held at the workshop with Eva Bellin, Lisa Wedeen, and Kimberly Morgan. Tarek Massoud sent in a set of extremely valuable written comments when a last-minute glitch prevented his attendance.

I also thank a series of institutions that provided support for various phases of my research. I began working on Islamist movements at the Carnegie Endowment for International Peace. A portion of my work there was supported by a grant from the United States Institute of Peace. (That work helped produce a different book, co-written with Amr Hamzawy and published by the Carnegie Endowment in 2010, titled *Between Religion and Politics,* on the activities of Islamist parties in Arab parliaments.) I also benefited enormously from the opportunity to work for a year at the Woodrow Wilson International Center for Scholars. My research has been quite generously supported as well by the Carnegie Corporation of New York under its Carnegie Scholars program.

At Cornell University Press, my experience has been very happy. Roger Haydon has simply been the most helpful and gentle editor I could have asked for.

I have dedicated this book to four nieces: Alexandra Brown, Lillian Brown, Aviva Pastor, and Elizabeth Lea. None has shown any particular interest in the subject of this book, but all four have traveled to other continents (and one was even born on one). This dedication is made in the hope that all four will live their lives in a world where any international travels and activities they choose to undertake will help enrich understanding across religions, cultures, and borders. Neither I nor any of my nieces is a Muslim, but that makes it especially appropriate to acknowledge in this context the wisdom of the oft-quoted Qur'anic verse (49:13): "We have created you out of a male and a female and made you into peoples and tribes so that you might come to know one another."

Those who know me might wonder why I do not mention any of my nephews in the dedication to this book. The reason is simple: they are part of my inspiration to write another book.

PARTIALLY POLITICAL MOVEMENTS IN SEMIAUTHORITARIAN SYSTEMS

Over the past generation, Arab politics has begun to open up. And some Islamist movements—particularly those modeled on Egypt's Muslim Brotherhood—have poured into the resulting gaps. How has politics changed them?

In a variety of Arab political systems, space for political speech and even activity has become more open but is still very constrained, and limits can be ruthlessly enforced. These changes were deeply entrenched long before the revolutionary upheavals of 2011; indeed, it is not yet clear how much would-be revolutionaries and reformers, as bold as their efforts have been, will overcome deeply institutionalized patterns of governance. Most Arab systems still inhabit a halfway house of semiauthoritarianism. Neither fully authoritarian in all the harshness that term has come to imply nor meaningfully democratic in allowing people to select their rulers, Arab political systems from Morocco to the Gulf passed in the last decades of the twentieth century into a semiauthoritarian era.

In this era, the opposition can organize to run in elections, but it cannot win them. Social services formally provided by the state have been taken on by a welter of movements, voluntary grassroots associations, and professionalized nongovernmental organizations, but regimes become suspicious and repressive when such social activity is linked to political opposition. The rules of political life are constantly rewritten, opportunities open and close irregularly, "red lines" are as brutally policed as they are mercurial in their meaning, and rulers seem steered rather than governed by laws they themselves have often written. But for all the limited and ambivalent nature of liberalization in the Arab world, there is still a notable change from a generation ago: some opposition activity is possible.

That space for political opposition helped launch some of the upheavals of 2011, but we are not primarily focusing on those events or on the possibilities for democratic politics that they have opened. Instead of speculation about the future, we are concerned with semiauthoritarianism as it has been operating, and we are especially focused on its effects on Islamist movements.

Islamists have sought to grasp the opportunities that result from semiauthoritarian politics, most publicly and dramatically in the electoral realm. Throughout the Arab world, Islamist political movements alarm some and excite others when they enter the electoral process. The thrill and fear have increased markedly in recent years. As new electoral horizons have opened, Islamist movements have moved toward them. But the new opportunities, while real, are kept within bounds. Elections are freer, because they include more serious contestants. But they are not fair, because only incumbents can win.

How are Islamist movements affected when they plunge into these freer but unfair elections? How much and how deeply are their organizations changed? What happens to their core ideological principles? This book shows that a specific but influential and widespread kind of Islamist movement (a broad and engaged movement modeled on Egypt's Muslim Brotherhood) will seize the political opportunities presented to it. Such a movement will invest seriously in politics, molding its structure and program in substantial ways in the process. But such investment will go only so far. Because the rewards of politics are limited, and because the movements are concerned with far more than politics, Islamist leaders try to leave a line of retreat. They invest, but they do not irrevocably commit.

When given uncertain and shifting opportunities, Islamist movements with broad agendas will invest much more in politics. They will develop their programs and their organizational capabilities in ways that are designed to take advantage of the more open environment, to an extent. They will form political parties when allowed to by law, but they will keep them on a short leash. And they will issue programmatic statements designed to assure potential supporters and calm potential opponents, but they will balk at giving detailed answers to some of the most difficult political questions that confront them. Islamist movements have broad and diverse agendas; semiauthoritarian politics encourages them to focus on political participation but gives them little reason to commit fully to a political path.

In short, we will see that Islamist movements reach for uncertain benefits by making uncertain changes. They adapt their organizations and bend their ideologies, but they are wary about the possibility that the political opening will fizzle or fail to deliver what they wish. The result is a cat-and-mouse game between dominant regimes and shrewd movements.

Our interest is in semiauthoritarianism, a political form very much alive in the Arab world. But even where it has fallen, its effects may linger. The upheavals of 2011 will likely have real and profound effects on the dynamic between regime and movement, but they may not have sudden ones. As scholars have long noted, the breakdown of an authoritarian system (and presumably a semiauthoritarian one as well) is not the same as the construction of a democratic one. Movements accustomed to cautious investment in semiauthoritarian politics may be tantalized by the opportunities presented by regime change but they may also be wary of the uncertainty. And they are also likely to find that converting their movements into structures designed for democratic politics a complicated project. In short, our findings about Islamist behavior under semiauthoritarian regimes might actually outlast those regimes.

The political activity of Islamist movements in the Arab world hardly wants for attention. But much of the public discussion—not only in Western policy circles but also in Arab intellectual debates—focuses on their democratic credentials: how sincere are Islamists about playing the democratic game? The question is an odd one: there simply has been no democratic game to play. We need to focus less attention on how much democracy lies in the hearts of Islamist leaders. And indeed, recent scholarly approaches have developed an alternative approach: rather than use the beliefs or ideologies of Islamists as the starting point for explanation, they turn matters around and ask what effect the political system has on Islamist movements. In its simplest form, this leads to what is often called the "inclusion-moderation thesis"—that including Islamist leaders in the political process will produce democratic Islamist movements.

Thus, while policy discussions often see Islamist ideology as a cause, scholars are more likely to see it as an effect—and to see elections and political participation as a particularly important way of modifying ideologies and programs. As Güneş Murat Tezcür claims, "the crucial variable affecting prospects for democratization in hybrid or authoritarian regimes in the Muslim world is the institutional characteristics of the ruling regimes rather than the ideological commitments of the opposition."[1] The scholarly preference has begun to have some limited effect on broader public and policy discussions, with growing interest in Western capitals in what seems to scholars an overly crude version of the inclusion-moderation thesis (based, often, on an understanding of western European history and the conversion of groups on the radical left and right to tamer electoral parties). Thus, in 2005,

---

1. Güneş Murat Tezcür, "The Moderation Theory Revisited: The Case of Islamic Political Actors," *Party Politics* 16, no. 1 (2010), 83–84.

President George W. Bush publicly mused, however briefly, about the possibility of electoral participation moderating Hizbullah before seeming to revert to the position that the party had to moderate before it could be considered a participant:

> I like the idea of people running for office. There's a positive effect when you run for office. Maybe some will run for office and say, vote for me, I look forward to blowing up America. I don't know, I don't know if that will be their platform or not. But it's—I don't think so. I think people who generally run for office say, vote for me, I'm looking forward to fixing your potholes, or making sure you got bread on the table. And so—but Hezbollah is on the terrorist list for a reason, and remain on the terrorist list for a reason. Our position has not changed on Hezbollah.[2]

Viewing Islamist ideology (and organization as well) as effect will prove very useful, and most of this book will follow that path. There are limits to the approach—we will see that the general sense of mission for Islamist movements is still an important part of the explanation for their behavior; that Islamist actors with different missions follow different paths; and thus that Islamists are not only creations of their political environment. But if this book participates in a broader scholarly inclination to tilt toward viewing Islamists as effect, it must still be noted that the inclusion-moderation thesis, especially in many of its cruder forms, can lead us to overlook critical features both of semiauthoritarian politics and of Islamist movements. We will certainly draw on the findings of those who explore inclusion and moderation, but we will refine both the arguments and the terms in fundamental ways.

"Moderation" means many things that are not always clearly related and are too rarely specified (it can refer to changes in positions on women's rights, the willingness to recognize Israel, nonviolence either in practice or in doctrine, acceptance of electoral defeat, embracing liberal values, and cooperating with U.S. foreign and security policy). It is generally based on a fairly facile use of historical analogies rather than sustained analysis (and its opponents respond with equally facile historical retorts, leading to what I term "analogy mongering" in Chapter 3), and the mechanisms by which it might operate are often unexplained and unexplored.[3]

Most important for present purposes, it all too often makes two implicit assumptions: that "inclusion" is in democratic elections and that movements are

---

2. "President's Press Conference," 16 March 2005, http://georgewbush-whitehouse.archives.gov/news/releases/2005/03/20050316-3.html.
3. My discomfort with some of the more facile uses of the inclusion-moderation idea certainly does not extend to all attempts to draw on it. Perhaps the most thorough effort to overcome the problems I note is Jillian Schwedler, *Faith in Moderation: Islamist Parties in Jordan and Yemen*

enticed to change as part of an effort to win. Neither of these assumptions holds for the Arab world, where the elections have not been fully democratic and Islamists usually make quite clear that they are not seeking a majority. Thus this book will begin with an attempt to recast some scholarly approaches to make them more suitable for the current inquiry.

Rather than use terms that have shifting and often unspecified meanings, we will focus on the *politicization* of Islamist movements—the extent to which they focus their energies on participation in an existing political system, within the rules and boundaries set by that system. Terms such as "inclusion" and especially "moderation" are infused with hidden normative assumptions and often devoid of fixed meaning. Past writings using such terms are useful, and we will draw on them heavily. But rather than struggle to express ourselves in a set of categories invented for political parties in democracies, we will focus on "politicization" in a way that better captures the realities of semiauthoritarian political systems (which offer only a limited role for opposition movements). More important, the most intensive debates within Islamist movements are usually not over "moderation" but instead over how much to commit a movement to a political path. So again, "politicization" captures the reality experienced by the actors.

The politics that interests us is very focused in nature: participation in officially sanctioned institutions and procedures. This is how the movements themselves tend to use the term; the question for them is how hard to play by the rules of a game they have little control over. They argue that political activity is best viewed in service of their general mission; when participating in politics, they are pursuing the same goals as they do when they preach, educate, meet, study, or serve the poor. But if their mission is constant, they still view politics as a distinct realm, in part because regimes make it one by their restrictive rules and practices.

The issue of political participation is a surprisingly difficult one, both for the participants (Islamist leaders) and for the external observers (the scholarly community). Members of the first camp encounter difficult problems when they approach semiauthoritarian politics; those in the second camp have problems for a different set of reasons: they enter the quest for understanding with a set of conceptual and theoretical tools that were designed for very different settings. Let us begin by considering the difficulties for each in turn.

(Cambridge: Cambridge University Press, 2006). Schwedler gives specificity to "moderation" as "movement from a relatively closed and rigid worldview to one more open and tolerant of alternative perspectives" (p. 3). And she pays great attention to understanding the mechanisms by which it takes place. But because my interest is in the positions, organizations, and behavior of Islamist movements, and because "moderation" is still used in all sorts of other (generally far less explicitly specified) ways, I have instead preferred more precise terminology.

Why Is Islamist Politicization under Semiauthoritarianism Difficult in Practice?

In one sense, the phenomenon of Islamists running for office in the Arab world is a hoary one: the founder of the oldest and largest movement, Hasan al-Banna of Egypt's Muslim Brotherhood, filed for parliamentary election in 1942 before withdrawing and actually ran (unsuccessfully) in 1945. In other Arab countries—ranging from Jordan and Yemen to Syria and Kuwait—Islamist movements participated in elections almost as soon as they were able. Even in Iraq, Israel, and the Palestinian Authority, Islamists dubious about the moral authority of the political system have competed in elections.

But there has been a qualitative and a quantitative shift in Islamist electoral participation in recent years. Earlier generations of leaders and activists dabbled in elections as a sideline to their main activities; their ideological diffidence toward democratic institutions and practices was marked; and many leaders showed strong ambivalence even to the word "democracy" itself. By contrast, today's leaders speak routinely of "a strategic choice" to commit to democracy and claim not only to support democratizing reforms at the national level but to practice democracy in internal operations. And just as impressive is their performance at the ballot box. In many cases, the number of votes they receive and seats they win seems to be limited primarily by the existing regime's shamelessness in manipulating the rules and results and the movement's own interest (or lack of interest) in winning.

Indeed, for all their increased interest in participation, Islamist movements in the Arab world only rarely enter an election to win it. That would be naive; in many Arab countries, the most reliable and stable electoral rule is that the opposition cannot win. But Islamists run even though losing is foreordained. Actually, they go further: they generally do not even contest a majority of seats. Islamist leaders turn the necessity of losing into a virtue, citing the slogan "participation not domination" (*al-musharika la al-mughaliba*).

Nevertheless, using whatever spaces the admittedly feeble electoral mechanisms of the region offer has potentially deep implications for these movements, and even deeper ones for the societies in which they live. For the movements, politicization—the decision to dedicate resources to elections, the move to form structures that resemble electoral parties, the effort to craft platforms and appeal to new constituencies, the development of new appeals and programs, the attempt to comply with onerous and restrictive laws, and the almost inevitable emergence of new leadership groups grounded in parliaments—can have profound effects on both their ideology and their organization.

The broader society finds Islamist movements difficult to integrate as normal political actors, for two reasons. First, no matter how peaceful their means, the movements offer not only a set of alternative policies but also a different vision of society. Because of the deep gulfs separating them from regimes (and even from other opposition actors), the movements, as much as they may accommodate themselves to the existing political rules on a practical and ideological level, still pose a strong challenge. They appear to be anti-system parties no matter how obedient their behavior.

Second, the movements have not been operating in democratic systems. Instead, their commitment to electoral politics has taken place under regimes that do not allow the opposition to win and allow electoral mechanisms to operate in a highly restricted fashion. Ruling elites resist accepting any political actors they cannot control, co-opt, contain, or manipulate. The question so often posed—are Islamist movements truly democratic or really revolutionary?—is in a fundamental sense based on an inaccurate understanding of semiauthoritarian regimes: instituting democracy would itself be revolutionary. To put it differently, any genuinely democratic party in the Arab world is in many respects an anti-system party. It should therefore be no surprise that in a few cases Islamist movements, with their deep social roots, have found that intensifying their democratic commitments can actually make them more threatening to existing regimes.

Why Is Islamist Politicization under Semiauthoritarianism Difficult in Theory?

Scholars focusing on Islamist participation in semiauthoritarian settings have a different set of difficulties: the theoretical tools they have to examine parties and elections were developed for a different set of circumstances—or more precisely, for a deceptively similar set of circumstances. Classic works and current ones generally situate political parties and party systems within electoral democracies.[4] The systems we are interested in have some electoral mechanisms but are not democracies; the movements that draw our attention participate in elections but claim (and behave) as if electoral victory is not their primary goal. Thus, while political scientists have studied elections and parties for decades, they generally do so by making two assumptions that simply do not hold in many Arab cases: that the outcome of an election determines the policy direction of a country or the identity of senior office holders, and that political parties are organizations that seek to win elections. Islamist movements participate in elections they often cannot realistically win no matter how strong their support. And just as oddly, they often lose on purpose—or at least acquiesce in their own defeat.

---

4. For older scholarship, see Giovanni Sartori, *Parties and Party Systems* (Cambridge: Cambridge University Press, 1976). For a recent example, see Carles Boix, "The Emergence of Parties and Party Systems," in *The Oxford Handbook of Comparative Politics*, ed. Carles Boix and Susan Stokes (Oxford: Oxford University Press, 2009).

We will therefore need to reforge some of our theoretical tools. For instance, the scholarly literature on parties—which has focused on understanding how parties seek to win votes, gain office, and affect policy (and the relative importance of each goal)—will have to be assessed and recast carefully before it offers us much guidance. As Jillian Schwedler, a scholar who has worked to specify both the meaning and the mechanisms of moderation, has noted:

> the logic of strategic behavior within institutional constraints provided by a democratic system offers little for understanding moderation within the gray-zone regimes characterized by weak institutions, as are common in much of the world. In this regard, analogies to Christian Democratic parties in Europe thus have limited comparative value in exploring the effects of inclusion when the political systems in question fall far short of democracy, as they do in most of the Middle East. . . . Can we assess moderation if the liberalization process in general has not gone forward?[5]

Not all analogies should be dismissed (if so, comparative politics would have to cease). But they must be explored through careful and rigorous analysis rather than used as a shortcut to understanding. If they are, we will find that the experience of Islamist movements is not as unusual or anomalous as initially appears. In fact, contemporary history is rich with examples of movements that stood on the margins of accepted forms of politics in settings of limited, partial, facade, or unstable democracy. Here Schwedler's insistence that we pay attention to the political context is extremely helpful, but her discounting the Christian Democratic analogy may be too hasty. Socialist, Christian Democratic, and fascist movements arose in European political systems whose democratic mechanisms were limited, untested, or sharply contested. And the movements themselves often showed deep ambivalence about elections. Further, they had wider agendas that were not restricted to the electoral or even the political realm. The problem (which presumably motivates Schwedler's cautionary note about the comparison) in drawing on the lessons of these parties is that their experiences are generally cited in almost a bumper-sticker fashion either to minimize the difficulties posed by Islamist parties (by likening them to current-day tame Christian Democratic parties) or to maximize the challenge (by favoring analogies instead to fascist parties). But such sloganeering should not lead us to abandon comparative inquiry. We need to be better students of history (and comparative politics), moving beyond citing quick analogies as a surrogate for analysis.

---

5. Schwedler, *Faith in Moderation*, p. 20.

Chapter 3 will explore the literature on political parties, working to move beyond crude analogy mongering and probing what our knowledge about political parties suggests may be relevant to the experience of Islamist parties. That chapter will reveal the Christian Democratic analogy to be helpful, though only when properly understood. But it will also make clear the need to shift some of the focus beyond the goals of the political parties. Political scientists have long been aware that parties operate within political systems that have great effects on parties and are not merely products of those parties. In short, even if we were interested only in the parties themselves, it would make no sense to concentrate only on the ideology of one sort of opposition movement. We also need to know something about the elections that are being held and the political systems holding them if we wish to explain what effect they have on Islamist movements—and how Islamist participation can affect the systems in which they operate.

There is another underappreciated complication in the use of existing scholarly approaches: not only are the systems much less than democratic, but Islamist movements are also much more than political parties. Indeed, the movements claim to pursue politics as only one aspect of a far broader project of remolding individuals and societies according to principles and practices inspired by Islamic teachings. Leaders constantly reiterate that political activity is a means but not an end; entering political life is only one possible avenue for pursuing the movement mission. To the extent that such statements reflect movement behavior (and not merely aspirations), electoral and political logic will explain only part of Islamist strategy and tactics. And indeed, we will see that one of the reasons Islamists hesitate to commit more fully to political life (for instance, by creating a political party that is completely free of the movement in its decision making) is the fear that they will be sucked into emphasizing politics too exclusively and lose sight of the broader mission.

Thus we must constantly remind ourselves that we are not asking about the effect of democratic politics on political parties; instead, we are interested in the effect of semiauthoritarian politics on broad movements. We need not abandon the insights that generations of students of democracy and political parties offer us. But we need to be cautious and qualified in drawing on those insights. In particular, as we will see in the next two chapters, we need to modify a strong tendency that scholars have noticed (a version of the inclusion-moderation hypothesis)—that over time, given a political process that offers substantial rewards for participation and substantial risks for other strategies, movements on the edge of a system will indeed be incorporated within it. Or rather, we will not need to modify this insight so much as realize that when we study Islamist movements in semiauthoritarian settings, we must shift our attention from the overall trend to the hedges and qualifications that are packed within this generalization, asking what kinds of rewards and risks are at issue, over what period does change take place, and about the degree, nature, and permanence of the incorporation.

The Cases

In this book we focus on Islamist movements in four Arab societies: Egypt, Jordan, Kuwait, and Palestine. While the societies and political systems vary greatly, the mission and approach of the Islamist movements under consideration in the four cases do not: all have broad agendas, aspirations to pursue a wide range of activities, diffuse but disciplined organizations, and general but uncodified (and practical rather than abstract) ideologies.

We will ask what happens to these movements as they are invited to invest in politics—in other words, we will examine the effects of politics on the movements. We are interested in the effects of the shift to semiauthoritarianism but even more in its ongoing operation. In that sense, we are probing change within semiauthoritarianism more than its emergence or demise. While we will not be able to resist a peek at the likely effects of (and contributions to) democratic politics by Islamist movements, the vast majority of our attention will be on semiauthoritarian conditions. And we will argue that this kind of broad Islamist movement will react to shifting semiauthoritarian opportunities by investing in them without making full commitments.

The relationship between the four movements receiving special focus in this book and the "mother movement" is often complicated; it is also sometimes loose and informal. In all four cases, the movement in question was inspired by Hasan al-Banna's Muslim Brotherhood, and all four claim to follow al-Banna's thought (*fikr*) and method or model (*manhaj*) to this day. By this they mean that they have a comprehensive agenda inspired by Islamic teaching and strive to realize it through personal, social, and political work. For movements following the Brotherhood model, neither the vision of personal improvement nor the dedication to building an organization of righteous Muslims leads them to cut themselves off from the broader society. Instead, such tasks are seen as integral parts of the broader project of social and political reform. But the Islamist movements have operated with a variety of political stances; they have also varied over time in their level of commitment to politics. The movements sharply disavow any intention to abandon political involvement, but they have been forced to bow to reality and acknowledge at times that political activity is too risky for the moment. Even when the emphasis on politics has been at its height, none of the movements studied here ever tried to win a national election. (Hamas's electoral victory—the exception that proves this rule—came after the movement held an extended debate about the advisability of participating, based on the assumption that it would do well but was unlikely to secure a majority.) The Moroccan Party of Justice and Development, similar to the parties studied in this book, was even described after elections in 2002 as "the party that did not want to win."[6]

The founders of the Muslim Brotherhood were not consciously engaged in an act of social science quasi-experimental design when they inspired branches of their movement to form in different Arab countries, but by doing so they facilitated the work of later scholars in two ways. First, we can compare the four cases in order to understand the effect of the political system on the movements. While all four societies are Arab and have political systems that have evolved markedly in a semiauthoritarian direction in recent years, they are different in almost all other respects—in political system, social composition, party system, socioeconomic level, and international position. This great variety in the societies and political systems covered is a welcome asset: if we find that the degree of semiauthoritarianism and the forms of the opportunities that it presents shape much of the Islamist response—that is, if we find a robust relationship between semiauthoritarianism and the organization and ideological responses of Islamist movements—that holds in the face of kings, amirs, presidents, salafis, Shi`a, liberals, prosperity, poverty, state strength, and statelessness, then we have discovered something important about how Islamists (and broad movements more generally) react to their environment.

Second, we can compare the same movement over time in the same society as the system changes. Indeed, in this book we will be more attentive to variation *within* each of the countries—the emergence of semiauthoritarianism, the degree and forms it takes, the openings it provides, the changes in its rules—than to variation *among* them. All four societies have moved toward semiauthoritarianism, a regime type that (as we will see in Chapter 2) by its very nature fosters instability in institutional arrangements, particularly those governing electoral competition. Thus, not only will we witness four cases of Islamist movements reacting to the emergence of semiauthoritarianism, but even more we will study a wide variety of political openings that arise (and close).

The cases show tremendous variation over time. Egypt, for instance, after its regime transformed itself into a semiauthoritarian one in the 1970s, alternated hauling Muslim Brotherhood leaders before military tribunals and inviting them

---

6. Michael J. Willis, "Morocco's Islamists and the Legislative Elections of 2002: The Strange Case of the Party That Did Not Want to Win," *Mediterranean Politics* 9, no. 1 (2004), 53–81.

into parliament. Jordan's erratic bouts of liberalization and crackdown have led to Islamists being invited into the government and allowed to form a legal political party—and also to the seizure of the movement's leading NGO. The Kuwaiti regime, like the Jordanian, has invited Islamists into the cabinet but has also singled them out for hostile treatment. In Palestine, the Israeli occupation (admittedly an unusual kind of authoritarianism but one that certainly suppressed political opposition) gave partial ground to the Palestinian Authority, a nonsovereign political entity that was born semiauthoritarian but in which liberalizing and democratic features were inserted. Hamas was encouraged to participate but was threatened with a constitutional coup after it did.

In none of these cases has the liberalizing features of semiauthoritarianism led to full democratization. To be fair, on a few occasions they have threatened to do so. In 2011, an Egyptian semiauthoritarian regime was brought down by a democratic opposition but not through the tools of semiauthoritarian politics—and the challenges of building a democratic system remain formidable. Kuwait has come closest to a sustained democratic opening because opposition political forces have brought down powerful ministers and used parliamentary tools effectively to veto some policy initiatives. But what is sometimes referred to as a "popular government"—a cabinet that is fully responsible to an elected parliament—remains beyond grasp. And in the Palestinian case the opposition actually won an election and briefly formed a government—but the system, rather than give way to democracy, broke down (or was actively destroyed) in the process. We will explore each case more fully in Chapter 5.

In working at understanding the effect of politics on the movements, we will first try to understand the systems in which they operate. That task will require some attention to detail: once the break from authoritarianism to semiauthoritarianism is made, the regimes change the rules of the political game frequently but hardly in a linear fashion; they do so in ways that are sometimes subtle; and they regularly mask authoritarian retrenchment as liberalizing reform. But armed with a reliable understanding of semiauthoritarianism and its openings, we can proceed to a study of the subsequent organizational and ideological responses of the movements. In this we will be aided by the tendencies of the movements to document themselves and also the inclination of many key leaders to make themselves available for interviews and frank discussions.

The Book

Our next two chapters will lay the theoretical groundwork for the remainder of the book. In Chapter 2, we will consider semiauthoritarianism in general but focus more specifically on how elections are held and how regimes and oppositions use them. In Chapter 3, we will turn our attention to the movements, asking what the experience of Social Democrats, Christian Democracy, and other broad reform movements lead us to look for in the Islamist experience. In both chapters, our efforts will be aimed at reforging the theoretical tools that political scientists have used to understand democratic politics and other social movements to make them more suitable to semiauthoritarian politics and Islamist movements.

In Chapter 4, we will examine the model of Egypt's Muslim Brotherhood. After briefly reviewing its history, we will analyze the model's basic characteristics and probe what those characteristics would lead us to expect in terms of likely reactions to semiauthoritarian conditions. Chapter 5 will bring in a more focused coverage of the four cases. There will be a reportorial element to this chapter (to provide the factual basis for understanding the subsequent analysis), but the broader purpose will be to understand how the movements have evolved in a semiauthoritarian context.

Chapters 6 and 7 will continue the detailed analysis of the four cases. Chapter 6 will examine political organization with special attention to the formation and operation of political parties as well as the degree that such parties are allowed to develop autonomously of the broader movements. We will seek to understand what organizational decisions are most difficult for Islamist movements to make, why they make the choices they do, and what this tells us about the effects of semiauthoritarian politics. Chapter 7 will turn to the ideological evolution of the movements, probing where movements come under pressure to adapt their ideologies, how they respond, and where they fail to respond (or do so only incompletely).

Throughout almost all the book, therefore, we will stave off the question as it has been more generally posed: instead of asking about the effects *of* Islamists and about change *of* regime (through democratization), we will focus on the effects *on* Islamists and on change *within* semiauthoritarianism. But in Chapter 8, we will succumb to the temptation to examine whether Islamists can make their states and societies more democratic. Having worked to understand the world as it is right now, we will probe how the world might be different; instead of studying how semiauthoritarianism affects Islamist movements, we will ask how the responses of Islamist movements in turn shape semiauthoritarianism. We will discover that Islamist political activity is unlikely to lead to regime change (and that when a semiauthoritarian regime does indeed fall, as happened in Egypt and Tunisia in 2011, Islamists play at most a supporting role) but contains several elements that can foster democratic practice (and a few that can discourage it) even within a semiauthoritarian setting.

Finally, in Chapter 9, we will conclude by returning to the issue of how semiauthoritarian politics and its vicissitudes affect Islamist movements. We will widen our field of vision somewhat, however, by comparing what we have found about Islamist movements in semiauthoritarian settings with Islamist movements in different settings and with different kinds of movements in semiauthoritarian settings.

RUNNING TO LOSE?

Elections, Authoritarianism, and Islamist Movements

We have complete domination by the executive. We cannot change that. But we can reach the public.

—Hamdi Hasan, Muslim Brotherhood member of the Egyptian parliament, April 2006

Semiauthoritarian regimes in the Arab world tempt, entice, repress, and frustrate Islamists in constantly shifting and often undependable ways. Semiauthoritarian politics is characterized by much more motion than movement. But fairly consistently, the pattern of rules constructed by such regimes invites Islamists to compete in—and lose—elections. What are the rules under which Islamists agree to run? Why do they bother? And how does participation in such a system affect them?

We are interested in this book in the effect of semiauthoritarianism on Islamist movements. In this chapter we will focus on understanding what semiauthoritarianism is, the political openings it provides (however unevenly and unreliably), especially in the realm of elections and formal politics, and the ways in which regimes and oppositions use the institutional tools that semiauthoritarianism offers. We will pay particular attention to the way in which the political rules seem to shift constantly in semiauthoritarian systems. In subsequent chapters we will explore what effects the use of these tools has on the movements.

Semiauthoritarian systems are those that allow the opposition some ability to organize and compete but deny them any possibility of forming the government.[1] Fully authoritarian regimes do not allow the opposition to operate even in these ways. Under authoritarianism, autonomous social organizations may exist and

---

1. I have written about these definitions in more detail in "Dictatorship and Democracy through the Prism of Arab Elections," in *The Dynamics of Democratization: Dictatorship, Development, and Diffusion*, ed. Nathan J. Brown (Baltimore: Johns Hopkins University Press, 2011).

even flourish, but they are not allowed to tread far into the political realm without risking repression. The opposition cannot speak, organize, or act in the political sphere.[2] Democracy, by contrast, allows the opposition to win. It has been paradoxically defined as a system in which political parties can lose elections; if there is a party that cannot lose, the system is not democratic.[3]

In between democracy and full authoritarianism, scholarly explorations of various "gray area" systems have stumbled on a distinct category of regimes whose defining characteristic is that opposition parties can organize, propagandize, canvass, convene, publish, and complain but not win. We refer to this category of system as "semiauthoritarian." And in exploring semiauthoritarian politics in this chapter, we are aided greatly by a burgeoning interest in nondemocratic regimes in general and nondemocratic elections in particular. But there are some blind spots in our emerging understanding of such semiauthoritarianism and nondemocratic elections. We are coming to understand how semiauthoritarian regimes maintain themselves and how they fail, but we often miss the ways in which they improvise and constantly change the rules of the political game. We have few tools to understand change within semiauthoritarian systems.

Indeed, in this book we will deemphasize the overarching questions that dominate many efforts to understand semiauthoritarianism and semiauthoritarian elections, questions that focus on long-term motives: Why were these regimes built the way they were? And why do they hold elections in the first place? These questions are important, but they can be misleading for our purposes. First, they are distracting: we are interested in the effects the regimes have, not in how and why they got there. Second, such questions risk overstating the importance of elections for both regimes and oppositions (indeed, we will see that those opposition parties that do well in elections are generally those that focus on them less). And third, they misstate the way the question is posed by the participants who do not betray the same interest in the existence of the elections and indeed largely accept and expect elections as a normal part of the political landscape. Both government and opposition in the Arab world show little sign of asking many questions about whether and why to hold elections, but instead think hard about how to use them.

---

2. I am not depending on a highly distinct line between semiauthoritarian and authoritarian regimes in this book. Were I to need one, I might suggest that a good working distinction might rely on the representation of the opposition in parliament. If opposition deputies hold more than 5 percent of the seats (enough to raise motions, question ministers, place draft laws on the agenda, and undertake some meaningful committee work), then a regime might be seen to have passed from authoritarianism to semiauthoritarianism. The Arab experience also suggests focusing on media, since the rise of prominent media outlets not under the control of national governments has been a critical element in opening up political space.

3. This is Adam Przeworski's fairly minimalist but also analytically useful definition, designed to help scholars distinguish between what is a democracy and what is not. See his *Democracy and the Market* (Cambridge: Cambridge University Press, 1991), p. 10.

More profoundly, we will need to take care in this and subsequent chapters not to let such questions lead our inquiry seriously astray into overemphasizing stability or being overly distracted by the possibility of systemic change. Students of politics have noted in recent years how widespread some democratic mechanisms are—most notably multiparty or multicandidate elections—in political systems that are not democratic.[4] Scholars have reacted by seeking to understand the emergence and persistence of "hybrid," "semiauthoritarian," "electoral authoritarian," or "liberalized autocratic" regimes, categories that often overlap but are still distinct. Indeed, typologies and terminologies have multiplied rapidly as scholars have worked to come to terms with the messy realities of electoral politics in much of the world that is not categorized as reliably democratic.

The problem with these typologies is not simply conceptual and terminological cacophony; instead, the problem is that they risk leading us to focus too much on the possibilities for systemic change or, alternatively, on control and stability. As we proceed in subsequent chapters, we will need some understanding of change within semiauthoritarian systems—and change there is, especially in the electoral realm, where fundamental procedures are constantly rewritten.

We thus wish to avoid both an overly teleological approach (viewing semiauthoritarian systems as democracies waiting to break out) and an overly functionalist one (regarding the various mechanisms and structures of semiauthoritarian politics as individually and collectively serving—and even designed—to maintain the system).

Regarding the first, most recent writings on semiauthoritarianism have not overcome the democratic teleology they are generally reacting against. Scholars writing on authoritarianism, democracy, and transitions in the 1980s and 1990s rarely sought to mask their championing of democratic outcomes; they were interested in how their preferred outcome, democracy, might be realized. Writings from the past decade have drawn back from the democratic advocacy (and optimism), but a heavy residue of democratic teleology remains: they still probe nondemocratic elections to understand how they might lead to democratic outcomes.[5] And it seems quite likely that the revolutionary upheavals in the Arab

---

4. For some leading examples of this burgeoning literature, see Steven Levitsky and Lucan A. Way, "The Rise of Competitive Authoritarianism," *Journal of Democracy* 13, no. 2 (2002), 51–65; Andreas Schedler, ed., *Electoral Authoritarianism: The Dynamics of Unfree Competition* (Boulder, Colo.: Lynne Rienner, 2006); and Marina Ottaway, *Democracy Challenged: The Rise of Semiauthoritarianism* (Washington, D.C.: Carnegie Endowment for International Peace, 2003). A useful recent work that focuses on Egypt is Lisa Blaydes, *Elections and Distributive Politics in Mubarak's Egypt* (Cambridge: Cambridge University Press, 2010).

5. For a recent collection of articles that examine the relationship between elections and democratization—including a variety of perspectives on a teleological approach—see Staffan I. Lindberg, ed., *Democratization by Elections: A New Mode of Transition* (Baltimore: Johns Hopkins University Press, 2009).

world of 2011 will restore some of the impulse to search for signs of emerging democracy. We do not want to abandon such a search completely, but we should remember that "semiauthoritarian," "hybrid," and "electoral authoritarian" regimes were categories invented in order to portray such regimes as stable rather than as way stations on the road to democracy. And even these concepts have still been defined very much in terms of what they are not and what they might become rather than what they are.[6]

But when the emerging scholarship on in-between regimes avoids such teleology, it can tempt us with the opposite problem of excessive functionalism. Many recent writings turn the focus from how such regimes fall (which they occasionally do) to how they continue (which is far more common). In the process, they break the connection (however imperfectly) between elections and democracy; as a leading scholar of electoral authoritarianism has put it, "Historically ... elections have been an instrument of authoritarian control as well as a means of democratic government."[7] This has the welcome effect of revealing that much of the important political struggle over elections in semiauthoritarian settings occurs not so much over the results (which are often foreordained) but over the mechanisms and rules by which elections operate, an insight that will emerge as particularly significant in the Arab world.

Such approaches, however, risk portraying semiauthoritarian regimes as expertly designed systems that differ from authoritarian ones primarily in their subtlety: every one of their seemingly democratic features is characterized as furthering authoritarian rules, sometimes in ways difficult to detect. A functionalist approach might lead us to dismiss semiauthoritarian politics as an authoritarian ploy and scour it for the hidden purposes of apparently liberalizing measures; a teleological approach would lead us to scour any liberalizing features of semiauthoritarian regimes for democratic time bombs and ask how and when semiauthoritarian rules bring into being democratizing forces they cannot control. The first approach generates the image of a master sorcerer; the second, of a sorcerer's apprentice. Neither of these images is helpful to us now; for reasons that this chapter will make clear, a better metaphor might be to see each regime as a group of resourceful but improvising mechanics. The systems are not so much designed as jury-rigged; if there was a moment of grand design, it has receded into the distant past.

---

6. "Hybrid" regimes are defined largely in terms of how close they come to a fully liberal democracy. See, for instance, Levitsky and Way, "Rise of Competitive Authoritarianism."

7. Andreas Schedler, "Elections without Democracy: The Menu of Manipulation," *Journal of Democracy* 13, no. 2 (2002), 36. Scholars of the Middle East have been in the forefront of working to understand elections freed of any democratic teleology. See, for instance, Ellen Lust-Okar, *Structuring Conflict in the Arab World: Incumbents, Opponents, and Institutions* (Cambridge: Cambridge University Press, 2005), and Lisa Wedeen, *Peripheral Visions: Publics, Power, and Performance in Yemen* (Chicago: University of Chicago Press, 2008).

Such an image will aid our inquiry tremendously. Semiauthoritarian elections are generally governed by unstable rules. Thus, when we investigate the effect of semiauthoritarianism on Islamist movements, we are investigating not only what it means to play by the rules but also what it means to play by many shifting rules. There is, to be sure, one overriding rule of electoral politics in semiauthoritarian regimes: the opposition loses. (More precisely, it can never win a majority.) If the opposition is capable of winning, then the system is no longer semiauthoritarian. But aside from that overriding rule, all else is open to contestation and incessant tinkering. It is this combination of uncertain rules and certain results that this chapter is designed to explore.

We will first look at semiauthoritarian elections and then examine how they appear (and what they offer) to regimes and oppositions. Finally, we will probe the implications of semiauthoritarian elections for the relations between regime and opposition.

Elections and Semiauthoritarianism

Throughout the Arab world, citizens are regularly summoned to the polls. They are asked to vote for presidents, parliaments, constitutions, and constitutional amendments. On rare occasions, elections have been canceled or electoral processes suspended, but in most states, elections are carried out with predictable regularity. And the results are generally predictable as well: political power almost never changes hands as a result of an election. (Indeed, on the two occasions in which such an outcome seemed possible, the result was civil war. When Hamas won an outright majority of parliamentary seats in 2006, the political system split in two; when Algeria's Islamic Salvation Front was poised to win in 1992, a military coup prevented such an outcome.) The seeming anomaly in the Arab world is that rulers determine election results, not the other way around.

But is this really anomalous? The situation in the Arab world—where residents are regularly asked to vote in elections in which the outcome is not in doubt—is not as unusual as it initially appears. Beatriz Magaloni's influential study of Mexico shows how a dominant party perpetuated itself and its dominance by retaining a legislative supermajority that allowed it to write the rules as it wished, tinkering with them in order to produce the desired result; through largely constitutional means it was able to ensure that there was "no binding set of constitutional rules."[8]

Elections occur with some regularity in most Arab countries. A few, like Saudi Arabia, have held off and refused to hold national elections. A few others, like

---

8. Beatriz Magaloni, *Voting for Autocracy: Hegemonic Party Survival and Its Demise in Mexico* (Cambridge: Cambridge University Press, 2006), pp. 260–261. When a series of incremental decisions led to the dominant party's loss of control over the constitutional rules, the system underwent a fundamental transformation, essentially a transition from semiauthoritarianism to democracy.

Iraq and Bahrain, have suspended elections for a considerable period. But such suspensions—a more regular feature of Arab politics from the 1950s through the 1980s—have become quite rare. In most countries, elections have simply become part of the institutional landscape. Inertia and the very mild dose of legitimation they provide have allowed elections to settle in, leading political forces in government and outside it to ask how they can use elections to their advantage far more than they ask whether they should be held at all.

It should be stressed that there is not much evidence that the legitimating role of elections is tremendously significant in Arab politics. Part of the legitimation that occurs is both limited and designed so that elections frustrate rather than persuade skeptics. The ritualistic victory of rulers shows that even formally democratic challenges are futile.[9] After two generations of experimenting with various manipulative techniques, rulers have rendered elections incapable of leading to a change in senior office holders. Any move toward making elections a more positive and democratic source of legitimacy would require abandoning these techniques and accepting the set of institutional safeguards that is becoming the norm for democratic elections in transition societies: truly independent electoral commissions, open and professional monitoring, and procedural fairness extending to all phases and aspects of elections (including party finance, use of state resources, and access to media). Many regimes in the Arab world have feinted in the direction of adopting portions of these safeguards, but none have done so convincingly. The one instance in which a regime instituted some of the standard international structures and guarantees—the Palestinian Authority parliamentary elections of January 2006—is likely to persuade semiauthoritarian regimes to avoid such a path at all costs. Indeed, even some of the limited forays toward such measures have been abandoned with breathtaking shamelessness if they were leading to unacceptable results (as in Algeria in 1992, when elections were forestalled by a coup, or Egypt in 2005, when security forces intervened massively to limit the size of the opposition showing; after the Egyptian polling, the few constitutional safeguards that existed were removed by amendment).

Existing oppositions can and do withhold their full acceptance of the regimes that place such sharp constraints on the workings and the effectiveness of the formally democratic elements in their constitutional orders, but proclaiming such a position has limited effect. International actors are also limited in the effectiveness of the democratizing tools at their disposal,[10] and the potential strength of

9. On this point, see Magaloni, *Voting for Autocracy.*

10. On the weakness of international "linkage" and "leverage" over electoral authoritarian regimes in the Middle East, see Steven Levitsky and Lucan A. Way, "Linkage and Leverage: How Do International Factors Change Domestic Balances of Power?" in Schedler, *Electoral Authoritarianism,* pp. 211–212.

Islamist movements has often persuaded them not to use the leverage they do have in some critical Arab cases. In short, elections fail to offer more than mild legitimacy to existing regimes, and the regimes have been willing to bear the domestic and international costs of this failure.

Although elections are held with increasing regularity, the rules that govern them—who can run, how campaigns can be conducted, who administers voting, the authority of the offices that are exposed to electoral contestation, access to official media, regulation of campaign activity, and the degree of contestation that is allowed—do shift. Electoral results in the Arab world may be written in stone, but the rules by which elections are held are written on water.[11] Indeed, it is not uncommon in some countries for major aspects of the electoral system to be reconfigured before every election. The fact of elections is well established, but nothing about their conduct is. This is why we should focus less on the question that has occupied some of the writings on electoral authoritarianism (Why are such elections held?) and instead ask, What are the various parties—regimes and oppositions—looking to get out of elections? And how does this shape the rules by which they will be conducted? We will address each question in turn.

What Do Regimes Want from Elections and How Do They Use Them?

In the Arab world, regimes remembering that electoral mechanisms exist (often having been constructed decades ago) have learned to use them, for two sets of reasons. First, both authoritarian and semiauthoritarian regimes have employed elections for internal purposes: to signal new ideological directions (with ritualistic referenda, for instance, on major policy questions, or new "national charters" or similar documents) and to construct and maintain patronage networks.[12] Such elections can proceed whether opposition exists or not and whether the organized opposition (if it does exist) boycotts, participates, unifies, or fractures. But the relative importance of such uses for elections has declined in the Arab world in recent years as authoritarianism has given way to semiauthoritarianism in many countries. In the 1960s, for instance—when one-party states were the norm in the Arab republics—these internal purposes were virtually the only use for elections. Over the past decade, one can certainly still find the ritualistic referendum endorsing a policy (such as in Algeria on truth reconciliation in

---

11. I treat this subject in more detail in "Dictatorship and Democracy."

12. Ellen Lust-Okar, "Elections under Authoritarianism: Preliminary Lessons from Jordan," *Democratization* 13, no. 3 (2006), 459.

2005) and the construction of politically supportive patronage networks (such as Egypt's sprawling National Democratic Party, an organization that seemed for all of its viable life to stand for little other than the authority of incumbents and the provision of services to those who supported them).

But with the rise of semiauthoritarianism, with its more pluralist party orders—in which republican regimes rule through a dominant party rather than a single one, and monarchies maintain themselves through outflanking, co-opting, and fracturing parliaments rather than subduing or even disbanding them—regimes have found a second purpose for the electoral mechanisms that exist: regulating relations between government and opposition. An earlier generation of Arab leaders tended to handle organized opposition movements by arresting their leaders (and sometimes their followers as well); the current generation has hardly abandoned harsh suppression but increasingly has turned to elections as a way of supplementing such draconian tools with more subtle ones.

Specifically, semiauthoritarian regimes use elections to govern oppositions in three ways. First, elections provide occasions to bring political opposition out into the open; elections can become a monitoring device. And in many cases, elections allow regimes to sort opposition movements as well, between those that are truly threatening (rejecting participation in the political process) and those that are more tame (playing by the rules laid down by the regime even as they complain about their fairness). Second, an electoral opposition can be co-opted on occasion. Here the regime moves beyond coaxing oppositions out into the open to seducing them to support the system.[13] Arab monarchies are especially fond of co-opting oppositions; with a monopoly on senior state positions and without their own party to support, ruling families tend to be more secure in reaching out to tame oppositions and offering them seats in the cabinet. Third, elections can be used not only to rule but also to divide. Certain constituencies can be rewarded (such as East Bankers in Jordan or Sunnis in Bahrain) by the drawing of electoral districts and allocation of seats. Certain ideological or political tendencies can be barred (most commonly those with a religious orientation). Such techniques serve not only to ensure that opposition strongholds are underrepresented but also to tempt some opposition leaders away from efforts to forge broad coalitions. Regimes have given limited concessions to Islamists (as Jordan did in the 1950s and 1960s and Egypt in the 1970s) in a bid to convince them that the left, not the regime, was their more important adversary; in the Mubarak

---

13. See Jennifer Gandhi and Adam Przeworski, "Authoritarian Institutions and the Survival of Autocrats," *Comparative Political Studies* 40, no. 11 (2007), 1279–1301.

regime's last years, the same technique was used to entice leftists and simultaneously frighten them away from alliance with Islamists. And electoral laws can be designed to favor certain kinds of identity—such as family, sect, or tribe—over ideological appeals in order to dampen the basis for a common opposition program (Jordan's current electoral law is a model in this respect).

If this is how regimes seek to use elections, we should expect constant tinkering with electoral rules and procedures. As regime priorities shift over time, we should expect restlessness with rules: when leaders are worried that opposition groups have mobilized too many supporters, they might be especially interested in preventing broad coalitions; when they are convinced that dealing with apparently less extreme leaders gives cover to (rather than isolates) extremists, the benefits of bringing opposition into the open will be less obvious. But even if regimes (and oppositions) were far more constant in their priorities, there is still a tremendous temptation to tinker: since the purpose of elections is less to produce a credible result and more to manage the opposition, there will be a constant effort to engineer the desired outcome through drawing and redrawing the rules, district boundaries, access to media, and other features of the electoral process. We should not fall into the functionalist trap here: regimes might make minor miscalculations all the time and more significant ones on occasion. But their efforts are still intended to calibrate the electoral process, however roughly, to produce the relationship with the opposition that they desire.

What Do Oppositions Want from Elections and How Do They Use Them?

Like regimes, opposition movements have generally come to view elections as a regular part of the political landscape in most Arab countries. But they are also accustomed (and contribute) to the instability in electoral rules and administration. Most opposition movements participate in elections, but some abstain totally and almost all persistently threaten to boycott. The terms they use in explaining their decision to participate or boycott generally refer to legitimation—the extent to which they are willing to lend credibility to a process they do not trust. Such language is misleading, however; even when they participate, most opposition movements still denounce the process as unfair. Their acquiescence can sometimes be bought but rarely their positive support. If elections are not about legitimacy in the Arab world, then what are regime opponents seeking? Why and how do they participate in elections that they would never admit to trusting?

Election campaigns offer opposition movements unusual opportunities in semiauthoritarian settings.[14] Opposition leaders striving to take advantage of semiauthoritarian openings generally find that elections allow them greater freedom to organize, more channels to proclaim their message, and increased access to the media and to public space. Such perquisites of electoral campaigns are never unfettered nor are they allocated equally, as armies of electoral observers in the region have documented in recent years. Opposition leaders who decry elections as unfairly administered are almost invariably correct—but they still find greater opportunities to speak and reach out to citizens than they do in ordinary times. This allows them to mobilize their old constituencies and even seek out new ones. Election campaigns are occasions to issue platforms in which opposition leaders can describe (sometimes in tremendous detail) their alternative vision for the society. Campaigns also grant them a greater level of attention from politically aware elites and even foreign media and diplomats, giving them a measure of protection from the repressive security agencies.

Parliamentary (as well as municipal) elections allow a second benefit as well: winning seats. Opposition activists who take seats in parliament find that they can transfer some of the advantages of the campaign season to ordinary political times. Deputies enjoy immunity; they can introduce legislation and question ministers; and they can even appear in broadcast and print media. In municipal councils it is harder to earn national attention, nor do those elected enjoy any kind of immunity, but opposition movements can demonstrate their probity and dedication to the everyday concerns of constituents.

None of these benefits is unlimited. Immunity can be (and has been) revoked; ministers can (and often do) ignore questions; draft legislation can be (and almost always is) shunted to committee to be quietly buried; official media can cover parliament as if few opposition deputies are present (or, more frequently, simply fail to report comments or individual statements that might provoke official displeasure); and local councils can be starved of resources. As limited (and revocable) as these benefits are, they still have real value to those who gain office.

---

14. For a rich discussion of the benefits (as well as some of the costs) of electoral participation for the Egyptian Muslim Brotherhood, see Tarek El-Meslhy Masoud, "Why Islam Wins: Electoral Ecologies and Economies of Political Islam in Contemporary Egypt" (PhD diss., Yale University, 2008), especially chap. 2. I find most of Masoud's analysis persuasive, though I differ in some emphasis. In particular, he focuses more on *why* the Brotherhood participates while I am more interested in *how* it participates. As we will see in Chapters 4 and 5, the decision to participate is old and well established, but the degree and nature of participation are subjects of continuous deliberation. Of course, understanding the underlying motives is still critical, since it deeply informs the incremental decision making.

But what about winning? Do opposition movements hope against hope to oust the regime through the ballot box? Of course, the Arab world has many opposition movements that see themselves as willing and able to govern. But while most would be delighted (if astonished) to win, they almost never enter any particular election expecting to win a majority. Few even try. Indeed, some have calculated (correctly) that even hinting at the possibility of an electoral victory is enough to unnerve rulers and provoke a repressive response. For the most realistic opposition leaders, elections are not about governing in the near future but about building a movement, articulating an agenda, and using the limited openings that elections can offer. For Islamist leaders in particular, patience is a divinely sanctioned virtue that helps them look beyond the frustrations and limitations of semiauthoritarian elections. In some cases, this may actually lead to their accommodating themselves to (without enthusiastically embracing) semiauthoritarian regimes in an ongoing way; Güneş Murat Tezcür observes that "electoral calculations, fear of state repression and organizational constraints all make them politically risk-averse. Consequently, they seek accommodation with authoritarian aspects of the regime."[15] This explains why many Islamist movements find themselves forced to contend with two sets of suspicions simultaneously—that they harbor a revolutionary agenda and that they are really interested in cutting a quiet deal with rulers.

This brings us to a truly anomalous feature of elections in the Arab world: those who invest most of their energies in elections are generally the ones who do most poorly. The political field is simply infertile ground and cannot be used effectively to build constituencies. This is in stark contrast to many established democracies in Europe and the Americas in recent years. There parties often seem to succeed to the extent that they jettison firm ideological missions and loosen any tethering that might have existed to a disciplined social movement; they thereby turn into virtual electoral machines as other aspects of their operations (ideological, mobilizational, etc.) atrophy. In the Arab world, by contrast, the semiauthoritarian environment has ensured that those who focus exclusively on elections have little to show for themselves and therefore have withered into small shells with few supporters. The Arab world's more formidable opposition movements are those that stress nonelectoral activities. Islamist movements in particular, with their mobilizational, educational, religious, charitable, and social-service agendas, have a deep social presence and enduring viability that can serve them well in open campaigns precisely because they are not designed

---

15. Güneş Murat Tezcür, "Moderation Theory Revisited: The Case of Islamic Political Actors," *Party Politics* 16, no. 1 (2010), 83.

primarily for that purpose. To put it differently, working too hard to win an election is the best guarantee of losing it particularly badly.

Like regimes that seek to tinker with electoral rules, opposition movements do not press for continuity and stability in how elections are run but instead constantly push demands for changes to make them more attractive. Almost all threats of boycotts come over procedural issues—who will administer an election, what sort of monitoring and observation will be allowed, how will votes be translated into seats, and how will the powers of the state be deployed in the campaign and voting.

With regimes and oppositions both constantly working to reconfigure electoral rules in order to manage their relationship with each other, it makes most sense to see elections in the Arab world not so much as contests for legitimacy (and much less for political power) as occasions for negotiating and renegotiating the boundaries and terms of political opposition.

Elections: Unequal Bargaining without Agreement

In the semiauthoritarian systems of the Arab world, the important electoral struggles to focus on—for both activists and analysts—are not the campaigns but the organization and administration of elections. Regimes and oppositions bargain continuously and without final resolution over who may run in elections, who will oversee the balloting, how votes will be translated into seats, who may observe the electoral process, how campaigns will be conducted, how candidates and parties can deliver their messages and what those messages may be, and what authorities of the elected body will be granted. It should be recalled that regimes are not only concerned with oppositions; they are also focused on international actors to some extent and often are especially sensitive to various groups within the regime (especially when patronage networks play a strong role). This set of concerns can make the regime a particularly mercurial (or perhaps frequently distracted) negotiating partner for oppositions.

As Andreas Schedler has written, "neither incumbents nor opponents will perceive manipulated elections as an 'equilibrium' solution that corresponds to their long-term interests. Rather they will accept the rules of the electoral game as a temporary compromise, a provisional truce contingent on current correlations of force and open to revision in the uncertain future." Or, more formally, "The ambivalent and thus (usually) contested nature of flawed elections implies that elections do not unfold as simple games but as two-level games.... At the same time as incumbents and opponents measure their forces in the electoral arena, they battle over the basic rules that shape the electoral arena. Their struggle over institutional rules is not extraneous to but an integral part of their struggle within prevalent institutional rules, as the game of electoral competition is embedded within the meta-game of electoral reform."[16]

In one way Schedler does not even go far enough, because his reference to a "truce" suggests that the contest over rules is suspended during the campaign itself. In fact, even provisional rules on such issues are continuously tested, probed, and pushed on both sides. There is no truce. What are often referred to as "red lines" are hardly stable and accepted. They are only the blurry frontiers in a fluid contest.

The contest may be constant, but it is not equal. Regimes in a semiauthoritarian setting have the capability, virtually by definition, to impose rules. Rulers are mildly limited—or better, steered—by four factors. First, inertia plays a role. Although regimes tinker with rules, they often use the last election as the starting point, since a significant legislative and bureaucratic residue generally remains. Second, the desire for legitimacy—while widely exaggerated—leads to feeble efforts to mimic some of the forms (if much more rarely the substance) of neutral (and increasingly internationalized) standards of electoral administration. Thus, in 2005 Egypt brought in an "electoral commission" that was designed to outflank demands for constitutionally mandated judicial supervision rather than allow truly independent oversight. Third, regimes wish to have at least some opposition movements participate in the election. A total boycott is a negative (though not intolerable) outcome. Finally, and most important, regimes do not wish to lose.

Opposition movements, by contrast, can generally affect the rules only by threatening to boycott. And this is precisely what they do—incessantly, loudly, and truculently, up to and even past the last minute. In 2007, the Jordanian Islamic Action Front pulled out of municipal elections on the morning of balloting—and then promptly resumed bitter internal arguments over whether to boycott the parliamentary elections scheduled four months later (a dispute that continued even long after the parliamentary balloting was over as party leaders squabbled over whether the party's secretary-general had accepted and

---

16. Andreas Schedler, "The Nested Game of Democratization by Elections," *International Political Science Review* 23, no. 1 (2002), 109–110. On elections as a two-level game, see also Scott Mainwaring and Timothy Scully, eds., *Christian Democracy in Latin America: Electoral Competition and Regime Conflicts* (Stanford, Calif.: Stanford University Press, 2003). I find Schedler's general portrait of semiauthoritarian elections extremely helpful, but I think he focuses too much on democratizing outcomes and legitimacy.

implemented the leadership's decision on participation). Just as a boycott is a negative but tolerable outcome for the regime, opposition movements (with some important exceptions) generally prefer to use whatever openings exist in order to pursue the aims described earlier in this chapter, but they can boycott without paying intolerable costs. And indeed, virtually the only tool they have to press for marginal increases in openness is to threaten to pull out of the process altogether.[17]

Thus semiauthoritarian elections in the Arab world are generally accompanied by prolonged and indeterminate bargaining, both explicit (in which leaders sit down, publicly or privately, to discuss rules) and implicit (in which bargaining takes place through posturing, press releases, veiled warnings, hints, and threats). And elections are often surrounded by rumors that the regime has cut deals with specific opposition movements (or even with specific leaders or factions within those movements). During Egypt's 2005 parliamentary elections and Jordan's 2007 polling, there was widespread speculation that the leadership of the Muslim Brotherhood had negotiated the number of seats it would contest and win. Such rumors are likely far more common than explicit agreements, but conspiracy theorists are still closer to the mark than may initially appear: the number of seats won by the opposition may rarely be determined by an explicit deal, but the result is almost always deeply affected by the constant explicit and implicit bargaining and maneuvering between government and opposition.

The nature of the bargaining aggravates the instability of any arrangements. Not only do the preferences and priorities of the various parties shift—as explained earlier in this chapter—but the explicit and implicit bargaining that takes place addresses only the short-term concerns of both regime and opposition. Over the long term, regimes want guarantees that whatever arrangements they make, they will not lose. And opposition movements willing to participate in an unfair process might want to know that eventually they could win. Both sides are quite able to find other short-term uses for elections, as explored above. But they are unlikely to agree to consider permanent any set of rules and procedures that do not meet these longer-term—and irreconcilable—goals.

It should be noted that Arab semiauthoritarian regimes are likely to be particularly unstable in their rules. They are generally highly centralized and built on foundations laid down by equally centralized but more authoritarian pre-

---

17. For an exploration of the boycott option, see Staffan I. Lindberg, "Tragic Protest: Why Do Opposition Parties Boycott Elections?" in Schedler, *Electoral Authoritarianism.*

decessors. That often leaves formal legal institutions (courts and parliaments) weak even by semiauthoritarian standards and allows a few figures in the regime unusual latitude in writing and rewriting the rules of the political game.

Rules may be more uncertain than results in semiauthoritarian elections, but we should not completely overlook the outcomes. Previous writings on semiauthoritarian elections betray an odd ambivalence on precisely this issue: while some stress the degree to which the elections are manipulated, others follow their fascination with electoral upsets. They both go too far. We need to revisit briefly the problems of functionalism and teleology that can lead some of our understandings astray.

On the one hand, writings on elections in an authoritarian setting explore very effectively the panoply of tools used by regimes to guarantee electoral outcomes.[18] Every aspect of the electoral rules—the licensing of parties, access to media, drawing of district boundaries, and so on—is designed by the regime to guarantee victory. While these scholarly lists provide useful descriptions of regimes' bags of tricks, they leave little room for the kind of unequal bargaining we are interested in exploring. And the list of techniques distracts us from exploring change over time or even distinguishing among regimes—and in particular from noting critical differences between fully authoritarian regimes, which are relatively intolerant of all opposition and pluralism, and semiauthoritarian regimes, which operate by manipulating and containing opposition but less evenly repressing it.

Some are attracted to images of omnipotent and omniscient regimes, but others are fascinated instead by the drama provided by rulers' fatal mistakes. There are good reasons for such fascination, since they have led to regime transition and even contributed heavily to democratization. In the Philippines in 1986, Poland in 1989, and Zimbabwe in 2008, and in the "color revolutions" of the former Soviet states early in the first decade of the 2000s, rulers accepted electoral arrangements that were tilted in their favor but could not absolutely guarantee a favorable result—and were shocked to discover that they had lost. There is now a considerable amount of scholarly research on such unexpected outcomes.[19] While these elections indeed deserve our attention,

---

18. Schedler, "Elections without Democracy" and *Electoral Authoritarianism;* Lindberg, *Democratization by Elections;* and Jennifer Gandhi and Ellen Lust-Okar, "Elections under Authoritarianism," *Annual Review of Political Science* 12 (2009), 403–422.

19. Axel Hadenius and Jan Teorell, "Pathways from Authoritarianism," *Journal of Democracy* 18, no. 1 (2007), 143–157; Joshua A. Tucker, "Enough! Electoral Fraud, Collective Action Problems, and Post-Communist Colored Revolutions," *Perspectives on Politics* 5, no. 3 (2007), 535–551; Lindberg, *Democratization by Elections;* and Michael McFaul, "Transitions from Postcommunism," *Journal of Democracy* 16, no. 3 (2005), 5–19.

they are very unusual. Moreover, our interest in Islamist movements in the Arab world should not lead us to overlook the vast majority of elections in which surprises occur that are far less disastrous—and ultimately manageable, if inconvenient—for regimes.

In short, for present purposes, the problem with current approaches to semiauthoritarian elections is not that they are wrong: the first camp is correct that most electoral authoritarian regimes have predictable results, and the second camp is correct that miscalculation can bring about dramatic change. Instead, the problem is that they can lead us to overlook the unequal but ongoing war of nerves between government and opposition that is the stuff of everyday political life in much of the Arab world. If we look at elections from this everyday perspective, they begin to appear not as minutely controlled charades or as democratic time bombs waiting to explode but as processes whose general outcomes are foreordained but whose specific results are managed and steered rather than dictated by regimes. Rulers are very much in control, but they are neither omnipotent nor omniscient. Elections therefore bring some surprises though very few shocks. Recent elections illustrate this picture. Anyone witnessing the Kuwaiti elections of 2006—which took place in the wake of a prolonged succession crisis in the ruling family—could not help but see the outcome as unpleasant for the rulers. But the ruling family, while dealt a setback, slowly regained its balance and found a way to deal with the new (and, from the rulers' perspective, extremely annoying) parliament. (And when it could no longer contain its frustration, it opted for yet another election.) In Egypt the previous year, the regime had to resort to increasingly blunt techniques in order to diminish what was still a strong electoral showing by the country's Muslim Brotherhood. In 2010, it reconfigured the rules in order to prevent a similar outcome—but it overcorrected and drove the serious opposition completely outside the parliament. (The result thus contributed to the regime's demise, but it met its end in the streets and not at the ballot box.) And in 2007, the Jordanian leadership placed enormous pressure on the opposition Islamic Action Front, finally succeeding in persuading the Muslim Brotherhood leadership to put forward a small and (from a regime perspective) relatively congenial slate, only to see the resulting recriminations within the party so hamper campaigning efforts that it ended up with a very weak electoral showing. And in 2010, the bitter residue of the 2007 elections led to an Islamist boycott.

Armed with an understanding of what semiauthoritarian politics is, how semiauthoritarian elections operate, how regimes and oppositions use elections in a semiauthoritarian environment, and, most important, how and why semiauthoritarian politics changes over time, we can now turn attention from the context to the movements themselves. What do we know about how ideological political movements react to electoral opportunities? As with semiauthoritarianism, we know a lot that is useful but we still must modify our conceptual and theoretical tools. That is the task of the following chapter.

BEYOND ANALOGY MONGERING

Ideological Movements and the
Debate over the Primacy of Politics

Islamist movements in Egypt, Jordan, Kuwait, and Palestine have dramatically if gradually increased their investment in electoral politics when they have found themselves in a semiauthoritarian environment. While they have always been interested in politics, their recent involvement is a qualitative and quantitative leap. It is not an unconditional one, nor has the payoff been unlimited. And they have been improvising in determining the level and nature of their commitment; the movements seem to be operating a bit in the dark, with no clear precedents to guide them.

Beatriz Magaloni has observed that "in the transition game, parties are viewed as unitary actors who seek to maximize votes and seats in elective office."[1] But what if (as we saw in the previous chapter) no clear transition to democracy is under way? (I do not wish to dismiss the possibility for democratization, but I do wish to maintain the focus on change within semiauthoritarian regimes and postpone discussion of the democracy until Chapter 8. In two of the cases presented in this book, there are some signs of transition: in Kuwait, there are limited possibilities to move toward a constitutional monarchy, and in Egypt after 2011 the possibility of a democratic transition suddenly and unexpectedly opened.) And what if movements are running to lose—or more precisely, as we saw in the previous chapters, participating in politics with goals other than maximizing votes and gaining office? Scholars seeking to understand such movements

---

1. Beatriz Magaloni, *Voting for Autocracy: Hegemonic Party Survival and Its Demise in Mexico* (Cambridge: Cambridge University Press, 2006), p. 229.

might also seem to be grasping in the dark, without clear precedents to guide their inquiry.

Perhaps the situation of such movements is a bit less unprecedented than initially seems the case. And perhaps scholars simply need to adapt the tools they already have rather than invent new ones. In this chapter we will attempt to shed comparative light on the issue of Islamist participation and further specify the terms of our inquiry.

We will begin with an attempt to identify why the quick and facile use of analogies to understand the politics of Islamist movements (are they more like Nazis of the 1930s or Christian Democrats of today?) can be misleading. But we will then go on to discover that a more careful comparative study of the experience of some of the same movements in late-nineteenth- and early-twentieth-century Europe is quite helpful. We will then widen our historical comparisons.

We will therefore proceed in three stages. First, we will examine the history of Christian Democracy and Social Democracy, focusing less on their tame current variants and more on the difficult process of their evolution under what might now be termed semiauthoritarian (or unconsolidated democratic) conditions. Second, we will consider the experience of movements of the radical right and left (including fascists and Communists), finding that they sometimes aimed for radical or revolutionary change but also were sometimes gradually politicized within stable systems. Finally, we will consider those parties that hold out fewer hopes for electoral majorities (often termed "niche parties") to see if their calculations and behavior are significantly different from those that hope to win elections.

The outcome of this set of comparisons will generally suggest a more specific version of the inclusion-moderation thesis: that *over time,* given a *political process that offers substantial rewards for participation and substantial risks for other strategies,* movements on the edge of a system will indeed *become politicized* and orient themselves toward securing their goals through peaceful and legal political activity. Even this more specified statement is less a conclusion than a framework; we need to shift our attention away from the general statement and pay far more attention to all the qualifications and nuances that it packs regarding time, rewards, risks, and politicization. The goal of this chapter is to use the historical comparisons—all of them showing some similarities to but also critical differences from Islamist movements in the Arab world—to develop a more sophisticated set of understandings of the effects of politics on broad ideological movements.

Thus we are searching in this chapter less for immutable rules and more for promising areas for investigation. Our purpose will not be to find an exact counterpart for Arab Islamist parties in the historical experience of different regions, but only to understand what political science scholarship has been able to uncover regarding how ideological movements in semiauthoritarian or imperfectly democratic environments evolve organizationally and ideologically. In the process of examining these other cases, we will see movements that respond to positive and negative sanctions, but often in a slow, jerky, and cranky manner; we will see that moving in the direction of acceptance of the prevailing system can be very different from moving toward the center on policy positions; and we will see that evolution involves not only ideological changes but organizational ones as well. In subsequent chapters we will use these insights to probe the effects of politics on Islamist movements in the Arab world.

Analogy Mongering

In May 2006, I served as a discussant when Sa'd al-Din al-'Uthmani, then secretary-general of Morocco's Party of Justice and Development (PJD), presented his views to a Washington audience at the Carnegie Endowment for International Peace. One of the tamest Islamist parties in the Arab world, the PJD seemed poised to finish first in the parliamentary elections scheduled a year later (in the September 2007 election, the PJD actually finished second). While quite self-confident, al-'Uthmani nevertheless found himself speaking under intense pressure from two sources. First, he was presenting the platform of an Islamist party in a city where the distinction between Islamist social movements and terrorist groups was still very hazy and often contested. Second, his party back home was divided on his trip: some activists viewed it as an inappropriate attempt to curry favor from a power that was generally seen as hostile to Islamist goals and even to Islam itself.

The moment that stands out most strongly in my memory of the event was when Michael McFaul, then a Carnegie researcher specializing in democratization, posed al-'Uthmani a difficult question: if his party went on to win the next election and al-'Uthmani was given a few moments on CNN to explain his party to an American audience only dimly aware of Morocco, what would he say? How could the PJD be presented not in the genteel atmosphere of a think tank but in the kind of sound-bite style permitted by satellite television? Al-'Uthmani grasped the need for a clear and concise message and therefore resorted to a quick analogy: the PJD was similar to the AK Party in Turkey. McFaul retorted that such an analogy would mean little to most CNN viewers. So al-'Uthmani tried again: the PJD was an Islamic version of a Christian Democratic party. Like Christian Democrats, he explained, Islamists of his stripe had a religious reference, but they were perfectly at home with the rules of democratic politics and pursued enlightened interpretations of Islam.

For al-'Uthmani's purposes, the choice was brilliant: while Christian Democratic parties have some religious roots as well as some socially conservative platforms, they are quite centrist in their politics. Better, they tend to be pro-American. If Americans were familiar with Christian Democratic leaders, they were likely to be stodgy postwar Germans; at worst, they were corrupt but cooperative Italians also from the postwar era. If the PJD was like them, then the party represented little threat to American security interests or values.

Of course, not everyone was easily convinced that al-'Uthmani was a slimmer version of Helmut Kohl. Many have been quick to view any Islamist political leader as more akin to a previous, far less genial German who led his country half a century earlier.

Indeed, it is striking how much argument about the nature of Islamist movements quickly degenerates into crude analogy mongering. Are Islamist electoral parties different from Christian Democrats (or other ideological—or formerly ideological—parties, like Social Democrats) only in the source of their ideology, but like them equally at home in the world of democratic politics? Or are they like Nazis or fascists who might occasionally use democratic mechanisms to pursue goals fundamentally at odds with the underlying principles of democratic life? Much analogy mongering is an attempt to make a quick assertion (as a substitute for argument or analysis) regarding the democratic credentials of Islamist movements.

Our focus in this book is broader and not centered on the issue of democratic credentials. But even if we were concerned only with democracy, the exclusive focus on the ideology of Islamist movements would be highly problematic: Islamists in the Arab world are asked to demonstrate their fealty to a set of democratic rules that simply do not exist and to embrace democratic ideals that others in their society (most of all, rulers) fail to practice. How can they prove their democratic credentials if there is precious little democracy to uphold?

Nevertheless, al-'Uthmani, despite his analogy mongering, may have provided more helpful guidance in a bit different manner than he intended. Our interest is in the effect of the political system on Islamist movements, as well as the effects of their participation on the semiauthoritarian environments in which they operate. Al-'Uthmani's analogy between Islamist parties and Christian Democracy is more apt than he likely realized—if we use it as the starting point for comparative inquiry rather than crude analogy mongering—for two reasons. First, the integration of Christian Democracy into European political systems was a more protracted and difficult experience than is often remembered. Second, serious pursuit of the comparison will suggest broadening our focus beyond exegesis of ideological and programmatic statements.

Al-'Uthmani was, in one sense, deeply misleading (or, to be fair, deeply misled): he was depending on (and quite likely a victim of) what Stathis Kalyvas has identified as a striking "amnesia" regarding Christian Democracy: "While the association between Catholicism and democracy may appear natural to contemporary Christian Democrats, this was not the case in the past. The ideology of the emerging Catholic movements in the 1860s and 1870s was informed by the Catholic Church's clear and unabashed opposition to liberal democracy."[2] Like Islamist parties today, Catholic and Christian Democratic parties were seen as being friendly to majoritarianism when they were in the majority but hostile to the underlying requirements of liberal democracy. An older study of Christian Democracy portrays its precursors (Catholic parties) as antiliberal and outside the bounds of accepted politics:

> Thus, the formation of Catholic parties ran afoul of the classic concepts of liberalism in three ways: by the obstinacy in which it brought to the fore a special interest (which, of course, had a most universal character), apparently incompatible with the unity of state and the national interest; by its application of the hierarchical principles of the church to politics (the old charge of "*parti-prêtre*"); and by the dangerous plebiscitarian direction of its political programs. All three points culminated in the accusation that politics for the Catholic parties was subordinate to religion. This, in view of the general state of thought, was an extraordinary and damaging accusation. For notwithstanding other differences, the liberal parties and their conservative opposition agreed on the primacy of politics; thus, a party whose real incentive came from beyond the political level naturally put itself outside the order created in 1789.[3]

Not only was Christian Democracy antiliberal; it was also not solely a political party. Instead, it was the political arm of a far-reaching social movement, connected to a powerful church and associated with a host of clubs, associations, newspapers, educational institutions, and other organizations.

As in the Arab world at present, it was not merely the religious movements whose liberal or democratic origins were questionable; the earlier European movements were born under regimes that also had at best uncertain democratic credentials. Those Christian Democratic parties active today in more stable democracies emerged out of broader social movements that often operated under what would now be called semiauthoritarian regimes. And when the parties themselves were founded as distinct organizations—often long after their

---

2. Stathis N. Kalyvas, "Unsecular Politics and Religious Mobilization," in *European Christian Democracy: Historical Legacies and Comparative Perspectives,* ed. Thomas Kselman and Joseph A. Buttigieg (Notre Dame, Ind.: University of Notre Dame Press, 2003), p. 298.

3. Hans Maier, *Revolution and Church: The Early History of Christian Democracy, 1789–1901* (Notre Dame, Ind.: University of Notre Dame Press, 1965), pp. 35–36.

broader parent movements had been established—they operated in systems that we might now term unconsolidated democracies, ones that were shaky, untested, or incomplete. Christian Democracy has a far edgier history than its currently stodgy image suggests.

Besides the Christian Democrats, many other important parties have emerged with uncertain democratic commitments out of broad social movements in political systems in which democracy was weak, unstable, sharply limited, or even fully absent. Socialist, populist, religious, and ethnic parties throughout the world may have suggestive experiences for our study of Islamist movements in the Arab world.

We will thus move on to consider a broad and diverse set of cases, from nineteenth-century Germany to twenty-first-century Turkey. Our coverage may strike specialists in these cases as cursory and almost breathless. We hope to be a little more nuanced than the analogy mongers, but more important, we intend to be far more modest. Our aim is to learn what to look for and what broader ideas to explore rather than to assert universal claims or write a comprehensive history of parties with ambiguous democratic credentials in semiauthoritarian or unstable democratic settings.

Christian and Social Democrats

Perhaps the two richest sets of cases are the Christian Democratic and Social Democratic movements. Both emerged at a time when liberalism was far from hegemonic, and democracy (universal suffrage and full accountability of the executive to electoral bodies and procedures) was seen as radical. Parliaments and elections were widespread in Europe, but the prerogatives taken today to be basic to parliaments—their role in legislation, state finances, and political oversight of the executive—remained weak, untested, or contested in most countries. The franchise was often limited as well. In much of Europe, universal suffrage and popular or parliamentary sovereignty were revolutionary causes. Christian Democracy and Social Democracy also arose in an environment in which political party systems were weak by current standards. Indeed, the Christian Democrats and Social Democrats were challenging precisely because they were well-organized political parties connected to large popular movements. Their social and political roots were broad and deep. Factions and tendencies had already risen wherever parliaments were allowed to operate, but political parties designed to win elections, staff executive offices, and make policy existed only in embryonic form. In some countries, the new Christian and Social Democratic parties thus confronted the political system with such difficulty in part because they were well-organized mass movements with comprehensive and controversial agendas but unsure how much to operate through existing institutions that were often unfriendly and certainly untested in their ability to integrate them.

For both broad movements, electoral and parliamentary politics was only one venue for their efforts, and activists debated contentiously about how much to emphasize it. Youth clubs, schools, mutual aid and charitable societies, sports leagues, and trade unions (and also, in the case of Catholics, the Church) organized large segments of the population. Christian Democracy and Socialist parties emerged as political organizations that drew on both formal and informal ties with these associations. In a sense, the parties were projects to ensure that how one lived, whether or how one prayed, what one played, which newspaper one read, and whom one turned to for help also determined how one voted.

Both kinds of parties sharply challenged the liberal order then still emerging, offering alternative visions of a society based not primarily on individual freedom but instead on particular conceptions of justice, family, God, community, solidarity, or equality. Although they were formed against liberalism, they often had a more favorable attitude toward democracy. Indeed, they seized on and poured into any political openings that appeared, though in the process they touched off strategic and ideological debates within their movements about the legitimacy, risks, benefits, and ideological enervation that might accompany the decision to contest elections.

How did political involvement affect Christian Democratic and Social Democratic movements?

Christian Democracy

The nineteenth century saw the gradual emergence of Catholic social organizations and political forces operating with some autonomy from the Church.[4]

---

4. For understanding the evolution of Christian Democracy, I have found the following works most helpful: Stathis N. Kalyvas, *The Rise of Christian Democracy in Europe* (Ithaca: Cornell University Press, 1996); Maier, *Revolution and Church;* Kselman and Buttigieg, *European Christian Democracy;* Carolyn M. Warner, *Confessions of an Interest Group: The Catholic Church and Political Parties in Europe* (Princeton, N.J.: Princeton University Press, 2000); David Hanley, *Christian Democracy in Europe: A Comparative Perspective* (London: Pinter, 1994); Michael P. Fogarty, *Christian Democracy in Western Europe, 1820–1953* (Notre Dame, Ind.: University of Notre Dame Press, 1957); Richard Webster, *Christian Democracy in Italy, 1860–1960* (London: Hollis and Carter, 1961); and Mario Einaudi and Francois Goguci, *Christian Democracy in Italy and France* (Notre Dame, Ind.: University of Notre Dame Press, 1952). Two other works helpful in understanding the context in which Christian Democratic parties arose are Otto Kirchheimer, "The Transformation of the Western European Party Systems," in *Political Parties and Political Development,* ed. Joseph LaPalombara and Myron Weiner (Princeton, N.J.: Princeton University Press, 1966); and Nancy Bermeo and Philip Nord, *Civil Society before Democracy: Lessons from Nineteenth-Century Europe* (Lanham, Md.: Rowman and Littlefield, 2000). A useful overview is Stathis N. Kalyvas and Kees van Kersbergen, "Christian Democracy," *Annual Review of Political Science* 13 (2010), 183–209.

Weak political parties arose episodically that explicitly identified themselves with Catholicism. But more impressive at first than any party was a developing social movement that sought to protect a sphere for religious institutions and values in the face of governments that were viewed as pursuing liberal, secular, or nationalist goals marginalizing religion. Authority over education and the content of instruction, for instance, was a common, often bitter, object of contention.

In the last quarter of the century, these movements began to spawn more sustained and organized political parties that often eschewed any explicit Catholic label but still sought to use the opening provided by electoral and parliamentary institutions to pursue the goal of a society friendly to religion and religious values. Some Protestant groups launched similar efforts (and in some countries Catholic and Protestant efforts eventually coalesced).

France and Italy had played prominent roles in the birth of the social movement, but the most successful Christian Democratic parties first emerged elsewhere, such as in Germany (the Center Party) and Belgium (where the party did not disavow the Catholic label until after World War II). Indeed, the Belgian party was so successful that it held an absolute majority of parliamentary seats from 1881 until the end of World War I. In Italy, France, Austria, and the Netherlands, Christian Democratic parties emerged more slowly, sometimes (especially in Italy) because the Church was not supportive of the effort, but in all these countries Christian Democrats became an important political force for large parts of the twentieth century.

Although the new Christian Democratic parties rejected secularism, they were not creatures of the Catholic Church. Indeed, the Church hierarchy was often suspicious of them, on both organizational and ideological grounds. Christian Democracy's rise entailed the emergence of a lay leadership representing Christian values and organizing the faithful in structures that remained outside Church control. Ideologically, Christian Democracy implied acceptance of parliamentary democracy and involvement in state institutions that often had a liberal, secular, or nationalist origin—and therefore Christian Democracy seemed to legitimate a political order that provoked strong reservations from the Church. In Italy, which was the most extreme case, the Church's formal opposition to all participation in the Italian republic was not fully dropped until after World War II.

The period between the two world wars at first seemed to offer Christian Democracy new possibilities because of the rise of more fully democratic political systems and the growing role of parliaments (especially because some Christian Democratic parties had developed an impressive ability to play electoral politics). But the deep ideological divide in most European societies—and the rise of parties on both the left and the right that refused to accept the legitimacy of the fledgling democratic institutions—led to the collapse of democracy in many states of the European continent. Christian Democracy was caught in this conflict between liberal democracy and its opponents. Most Christian Democratic parties supported the democratic order under attack, but they could muster little enthusiasm for some of the liberal and leftist forces that seemed associated with it. And they were frequently challenged on the right by parties less beholden to the democratic and constitutional order. The broader social movement from which Christian Democracy emerged often made its peace with (and in some countries, such as Austria, Spain, Hungary, and Portugal, actually supported) a growing right-wing nationalist and sometimes even fascist order. In Latin America, Christian Democracy did not jettison its democratic commitments quite so easily, but it retained its edgier ideological stance (taking its Christianity, and even its Catholic-inspired suspicions of liberalism, far more seriously), often until the end of the century.

The collapse of most of the undemocratic rightist systems that came with their military defeat in World War II led to Christian Democracy's greatest progress in Western Europe but also to its domestication. With democracy more firmly established, Christian Democracy's rivals on the right discredited, and the Communist left unable to present itself as an acceptable coalition partner in Western Europe, Christian Democratic parties could reposition themselves as broad-based parties of the center right. In Germany and Italy, they were more often in government than out of it throughout most of the Cold War period. Remarkably, their electoral success continued despite the steady progression and triumph of the very force that Christian Democracy had formed to combat: the secularization of European societies. And just as remarkably, a movement that had begun on the edge of legitimate politics took on an increasingly mild, even staid, character throughout this process. Far from seeking approval of others, Christian Democratic parties came to be able to bestow or withhold respectability (through forming coalitions or refusing them) with parties on either extreme of the political spectrum.

Social Democracy

Like Christian Democracy, Social Democracy emerged in the nineteenth century out of a movement motivated by principles that placed it sharply at odds with the prevailing political order.[5] Also similarly, those within the movement had

---

5. The academic literature on Social Democracy is extensive. Some works that I have found particularly useful for present purposes are Adam Przeworski and John Sprague, *Paper Stones: A History of Electoral Socialism* (Chicago: University of Chicago Press, 1986); Shari Berman, *The Primacy of Politics: Social Democracy and the Making of Europe's Twentieth Century* (Cambridge: Cambridge University Press, 2006); Gøsta Esping-Andersen, *Politics against Markets: The Social Democratic Road to Power* (Princeton, N.J.: Princeton University Press, 1985); and Herbert Kitschelt, *The Transformation of European Social Democracy* (Cambridge: Cambridge University Press, 1994).

severe doubts about (and many peremptorily rejected) the possibility of serving the movement's goals through the electoral process.

As the franchise was extended, however, the electoral arena proved too tempting for some leaders, who plunged enthusiastically into politics. Others grudgingly went along, believing it was necessary to give their movement an electoral face if only to prevent those outside the movement from organizing the same constituency. Drawing on the broader movement's impressive organizational success in the societal and trade-union realms, Social Democratic parties tended to do well in elections. But because they continued to challenge the economic and social order—and did not disavow revolutionary transition—their electoral success often stiffened ruling regimes' opposition to widening the franchise or empowering parliaments.

Where Social Democratic parties were able to translate their electoral prowess into parliamentary representation, and where parliaments were able to establish the principle of political accountability of the executive, governing fell tantalizingly within the Social Democrats' grasp—if only they could either gain a few more votes to form a majority or coax other parties into a coalition. But both these paths meant reaching beyond their electoral base and therefore downplaying or even abandoning critical ideological commitments. In the eyes of some supporters, this would mean subordinating principles to politics.

That is precisely what they did—but painfully, querulously, and only over the very long run. The parties generally did what they had to do in order to gain office, but because of the ideological nature of their movements, the steps down that path were difficult, hotly debated, and surrounded by arcane ideological disputations, recriminations, and charges of opportunism and revisionism by rivals on the left. Nor was the socialists' commitment to electoral change inevitable; in Spain they were sucked instead into a violent civil war. Each twist and turn in the transformation from serving as the political face of a revolutionary movement to posing as an electoral party willing to enter and leave the government was torturous. Social Democratic parties were often powerful performers in the electoral realm, and that made democratic triumph imaginable. But each success bred new pressures. Competing in elections, supporting the cabinet (or even agreeing to abstain in a major vote), forming parliamentary coalitions, and accepting cabinet positions: all these measures meant revising and even downplaying ideology. Perhaps party leaders could have maintained ideological purity better had they been consigned to a small share of parliamentary seats. Their success not only meant ideological revision; it also often meant finding new voters, thus diluting reliance on the working class and leading to a deemphasis of purely class issues.[6]

---

6. This process is most thoroughly explored in Przeworski and Sprague, *Paper Stones.*

Parts of the working-class movement made fewer concessions to an electoral strategy and maintained a stronger dedication to revolutionary transformation. Most of these elements gravitated toward the Communist section of the left-wing spectrum. While Communists ran for election (and indeed, in later years came to feel the same pressures to reach out to new constituencies and dilute their message that socialists had faced earlier), in the period between the two world wars Communists oscillated between being allies and rivals of Social Democrats. Communists challenged the ideological credentials of Social Democrats, competed with them for followers, and tainted them on occasion by association. Regimes varied in their responses to radical leftist groups (as they did to radical rightist groups), both between the two world wars and in the post–World War II period, but eventually Social Democrats managed to establish a strong separate identity—and the Cold War froze many Communist parties outside the legitimate political spectrum either by law or by informal understanding among other political actors. In that sense, the post–World War II order in Western Europe successfully imposed high costs for failing to accept the rules of democratic politics.

Thus, by the second half of the twentieth century, most Social Democratic parties had made the adjustments required of them to become mainstream parties of the center left. And as with the Christian Democrats, this meant that some of their greatest success in elections and governing came after the constituencies they had been formed to represent—and that had seen themselves as constituting the natural majority of the society—had begun to decline as a share of the population.

Lessons from the Politicization of Christian and Social Democracy

From a long-term perspective, the integration of Christian Democratic and Social Democratic movements into the political order of European states is impressive and complete. If there is a single lesson from their experience, it is that *over time*, given a *political process that offers substantial rewards for participation and substantial risks for other strategies*, movements on the edge of a system will indeed *become politicized* and work within legal and peaceful channels to secure their goals. This is a far more precise version of the overly general claim that inclusion can breed moderation.

Most critically, this framing of the sunny long-term view can be used to highlight rather than obscure the controversial, uncertain, and possibly even violent process of the movements' politicization. The difficulties become clear when one views the process not over the long term and retrospectively from the vantage point of stable postwar West European democracies but instead from the viewpoint of the year-to-year, even decade-to-decade battles over and within Christian Democracy and Social Democracy from the late nineteenth century forward. Seen this way, the experiences all draw our attention to the qualifications in the general statement: "*over time*" and "*a political process that offers substantial rewards for participation and substantial risks for other strategies*"; we also need to be far clearer about what we mean by "*politicization*" and not take refuge behind the slippery term "moderation."

If we seek to explore these qualifications—regarding timing as well as rewards and risks—solely in light of the experiences considered thus far, we may actually be steered toward quite pessimistic conclusions. Had things worked out differently, or indeed, where things did work out differently over the short to medium term, both movements suffered bitter defeats or accommodated themselves to antiliberal, antidemocratic orders. Even over the long term, it is difficult to understand the politicization of Christian and Social Democratic movements outside the context of the tremendous political convulsions and conflicts that shook Europe in the twentieth century: World War I and the revolutionary wave of 1917–1919 led to the demise of many regimes that had worked to restrict democratic politics; the suppression of that revolutionary wave often entailed brutal conflict; the interwar depression gave a strong impetus to socialism but also to far-right parties that were bitter enemies of the socialists and rivals of Christian Democrats; World War II destroyed those rivals, invalidated what they represented, and led to the restoration in many countries of democratic systems; and the Cold War helped support democracy in Western Europe, discrediting the far-left critics of Social Democracy in some European countries while helping Christian Democracy's turn toward tame conservatism.

This was not a set of experiences that anyone should wish to repeat. In the first half of the twentieth century, European politics was extraordinarily violent. Much (though hardly all) of this violence was among states, but the ideological and partisan struggles within states helped fuel that international conflict. In the second half of the century, the European political order claimed fewer victims but it was simultaneously sustained and threatened by the clear threat of global annihilation. The struggle over the politicization of Christian Democratic and Social Democratic movements was not the primary cause or issue of that violence (real and threatened), but it remains difficult to separate from those larger conflicts.

Even if we set aside the violence and difficulty of the process, it is hard to understand the politicization of Christian Democracy and Social Democracy without reference to long-term social, economic, and demographic trends: the secularization of the European population, the decline of the industrial working class, and sustained postwar prosperity. Thus, if what we mean by "over time," "substantial benefits and risks," and "politicization" can include a century of struggle, global conflicts, millions of deaths, the threat of nuclear war, and fundamental social and economic transformations, then we have an overly broad generalization. The experience of Christian and Social Democracy cannot be transferred comfortably to Islamists in the Arab world; we still need to proceed with great care and pay close attention to the qualifications and hedges in the general statement.

In order to explore what time period, benefits, risks, and politicization are at issue, it is helpful to review the experience of not simply those, like the Christian Democrats and Social Democrats, often cited as examples of successful politicization, but also unambiguously "anti-system" parties, especially Nazi, fascist, and Communist movements, that are used as iconic examples of the perils of "inclusion" or "engagement" with radicals. After some consideration of these other experiences, we can return to a more detailed consideration of the meaning of *"over time," "a political process that offers substantial rewards for participation and substantial risks for other strategies,"* and *"politicization."*

Movements on the Edge

The movements that concern us—the ones that spawn what are often referred to as "anti-system" parties—are diverse not only in geographical and temporal senses but also in the way in which they challenge the system. Giovanni Capoccia has introduced a useful distinction between "ideological" anti-system parties (those opposed to the core elements of a political system) and "relational" anti-system parties (those whose platforms or ideologies do not necessarily challenge the core elements of the system but place the parties at considerable distance from other political actors).[7] The distinction is not always completely clear: parties frequently leave substantial ambiguities in their programs in order to paper over internal divisions, assure critics, and appeal to diverse constituencies. And the line between reforming a system and overthrowing it can be difficult to draw. This is particularly true in the Arab world, in which rulers obscure any conceptual division between regime and state (so that in Egypt between 1952 and 2011, for instance, a call to give life to democratic mechanisms, even those that seemed to exist on paper, was tantamount to calling for radical systemic change). But Capoccia's distinction is still useful for our inquiry, for two reasons. First, as we will see, one of the main

---

7. Giovanni Capoccia, "Anti-system Parties: A Conceptual Reassessment," *Journal of Theoretical Politics* 14, no. 1 (2002), 9–35.

effects of politicization is to induce parties to become less ideologically opposed to the system. (The effect on relational anti-system orientation is less consistent; indeed, we will discover ways in which the politicization of Islamist movements has led parties into more strident opposition.) Second, the distinction helps us understand why even those Islamist parties that have never aimed to overthrow the political system (as Jillian Schwedler reminds us is frequently the case in the Arab world)[8] are still considered anti-system parties in the relational sense.

Nazis, Fascists, Communists, and Greens: Undermining Stable Systems, Being Tamed by Stable Ones

The most-cited examples of ideological anti-system parties are the Nazi and fascist movements that arose in Europe in the 1920s and 1930s. These parties used democratic openings where they were available, but their opposition to liberalism and their failure to accept democratic forms of legitimation (despite strong populist orientations) led them to treat democratic mechanisms in a highly instrumental fashion, shamelessly disregarding and overturning them when they wished. Where democratic mechanisms were new, weak, or extremely fragile (such as in Italy, Germany, Austria, and arguably Spain and Portugal), fascist or fascist-like movements (in the Iberian cases, actively supported by elements of the military) seized political power and built new, nonliberal orders. In other cases (such as France and Hungary), the movements seriously threatened the stability of the political system in the 1930s.

In short, these movements were hardly politicized in the meaning of the term employed in this book (of focusing more on political participation within an established framework). Their political involvement was aimed at overthrowing or seizing control of the existing system. It is thus not surprising that those suspicious of an inclusive approach to anti-system parties cite such worrisome analogies. More nuanced accounts of democratic breakdown (and democratic survival) in the interwar years examine not only the ideology of the challengers but also the actions of elites and the responses of other political actors. This suggests that we should take a less categorical view of whether anti-system movements can or cannot be politicized within the boundaries of an existing system: a different system or a different set of reactions can produce a different result even with such radical movements.[9]

---

8. Jillian Schwedler, *Faith in Moderation: Islamist Parties in Jordan and Yemen* (Cambridge: Cambridge University Press, 2006).

9. See, for instance, Nancy Bermeo, *Ordinary People in Extraordinary Times: The Citizenry and the Breakdown of Democracy* (Princeton, N.J.: Princeton University Press, 2003); and Giovanni Capoccia, *Defending Democracy: Reactions to Extremism in Interwar Europe* (Baltimore: Johns Hopkins University Press, 2005).

Indeed, a different kind of anti-system party emerged in Europe after World War II: sometimes referred to as "new right," "populist," or even "neo-fascist," such parties combine nationalism, anti-elitism, and appeal to issues (such as problems associated with immigrants and immigration) that critics charge hark back uncomfortably to the fascist era. But in one sense the analogy between new right and old fascist movements is misleading: the new parties may have illiberal features (and strongly intolerant, even racist overtones in their appeals), but they are not ideologically anti-system parties. Their positions place them at (or even beyond) the boundary of respectable politics, and thus they are often political pariahs, but they do not reject the basic elements of the democratic order. Most of these parties did not emerge until after functioning democracies established (or reestablished) themselves. The parties have had varying levels of effectiveness: generally, but not always, shut out of government at the national level, they still make their presence felt by demonstrating the electoral appeal of certain issues and positions, sometimes sucking more respectable parties in their ideological direction.

Thus participation may not have tamed many of the ideological fascist parties of the interwar era, but this was largely because their rise was accompanied by— and contributed to—the collapse of the political order. The rise of the movements may simply have been too strong and swift for fragile systems to bear. More stable systems induced postwar movements based on similar appeals to reject any revolutionary or ideological anti-system path. In that sense, the movements have become politicized. But that has not always softened their positions; only a portion of the relational anti-system parties emerging in the last few decades have moved toward the center on policy issues.[10]

This experience is suggestive rather than conclusive, but it is mirrored by the experience of the Communist and Green movements. Both began as ideological anti-system parties but eventually transformed into relational anti-system parties as they came to terms with the stability of the postwar political environment, Communists extremely gradually and Greens more quickly.

---

10. There is now considerable literature on the impact of parties of the far right (as well as other anti-system and niche parties) and how political systems and other political actors shape the opportunities presented to them. See, for instance, Paul Taggart, "New Populist Parties in Western Europe," *West European Politics* 18, no. 1 (1995), 34–51; Jens Rydgren, "Is Extreme Right-Wing Populism Contagious? Explaining the Emergence of a New Party Family," *European Journal of Political Research* 44 (2005), 413–437; James Adams, Michael Clark, Lawrence Ezrow, and Garrett Glasgow, "Are Niche Parties Fundamentally Different from Mainstream Parties? The Causes and the Electoral Consequences of Western European Parties' Policy Shifts, 1976–1998," *American Journal of Political Science* 50, no. 3 (2006), 513–529; and Bonnie M. Meguid, "Competition between Unequals: The Role of Mainstream Party Strategy in Niche Party Success," *American Political Science Review* 99, no. 3 (2005), 347–359.

Communist movements entered the electoral arena with far less conviction than the Social Democratic parties referred to above, and the political systems in which they operated returned the skepticism. Like Christian Democrats and Social Democrats, Communists could perform credibly at the ballot box because they were armed with the support of a host of organizations (especially trade unions) that could turn out supporters to vote. But accepting liberal democratic forms of legitimacy was ideologically far more difficult for parties that held to revolutionary goals. In the interwar years, Communist parties were often compared with fascist movements for the way they used democratic mechanisms opportunistically without dropping their anti-system ideology. After World War II, their anti-system positions became increasingly ambiguous, as they found themselves subject to the same calculations that had affected the behavior and stances of Social Democratic parties earlier. If they wished to perform well in elections, they needed to broaden their appeal; if they wished to think about participating in the government, they had to lessen their ideological opposition to the prevailing order. They did both, but with a gradualism and degree of ambiguity that left them relationally anti-system parties until (and sometimes even after) the waning of the Cold War. Communist movements—whose ideological debates could be Jesuitical—had more difficulty adjusting programs and jettisoning rhetorical commitments than virtually any other movement (a particularly ironic fact given their historical materialism).[11]

Green parties have faced a similar calculus, though they have tended to replicate the trajectory toward integration far more quickly. In some ways, they may be the closest ideological counterparts to Islamist movements because they were founded not simply on a political agenda sharply at odds with those of prevailing parties but also on a different social and moral vision. Like the Islamists, they have a tendency to integrate the personal and the political. Also like Islamists, Green party activists take their ideological commitments quite seriously but still find them a poor guide to tactical and even strategic decision making, since their ideologies are very general and do not exist in any codified or canonical form. For precisely this reason, the debates about participation in elections and government, though heated, have been resolved with greater ease and fewer fissures

---

11. The matter could be far more complicated for Communist parties than this short summary indicates. For instance, the parties sometimes faced a choice between a confrontational approach that might increase their reputations as anti-system parties but result in a net gain rather than a loss in votes. Alternatively, a cooperative approach with other parties that might offer it a share of respectability or even official office might disillusion enthusiastic supporters and depress vote share. The dilemmas may have been particularly acute for the Italian Communist party, which ironically found that the closer it came to "historic compromise," the fewer votes it received. For an interesting analysis, see Roberto D'Alimonte, "Party Behavior in a Polarized System: The Italian Communist Party and the Historic Compromise," in *Policy, Office, or Votes? How Political Parties in Western Europe Make Hard Decisions,* ed. Wolfgang C. Muller and Kaare Strom (Cambridge: Cambridge University Press, 1999).

than those that afflicted the working-class parties of the left. Green parties moved from being relationally anti-system (with ideological anti-system elements) when they began as movements in the 1970s (and formally as political parties in the early 1980s) to fully politicized and even well-integrated parties, sometimes participating in the government, in the 1990s.

The experience of new right, Communist, and Green parties in postwar Europe—especially when compared with anti-system parties in the interwar period—suggest that well-established and secure systems can pressure or entice ideologically anti-system parties into becoming relational anti-system parties. The effect on relational anti-system parties is less consistent: politicization smoothed the harsh ideological edges for some, but others found that plunging into electoral politics gave fewer rewards for the ideologically tepid.

Anti-system Parties in Shakier Systems

What of less secure or stable democracies? Or of parties that know they are consigned to electoral ghettos? Does the interwar European experience suggest that such systems are likely to be too insecure, unstable, or unattractive to have any taming effect? Before we rush to such a conclusion, we should consider some other experiences. Perhaps the most notable are those of the AKP in Turkey—the analogy preferred by al-'Uthmani—and the BJP in India. Both offer a highly qualified but also far more positive picture of the ability of less well established political systems to induce the politicization of movements on the edge.

The Turkish case suggests the importance of negative as well as positive incentives and shows that such inducements can operate even in a shaky and incomplete democracy. Over the life of the Turkish Republic, a variety of political parties have challenged the Kemalist secularist mandate, one that subordinates public expressions of religion to state authority.[12] Such parties have generally been suppressed, sometimes as a result of military intervention. The most recent period of direct military rule, 1980–1983, resulted in some shifts in Turkish secularism. Not only did the security establishment lay a strong claim to a nationalist-religious synthesis,[13] but the dominant politician for the following

---

12. On Islamist politics in Turkey generally, see Jenny White, *Islamist Mobilization in Turkey: A Study in Vernacular Politics* (Seattle: University of Washington Press, 2002); Gamze Cavdar, "Islamist *New Thinking* in Turkey: A Model for Political Learning," *Political Science Quarterly* 121, no. 3 (2006), 477–497; Fulya Atacan, "Explaining Religious Politics at the Crossroad: AKP-SP," *Turkish Studies* 6, no. 2 (2005), 187–199; William Hale, "Christian Democracy and the AKP: Parallels and Contrasts," *Turkish Studies* 6, no. 2 (2005), 293–310; and Berna Turam, *Between Islam and the State: The Politics of Engagement* (Stanford, Calif.: Stanford University Press, 2007).

13. See Sam Kaplan, *The Pedagogical State: Education and the Politics of National Culture in Post-1980 Turkey* (Stanford, Calif.: Stanford University Press, 2006), especially chap. 5.

decade, Turgut Özal (prime minister until 1989 and then president until his death in 1993), was friendlier to religious themes than his pre-coup predecessors. While these differences were fairly subtle, the post-coup order also saw the reemergence and growing electoral strength of parties with a far stronger Islamic coloration—first the Welfare Party, then the Virtue Party, and finally the Justice and Development Party (AKP). These parties realized strong success at the municipal level but provoked strong opposition from the military, other state institutions, and some portions of the more secular political elite on the national stage.

Nevertheless, backed by a wide-ranging social movement with deep roots, the new parties were able to do well in parliamentary elections. The Welfare Party, which drew on right-wing nationalist as well as Islamic roots, was sufficiently successful to form a coalition government beginning in 1996 but was forced from office by a heavy-handed threat of military intervention in 1997. In 1998, the Constitutional Court banned the party. The Virtue Party quickly stepped into the gap but was itself banned by the same court three years later.

Finally, the AKP, many of whose leaders came from the less strident elements of the Virtue Party, proved able to succeed where its predecessors had failed. It claimed to accept secularism and embrace only traditional and conservative values. It coupled this with a pro-European policy as well as a free-market orientation that helped assure Turkey's allies and business community that it represented no threat to their interests. The AKP formed the government in 2002, winning again in 2007. The repression of the AKP's predecessors—and threat of repression that was never absent from the Turkish political scene—worked deep if gradual effects on the kind of religious opposition parties that emerged. The AKP, the most recent iteration of the attempt to build a successful party, not only won elections but was allowed to rule. Yet it paid a price: it made so many adjustments to its ideology and program that it no longer fits the definition of an Islamist party in the formal sense of explicitly advocating that public life be predicated on an Islamic reference. While the AKP draws on religious symbols, espouses conservative social values, relies on an Islamic social movement, and is led by individuals known for personal piety, the party itself rejects the Islamist label. (By 2010, it had become clear as well that the AKP's success had progressed so far that its domination of the system rather than incorporation by it had become the issue. The party's electoral performance put it in a position to amend the constitution and directly challenge some of the actors that had forced its past ideological compromises.)

The AKP made ideological adjustments in response to sanctions and threats. But sometimes opportunities offered by politics lead a party to make adjustments in techniques and tactics rather than ideology. A leading example is India's Bharatiya Janata Party (BJP). Like Turkey's, India's democracy was imperfect, though it was marred not by military intervention but by long-term, one-party dominance by the Congress Party and even a brief period of dictatorship from 1975 to 1977. Before 1974, the BJP's predecessors were unable to crack either national or local government. In the 1977 elections that ended the dictatorship, the elements that later formed the BJP participated in a broad and victorious opposition coalition. The BJP itself was formed in 1980 and began to merge its strident nationalist appeal with a pro-business platform more attractive to elements of India's middle class.[14] Despite its extremist reputation, it was able to combine electoral success with coalition building sufficiently to form a cabinet briefly in 1996 and govern between 1998 and 2004.

The BJP showed an ability to recast its platform to earn votes (in this case by a pro–private sector tilt) and form coalitions with other parties. But as Sanjay Ruparelia has observed, this should not be taken as indisputable evidence that institutions can force a party to engage in self-limiting behavior. The party was supplementing its appeal, not modifying it. Like other movements on the edge of a political system, the BJP faced tensions between the pressures of its base and the need to form alliances with other parties. Like other parties, it chose to react not only by making difficult choices on occasion but also by attempting to avoid them—in this case, when it sought to rally its followers by taking actions that heightened communal tensions. The effect of such a tactic was to foster violence and polarize politics in a way that worked to the BJP's advantage.[15] The use of polarizing techniques for electoral purposes is hardly a BJP invention, of course—indeed, in some countries, political parties seeking to mobilize supporters might even conjure or politicize divisions that had not been salient before.[16] The effects of such techniques are probably particularly pernicious in less stable settings.

The opportunities opened by India's politics allowed the BJP to avoid, for the short term, jettisoning those aspects of its ideology that had led to its relational anti-system reputation. If the BJP is toning down its strident and intolerant nationalism, the process is happening gradually. The lesson of the BJP's experience is that creative party leaders can respond to threats and opportunities in a variety of ways; rather than make clear ideological commitments, the BJP's leaders managed to avoid them.

If we extend our focus a bit, we will see other kinds of parties and movements that try to taste the benefits of participation without making clear ideological commitments that might dilute their appeal or divide their constituencies.

---

14. Pradeep Chhibber, "Who Voted for the Bharatiya Janata Party?" *British Journal of Political Science* 27, no. 4 (1997), 631–639.

15. Sanjay Ruparelia, "Rethinking Institutional Theories of Political Moderation: The Case of Hindu Nationalism in India, 1996–2004," *Comparative Politics* 38, no. 3 (2006), 317–336.

16. See, for example, Adrienne LeBas, "Polarization as Craft: Party Formation and State Violence in Zimbabwe," *Comparative Politics* 38, no. 4 (2006), 419–438.

The parties examined thus far—socialists, fascists, Communists, Greens, nationalist, and religious—all share a common feature: each saw itself as representing the interests of the community as a whole, or at least the majority (whether it had the votes of most members or not). This heightened the attractions of electoral participation and ultimately of democracy as a principle: a party that sees itself as representing the majority will generally view majoritarian practices as serving its long-term interests. Politicization often led movements and parties to move away from an ideological anti-system position while sometimes remaining relationally anti-system.

Yet what of parties that seek to advance the interests of only a portion of society? Oddly, such parties often show the precise opposite pattern: their politicization leads them to decrease their relational anti-system character while they seek to retain their purity as ideological anti-system parties. In other words, they will reject a system in principle but participate in practice in order to secure benefits for their constituents. Minority and ethnic parties—such as those in Northern Ireland, Spain, and Israel—often show such a tendency to regard the political system in a cold but instrumental way. Such parties strike strong ideologically anti-system poses, especially when the political system seems to promise permanent subordinate status for their constituents. Sometimes this takes violent form (such as in the Northern Irish and Basque cases); other times strong but nonviolent oppositions (as with Arab parties in Israel); and still other times quiet contempt (as with ultra-Orthodox Jewish parties in Israel).[17] But offered real concessions to their constituents—welfare benefits, seats in the cabinet, constitutional reform, or devolution—some of these niche anti-system parties have taken the bait. In general, such parties will be far more likely to make tactical concessions than they will be to embrace the prevailing order as an explicit and strategic choice. Even hints of an ideological shift are difficult for those parties that have armed wings (or that represent constituencies that have such bodies) since they will be caught between a militant group able to disrupt any inclusionary approach and a broader constituency that sometimes hopes for practical gains.

Climbing in from the Edge?
International Lessons

We may now return to further specifying the statement that "*over time,* given a *political process that offers substantial rewards for participation and substantial*

---

17. For attempts to understand such parties, see Sultan Tepe, "Religious Parties and Democracy: A Comparative Assessment of Israel and Turkey," *Democratization* 12, no. 3 (2005), 283–307; and Peter R. Neumann, "'The Bullet' and the Ballot Box: The Case of the IRA," *Journal of Strategic Studies* 28, no. 6 (2005), 941–975.

risks for other strategies, movements on the edge of a system will indeed become *politicized* and orient themselves toward securing their goals through peaceful and legal political activity."

It bears emphasizing again that our purpose in this chapter is only to highlight possibly relevant factors in understanding the evolution of movements. Capoccia, author of one of the most rigorous studies of the subject, concludes resignedly that "comparative politics has not yet achieved even a minimally systematic knowledge of the complex phenomenon of reactions to extremism in democracies."[18] And even if there were definitive lessons from these experiences, they would be imperfect guides to exploring the particular conditions of the Arab world.

Yet if we have learned nothing definitive, we have uncovered much that is highly suggestive. What explains the timing of change? How are risks and benefits calculated? And what is the nature of the politicization we have so often referred to?

Over Time: The Stickiness of Ideology and Experience

We now should suspect that ideology can matter, especially when it comes to the timing and pace of change.

This goes against the grain of many recent writings. Scholars who study the integration of movements on the edge of a system generally view ideological change as following rather than causing changes in behavior. Writing about religious parties, Stathis N. Kalyvas explains:

> It is my contention, therefore, that the study of religious mobilization requires that we take religious doctrines for what they are, that is, flexible and malleable statements of often ambiguous political intent, as opposed to rigidly predictive policy platforms. Hence we need to move beyond political theologies, semantics, ideology, and the search for the "essence" or the "correct interpretation" of religious doctrines and focus on actors and institutions.[19]

Kalyvas is right. As seriously as their adherents take them, ideologies are often general and plastic and thus very uncertain guides to action.

But ideology can still make a difference: a careful examination of the experience of parties presented here suggests that even if ideology ultimately changes under pressure, it does so slowly and unevenly. Creeds, programs, and statements

---

18. Capoccia, *Defending Democracy,* p. 242.
19. Stathis N. Kalyvas, "Unsecular Politics and Religious Mobilization: Beyond Christian Democracy," in *European Christian Democracy,* ed. Kselman and Buttigieg, p. 297.

can make behavior a bit sticky for ideological parties; they may frequently bend and evolve, but they tend to do so reluctantly and erratically. Ideology is not merely something that can be molded to woo skeptics. The ideological and pro-grammatic statements issued by a party are used to guide leaders, resolve de-bates among factions of a movement, and motivate and recruit followers. While general statements can be applied in many different ways, they are not infinitely elastic, nor can they be changed on short notice without a severe risk of schism or alienation of key groups; frequent or radical shifts will earn charges of opportun-ism among followers and critics alike. Further, leaders of ideological movements will hesitate to jettison the strong commitments that attracted them in the first place to the movement.

Thus, when the parties examined in this chapter did respond to opportunities and threats—and they almost always did—they moved cautiously, step by step. Or more precisely, perhaps, they took a long series of half steps: running for par-liament while eschewing participation in the cabinet, securing policy concessions in return for abstentions in key parliamentary votes, justifying shifts in tactical rather than strategic terms, and seeking to square old ideological commitments with new positions. Christian Democracy and Social Democracy, for instance, never repudiated their separate critiques of liberalism but increasingly aimed less to combat the liberal order than to correct its perceived excesses (with social wel-fare policies, for instance, or pro-family measures). After World War II, Christian Democracy came to embrace a form of "personalism" that seemed quite tame in its attempt to correct liberalism's "individualism."[20] Social Democratic parties, growing out of an intensely ideological environment, similarly adapted to the postwar order. The degree and pace with which the parties repositioned them-selves varied with the nature of their rhetorical and ideological commitments.[21]

We now have some understanding of how ideology may affect the timing and pace of a party's evolution, but what about its direction?

Rewards and Risks: The Complex Calculus of Movements on the Edge

Let us now turn to the second hedge, that parties will be politicized within a political process that offers substantial rewards for participation and substan-tial risks for other strategies. In the cases considered thus far, most of the re-wards were obvious: opportunities to take office and affect policy. And those

---

20. Emiel Lamberts, "Christian Democracy and the Constitutional State in Western Europe, 1945–1995," in *European Christian Democracy*, ed. Kselman and Buttigieg, p. 124.
21. Kitschelt, *Transformation of European Social Democracy*, p. 278.

opportunities were determined by the political rules and structures (the openness of democratic procedures and the nature of those procedures) as well as the nature of the society (movements representing potential majorities naturally finding democratic procedures especially attractive). Risks, such as repression or competition, as well as rewards served to affect a movement on the edge of political respectability. Yet while these risks are real, movements have varied in their responses. Repression, for instance, is often held to backfire against regimes when it undercuts opposition leaders who favor a political strategy. In some cases, harsh state measures have indeed radicalized movements. Repression can also work, however, especially when combined with other, more ameliorative strategies aimed at splitting a movement's leadership or siphoning off its supporters.[22] Indeed, there is little way to explain the gradual taming of Turkish Islamism without reference to the waves of repression, military interventions, threats of intervention, and heavy-handed action by courts.

While there has been variation in the effects of rewards and risks, the actual process by which movements climb in from the edge has been fairly similar when it has taken place. The availability of viable opportunities to gain office or influence policy through the democratic process affected a movement by fostering the rise of a group of activists (often ensconced within a political party linked to the broader movement) committed to the political process and by strengthening their hand in internal movement debates. To be sure, there were many kinds of formal and informal linkages between the political parties discussed here and the broader movements from which they sprang. But there was surprising consistency in the debates that occurred among activists in those movements and parties over political participation. There were reliable flash points: over whether to field candidates in elections, over the relationship between parliamentarians and the broader movement leadership, and over whether to enter the government. In all these decisions, over the long term (for the reasons explored above, there was often considerable delay), the parties discussed here tended to rise above their pariah status—whether self-imposed or not—as the political leadership increased its autonomy and influence within the movement.

Gaining office and influencing policy were the chief reward, but more open political systems could offer a less immediately obvious reward as well whose benefits were clear to the entire movement and not merely the politically inclined: the ability to organize and find channels of communication with critical constituencies. Indeed, this reward was available not only in stable democracies but also

---

22. Capoccia, *Defending Democracy.*

in incomplete and unstable democracies—and to a significant degree in semi-authoritarian systems as well. A political system that is partially pluralistic—or that wishes to appear pluralistic—will allow opposition movements the opportunity to organize within certain boundaries. A movement seeking radical political or social change might take advantage of such openness to present itself as a political party seeking only legal protection and recognition of its status.

We have uncovered as well that movement away from ideological anti-system postures is very separate from movement on relational anti-system positions. Indeed, movement on the first often discourages movement on the second as leaders strive to retain and motivate followers during periods of ideological adjustment by taking strident policy positions. For instance, socialists and right-wing movements that have seen little possibility of governing often found that political openness offered their movements real benefits that they were anxious to protect—but few incentives for programmatic evolution. Indeed, in such an environment, movements have been beholden to core constituencies and grassroots activists who resist substantial changes in the movement's positions. Mobilizing such followers often depends not on softening the message but on confrontational appeals and rhetoric.[23]

Politicization: What Does It Mean to Climb in from the Edge?

This mixture of rewards and risks—and striking parallels in how movements assess and debate them—helps us specify what we mean by "politicization" and allows us to avoid the term "moderation," with its host of associations that vary from one user to the next. We have discovered that politicization is as much an organizational as an ideological subject. A movement can be viewed as politicized to the degree to which it emphasizes a political strategy that works through existing institutional and constitutional arrangements.

That is precisely how matters have been understood by Social Democrats, Christian Democrats, Communists, and Greens, as well as Islamists: What is the relative importance of politics? How should a party be organized, and what should be its relationship to the broader movement? How much should a movement invest in politics, and how does political work supplement or distract from other strategies? Often the most bitter debates take place over how much to stress politics and how seriously to take political (especially electoral) participation. Leaders worry about what the degree and form of participation mean for being

---

23. For cases in which parties deliberately followed polarizing strategies, see Ruparelia, "Rethinking Institutional Theories," and LeBas, "Polarization as Craft."

co-opted, banned, excluded, sucked in, gaining supporters, losing adherents, diverting energies, growing resources.

This debate takes organizational form, sometimes with the rise of a professional or politically oriented group within the leadership and sometimes in the form of political parties that have some autonomy from the broader movement. Allowing the emergence of political leaders and structures has attractions for movements that see opportunities in the political realm, but it also carries costs for those that see such opportunities as distracting or inherently limited.

Even in a movement committed to some political activity, the question becomes how much to stress politics—or sometimes why to stress it. Is the primary purpose of politics to govern or spread the word? The two are not mutually exclusive, but especially in semiauthoritarian systems or uncertain democracies they pull in different directions. For an ideological or religious party, or one tied to a broader movement, there are often different orientations within the party. Kenneth Greene has written of "office-seekers" who believe "you cannot change policy unless you first win elections" and "message-seekers" who instead insist that "winning is only valuable if it reflects social transformation from the bottom up."[24] Semiauthoritarianism leaves few openings for pure "office-seekers," but it often generates tensions between those who wish to build the political party and those who seek to concentrate on the overarching goals of the social movement. The two camps can, and do, protest that their goals are the same, but their tactics can differ.

Besides capturing the process as movements often experience it, the term "politicization" has the benefit of alerting us to the dual nature of the process: it is necessary to ask not only if movements are reorienting or reorganizing themselves (as "moderation" implies) but also whether the system in which they operate is enticing them to do so.

Turning to Islamist Movements in the Arab World

The range of experiences considered thus far suggests many parallels to Islamist movements and parties in the Arab world, though all the comparisons are imperfect. We have learned that movements on the edge of a political system respond

---

24. Kenneth F. Greene, "Creating Competition: Patronage Politics and the PRI's Demise," Kellogg Institute Working Paper 345, December 2007, http://citeseerx.ist.psu.edu/viewdoc/download?doi=1 0.1.1.126.5276&rep=rep1&type=pdf.

to positive and negative incentives but often slowly and with difficulty; that there is variation among and within movements about how much to value positive incentives and avoid negative ones; that movement toward politicization does not necessarily mean relaxing other positions; and that politicization has important organizational and not merely ideological aspects.

Like many examples cited thus far, Arab Islamist parties exist in a context of popular movements with broad (and not merely political) goals; the political leadership is frequently challenged by those who wish to emphasize nonpolitical aspects of the movement's agenda as well as by those suspicious that participation under prevailing conditions will lead to co-optation. The movements have sometimes taken significant strides toward accepting democratic mechanisms (aided by their self-image as representing natural majorities) and even liberalism (though perhaps more in the direction of a stance similar to the "personalism" of Christian Democrats mentioned above). But these steps are controversial within both the party and the broader movement.

Not only are the parties viewed suspiciously by many in or vaguely allied with the broader movement, but the party and the movement are both viewed suspiciously by other political actors. These suspicions stem partly from the universalist ideologies of the movements—their claim to represent the interests of the entire society and the alleged hostility this provokes in such movements to any who do not share their objectives. Indeed, Islamist parties, like many of the parties considered here, seem to their critics to combine two contradictory vices: they are niche parties, pursuing a highly particularistic agenda. At the same time, they are denounced for claiming a privileged relationship with universal and eternal truths.

We have seen in this chapter how a rich variety of experiences shows what politicization means, how it takes place, what encourages it, and what discourages it. Only a portion of the systems examined were semiauthoritarian, but the variety of cases still revealed how we have to focus on protracted processes, the sticky nature of ideological change, the particular mix of threats and benefits, the ways in which evolution has organizational as well as ideological aspects, and the importance of considering how these threats and benefits are perceived and weighed by the movements.

Armed with this understanding, we can now proceed to our study of Islamist movements to understand how they have evaluated and reacted to the opportunities and threats that semiauthoritarian Arab regimes present to them. Our coverage of these movements will proceed in two parts. First, in Chapters 4 and 5, we will focus on the Muslim Brotherhood model in general and in four settings. What is the model and how it is likely to operate in a semiauthoritarian context? In Chapter 4, we will study the original model and consider how it seems (accidentally) designed to cope very effectively with semiauthoritarianism. In Chapter 5, we will see how it has actually operated in Egypt, Jordan, Kuwait, and Palestine as those systems became semiauthoritarian and opened and closed various opportunities. We will then look more thematically at the way the movements have adjusted their organizations (Chapter 6) and ideologies (Chapter 7) in reaction to semiauthoritarian conditions.

THE MODEL AND THE MOTHER MOVEMENT

Be prepared!

—Motto of the Muslim Brotherhood

O Brothers: You are not a charitable society nor a political party nor a body established for the purposes of limited goals. But you are a new spirit flowing in the heart of this community [*umma*] and revived by the Qur'an, a new light rising and dispelling the darkness of the material with knowledge of God. . . . Say that we call to the Islam brought by Muhammad, God's blessing and peace be upon him. Government is part of that and freedom is among its duties. It will be said to you that this is politics! So say that this is Islam and we do not know such divisions. If it is said to you that you are preachers of revolution, then say that we are calling for truth and peace which we believe in and hold dear.

—Hasan al-Banna, "Between Yesterday and Today," 1941

We have seen how semiauthoritarianism operates, and we have begun to build some ideas about how social movements with ambitious agendas might react to the opportunities semiauthoritarian politics leaves open. In this chapter, we turn our attention more specifically to the model of the Muslim Brotherhood, the central focus of this book. Semiauthoritarian regimes and the Muslim Brotherhood model seem virtually (if partly unintentionally) made for each other. Semiauthoritarian regimes provide the circumstances in which Islamist movements can flourish, at least by the anemic standards set by other opposition forces in such circumstances. Islamist movements are often willing to provide the self-limitations and assurances that semiauthoritarian regimes demand from the opposition; they have the organizational resilience and adaptability to reconfigure themselves to take advantage of the opportunities and survive the limitations that the vagaries of semiauthoritarian politics impose on them; and they combine a firm sense of mission with programmatic flexibility, making them appear both principled and responsive to a potential opposition audience in a semiauthoritarian polity. We will examine this model first with a quick review of its emergence and then with a study of the model in more detail, paying special attention to these features, which seem to fit semiauthoritarian conditions so well.[1]

This chapter is divided into four parts. The first is a historical examination of the emergence of the Muslim Brotherhood. The history of the Brotherhood's first three decades is fairly well known; our effort here will be to draw on and develop those understandings in order to explore (implicitly in this chapter and more explicitly in subsequent chapters) why the movement is able to react with agility to semiauthoritarian conditions.

The second and third parts of the chapter are analytical rather than historical, but the purpose is the same: to explore first the distinct organizational form and second the general ideological stance of Brotherhood-type movements, with an eye to how these characteristics position the movements to react to political conditions. Finally, in the fourth part, we will bring these general characteristics into sharper focus by comparing them with other Islamist movements built on different models.

In the next chapter, we will turn our attention to the different chapters of the Muslim Brotherhood in the Arab world. The purposes of the two chapters taken together are to show how the movements operate in semiauthoritarian conditions and to understand the politics surrounding movements based on this distinct organizational form. But in the process we will also be able to lay the basis for the analysis of the subsequent chapters, which will shift the focus from specific movements to a more thematic analysis of the organizational and ideological effects of participation in semiauthoritarian conditions.

Islamist movements modeled on the Muslim Brotherhood have an unusual set of organizational characteristics and often display a similar set of paradoxical traits. They are resilient and adaptable but also reactive and slow moving. They display the first trait by surviving in many different and difficult settings; they display the second when they spend inordinate amounts of time on simple

---

1. Tarek Masoud's superb study of the Muslim Brotherhood in recent Egyptian parliamentary elections makes a similar but more specific argument, that the electoral system that emerged in Egypt in recent years was ideally suited for the Muslim Brotherhood as an organization. I find his argument persuasive, but I also note that aside from the way the law operates (accidentally—and, as befits a semiauthoritarian regime, because of a series of incremental modifications in the legal framework), Brotherhood movements still perform relatively better than most other opposition forces. Countries with different systems (such as Jordan, which Masoud analyzes) reward the Brotherhood less than the system that emerged in the first decade of the 2000s in Egypt but still provide opportunities in a way that allows Brotherhood-type movements to outperform opposition rivals. See Tarek El-Miselhy Masoud, "Why Islam Wins: Electoral Ecologies and Economies of Political Islam in Contemporary Egypt" (PhD diss., Yale University, 2008).

decisions and cast their slow reactions as the virtue of patience. Brotherhood movements have the organizational discipline of a Leninist party but the diffuse looseness and heterogeneity of a broad social movement. They show the first characteristic when movement leaders clearly operate in accordance with the principle of democratic centralism and defend decisions they opposed in internal deliberations; they exhibit the second by reaching into many diverse fields and operating through a welter of organizations that have some autonomy from the main movement. The Brotherhood is a highly ideological organization with prescribed texts and study sessions, but it rarely enforces any particular ideas nor does it allow ideological debates to spiral into schisms. While the various country-based movements of the Brotherhood are based on the idea that religion is a unified and unerring source of truth, they tolerate a wide range of interpretations of that truth within their ranks. With only a few exceptions, Islamist movements combine a fierce demand for loyalty with a collective and consensual decision-making structure that obstructs the emergence of charismatic leaders.

Brotherhood movements are unusual in some respects, but they also are not unique: they share many of these features with other religious, political, ideological, and social movements. The two quotations used as an epigraph for this chapter point us in some helpful directions in understanding what is distinctive and unusual about Islamist movements and what is not. The first quotation—"Be prepared!"—has been the motto of the Brotherhood since the movement's early days. It is shared, of course, with the Boy Scouts.[2] The resemblance between Brothers and Scouts goes beyond wording. Hasan al-Banna, the Brotherhood's founder, began his organizational work in an environment in which the Scouts and similar youth movements were widely known, and he was certainly influenced and inspired in part by them (indeed, the Brotherhood formed its own Scout wing).[3] But the resemblance is only partial. Al-Banna worked to construct an even more broadly focused organization than the Scout model suggested. The parallel between Brothers and Scouts remains helpful, however, since it draws attention to the Brotherhood's focus on personal development and other activities that can fall far from the interests of conventional political parties.

---

2. The far more well known slogan of the Muslim Brotherhood, especially for election campaigns, is "Islam is the solution." I have not been able to trace use of that slogan back before the 1980s. The motto "Be prepared!" (*wa-a'iddu*) appears on the movement's seal; it certainly invites comparison to the Boy Scouts that may not be completely coincidental, but it is taken from the Qur'an (8:60). I am grateful to Clark Lombardi for bringing the motto to my attention.

3. On al-Banna's experiments with scouting, see Gudrun Krämer, *Hasan al-Banna* (Oxford: Oneworld, 2010), pp. 54–57.

The second quotation, by contrast, was uttered over seven decades ago but is much better known than the movement's actual motto. It (or similar statements issued by al-Banna in the movement's first decade) is cited in many, if not most, Arabic-language writings on the Brotherhood and pops up in a good number of English-language writings as well. But what did al-Banna mean by defining the Brotherhood as "a new spirit flowing in the heart of this community and revived by the Qur'an, a new light rising and dispelling the darkness of the material with knowledge of God"? Why is such a maddeningly Delphic declaration so useful in shedding light on the Brotherhood's nature? As political scientists, we may know how to study political parties, social movements, and religious orders. But whatever are we to do with "new spirits" or "new lights"—especially ones that "do not know" divisions or distinctions?

Al-Banna's proclamation is useful precisely because it suggests an organization with many forms: it shows the many things the Brotherhood works to be. The statement illustrates the broad and flexible agenda of the movement and suggests a diverse range of organizational expressions. For our purposes, since we wish to understand something about Islamist movements in politics, we will need to probe how they attempt to be political parties and not political parties at the same time. And we will need to be alert to variations in both the nature and the amount of their involvement in politics over time, the ways that political goals overlap with but also may operate at cross-purposes with nonpolitical goals.

The Mother Movement: The Model of the Muslim Brotherhood in Egypt

Egypt's Muslim Brotherhood has set the pattern for the other Islamist movements discussed in this book, and many of the various movements it spawned in other countries continue to refer to the original Egyptian organization as the "mother movement." Its flexible organization and its general (sometimes vague) emphasis on reform have set the example and tone that other movements have tried to follow. That organization and ideology led the movement to increase its political involvement slowly over time, and it is therefore to the formation and gradual (if partial) politicization of the Brotherhood that we now turn.[4]

---

4. There is an extensive literature on the Brotherhood's history in both English and Arabic. English-language readers have several strong book-length studies that overlap to some degree but emphasize different periods. For the founding of the Brotherhood and its first two decades, the leading work is Brynjar Lia, *The Society of the Muslim Brothers in Egypt: The Rise of an Islamic Mass Movement, 1928–1942* (Reading, U.K.: Ithaca Press, 1998). Also covering the founding but focusing more on the

The Muslim Brotherhood was formed in Egypt in 1928 and spread rapidly, first in Egyptian society and then more broadly in many Arab countries (and eventually outside the Arab world). The movement began in Isma'iliyya, a provincial city, but its headquarters moved along with Hasan al-Banna, the founder, to Cairo in 1931. Even at its founding, the Brotherhood's focus was extensive and ambitious. It mimicked not only the Boy Scouts but also Christian missionary organizations and soon plunged into charitable, educational, and religious work.[5] The leading account of the organization's origins stresses that al-Banna was motivated from the beginning precisely by the desire to form a very broad organization that transcended more focused and restricted existing organizational forms (such as youth movements or charitable societies).[6]

Indeed, members of Brotherhood movements in various countries continue to this day to describe their goal as reform of the individual and reform of the society—naturally, along Islamic lines. Such an ambitious agenda suggests a wide range of activities, from the formation of small study groups to educational work to charitable activity to public advocacy of religious values (through preaching and publishing, for instance) to running for office. And the Brotherhood's rapid rise in membership (after a mere decade and a half, it had attracted anywhere from 100,000 to half a million members)[7] allowed it to pursue more and more of these activities.

1940s and 1950s is Richard Mitchell, *The Society of the Muslim Brothers* (Oxford: Oxford University Press, 1993). Krämer's synthetic *Hasan al-Banna* is very useful. For an explicit analysis of the Brotherhood as a social movement, see Ziad Munson, "Islamic Mobilization: Social Movement Theory and the Egyptian Muslim Brotherhood," *Sociological Quarterly* 42, no. 4 (2001), 487–510.

For the 1960s and 1970s, a recent work is Barbara Zollner, *The Muslim Brotherhood: Hasan al-Hudaybi and Ideology* (Abington, U.K.: Routledge, 2009). For the reemergence of the Brotherhood in the 1970s and 1980s, Carrie Rosefsky Wickham, *Mobilizing Islam: Religion, Activism, and Political Change in Egypt* (New York: Columbia University Press, 2002), is perhaps the most useful. Also valuable on recent decades is Hesham al-Awadi, *In Pursuit of Legitimacy: The Muslim Brothers and Mubarak, 1982–2000* (London: Tauris Academic Studies, 2004). On the international movement, see Alison Pargeter, *The Muslim Brotherhood: The Burden of Tradition* (London: Saqi Books, 2010). On an important radical offshoot, see John Calvert, *Sayyid Qutb and the Origins of Radical Islamism* (New York: Columbia University Press, 2010).

Al-Banna's ideological and programmatic writings have provoked considerable analysis and commentary from a wide range of intellectuals in the Arab world. I make no pretense of covering this discussion extensively here. For a representative example from an influential Egyptian intellectual, see "This Is How Tariq al-Bishri Reads the Writings of Hasan al-Banna," October 2007, http://islamyoon .islamonline.net/servlet/Satellite?c=ArticleA_C&cid=1193049268827&pagename=Islamyoun%2FIYALayout.

5. On the Brotherhood's patterning itself after missionary activity, see Heather J. Sharkey, *American Evangelicals in Egypt: Missionary Encounters in an Age of Empire* (Princeton, N.J.: Princeton University Press, 2008), p. 107. I am also grateful to Beth Baron for conveying to me the preliminary results of her research on the subject.

6. This is a central theme of Lia, *Society of the Muslim Brothers in Egypt*. Lia stresses this point perhaps more than Mitchell (*Society of the Muslim Brothers*), but his portrait is certainly consistent with Mitchell's earlier account.

7. Lia, *Society of the Muslim Brothers in Egypt*, p. 154, reporting British intelligence estimates from 1944.

The Brotherhood's entry into political activity began early but appeared cautious and almost diffident at first. In the 1930s, the movement eschewed tight political alliances but still found itself involved in rivalries among Egyptian political forces (sometimes earning itself a reputation for being close to the palace or to particular politicians). In addition to navigating political alignments, the leadership focused on a few specifically Islamic causes that had sharp political overtones: Christian missionary activity, British imperialism, and the brewing conflict between Arabs and Jews in neighboring Palestine.

At first the Brotherhood's political activity involved merely advocacy in public debates on these issues, but the temptations of more direct and active political participation beckoned at times when there were competitive elections. (In interwar Egypt, such elections were somewhat irregular; the constitution was effectively suspended for most of the Brotherhood's first decade.) The steps toward politics involved both push and pull. The Brotherhood was impelled to politics for its own agenda; at the same time, political leaders of various stripes found the Brotherhood's ranks a potentially important constituency to attract.

For all the incentives to participate, however, the political field provoked ambivalent and hesitant Brotherhood involvement. Famously averse to "party politics" (*hizbiyya*) and sometimes wary of being overly identified with any particular political actor, the Brotherhood tended to take one step forward and one step back as the question of political involvement arose. The hesitating and erratic moves toward political participation were not only a result of internal Brotherhood deliberations. Egypt's political system seemed to alternate between encouraging and sharply limiting the Brotherhood's role. Bouts of authoritarian and emergency measures, some arising from internal Egyptian political struggles and others stemming from World War II, left the Brotherhood's leaders uncertain about the movement's position given the shifting rules of political life. And political restrictions often led to sharp constraints on Brotherhood political activity (and even to harsh administrative measures and arrests of movement leaders). The leadership tended to react to such moves by reaching out to potential allies, toning down political rhetoric, and turning attention to less controversial, nonpolitical activities. The Brotherhood rushed, for instance, to register with the Ministry of Social Affairs in order to obtain a legal umbrella for its social and charitable activities and to communicate an emphasis on such work rather than electoral politics.

By 1941, the organization decided that it would run for parliament if the opportunity arose but not under any party banner. Yet its candidates withdrew when elections were held the following year after the movement came under intense pressure from the leader of the (ultimately victorious) nationalist Wafd party.[8] For the next decade, the Brotherhood's involvement in politics grew markedly throughout a time of escalating international crises and mounting domestic instability. But its horizon now extended beyond parliament; it formed a "special apparatus," partly to provide training for those wishing to fight for the cause of Muslims in Palestine and partly to prepare followers to fight British imperialism in Egypt. Members were involved in domestic violence as well, though ever since, it has remained a matter of sharp controversy how much the senior leadership of the Brotherhood sanctioned such violence.

The Brotherhood's relations with some of those in political authority grew increasingly tense, and the Egyptian government eventually used martial law to ban the organization. The prime minister carrying out that measure was assassinated by a Brotherhood follower in 1948, and shortly thereafter al-Banna himself was killed (a political murder generally attributed to Egyptian police).

Without legal status and with its charismatic founder dead, the Brotherhood hesitated in determining how to react. Eventually, it brought an outsider, a respectable senior judge, Hasan al-Hudaybi, to head the movement. Al-Hudaybi attempted to take a conciliatory approach and moved to rein in and abolish the special apparatus. His efforts were resisted by some within the organization. While official suspicion and hostility diminished, they hardly disappeared.

In 1952, a group of army officers, many with ties to the Brotherhood, overthrew the monarchy and abolished the constitution as well as all existing political parties.[9] For a short time, the Brotherhood saw a possibility for a more cooperative relationship with the government and indeed was even invited briefly into the cabinet. Since it was not a political party, the Brotherhood was not at first shut down and therefore seemed to be singled out for favorable treatment. But after this short honeymoon, the new regime soon proved even more suspicious than its predecessor of the Brotherhood. When a Brotherhood member was charged with attempting to assassinate Gamal 'Abd al-Nasir, one of Egypt's new leaders, the new regime launched a ferocious campaign against the movement. The Brotherhood's leaders were arrested, and a rather dodgy special tribunal was constructed to try them. Eventually, six members were executed and many others were imprisoned or fled Egypt. While the Brotherhood maintained a skeletal

---

8. While Mitchell (*Society of the Muslim Brothers*, p. 27), relying on accounts of Brotherhood leaders, emphasizes the concessions al-Banna won in return for withdrawal, Lia (*Society of the Muslim Brothers in Egypt*, p. 269) portrays the decision as the result of official coercion. Lia also gives an earlier date (1938) for the decision to run for parliament.

9. On this period generally, see Joel Gordon, *Nasser's Blessed Movement: Egypt's Free Officers and the July Revolution* (Oxford: Oxford University Press, 1992).

existence through the Nasir years (and even showed brief signs of a resurgence in the early 1960s), the movement was not able to reemerge in Egypt until the 1970s and since then has operated under a shifting set of largely unfavorable (and generally unwritten) rules. Only in 2011 did it regain any legal status when its party received a license.

If the period after the 1940s saw instability and problems in Egypt, it also saw expansion of the Brotherhood outside the country. Already in the second half of the 1930s, the Brotherhood showed interest in spreading overseas; in the 1940s, full organizations began to emerge in several other Arab countries. These movements were often inspired by the efforts of Egyptians visiting or resident in the Arab countries; in addition, the rise of the Muslim Brotherhood in Egypt attracted attention and admiration from citizens of other Arab countries who then launched local efforts, generally with the encouragement and support of the mother movement. From the beginning, these various efforts developed their own local leadership; while they usually remained formally linked to the Egyptian Brotherhood (the movement's "general guide" in Egypt doubles as head of the international organization to this day), in practice the various country-based movements (each with its own local leadership and "general supervisor") operated extremely autonomously by adapting the malleable Egyptian model to their particular setting.

Organization and Forms

Islamist movements based on the model of the Muslim Brotherhood exhibit common organizational and ideological features. But those features are not mechanically duplicated by each of the country-based movements; instead, the various national movements are characterized by flexibility, responsiveness to the external environment, and an avoidance of rigid replication. Thus the common features, while quite noticeable, are also very general. Before describing the specific organizations under study, let us explore these general organizational forms and ideological themes in this family of Islamist movements.

Movements inspired by the Muslim Brotherhood show three distinctive organizational features: formal organization, social and political engagement, and flexibility verging on opportunism.

Formality

Perhaps the most notable feature of Islamist movements following the Muslim Brotherhood model is their formality: for all their problems attaining legal status, they still strive to have bylaws, clear criteria for various gradations of membership, regular internal arrangements, established procedures for selecting officers and determining policies and positions, collegial and consultative decision-making organs, and specialized bodies with clear functional tasks.[10] The more successful and legally recognized movements manage to institute all these features, but even those that operate outside a legal framework (with some movements forced partly or largely underground) still strive for some degree of formality and fidelity to internal procedures. Indeed, the movements not only work hard to follow formal procedures; they take great pride in doing so. Decision making is sometimes lumbering and cumbersome, but leaders often see this as a strength: "Every step is deliberate (*kull khatwa madrusa*)," they frequently intone to communicate the seriousness and care of their decision-making processes. Formality does not start at the top. Since al-Banna's day, the organizational emphasis has been far more on the grass roots. Membership at the base level is not a trivial affair: some degree of loyalty and regular activity is demanded of all who join, and responsibilities increase with status in the organization. Indeed, the closely knit fundamental unit of many movements—a small cell of a few individuals—is the secret of the organizations' strength and continuity.[11]

The original movement, based in Egypt, was organized and led by al-Banna, its charismatic founder. The Egyptian mother movement still tends to be fairly hierarchical and perhaps a shade more personalistic than its offspring; most of the other country-based movements show a much greater tendency toward collective leadership, turnover in top offices (though often only after a founding generation has passed from the scene), and a dearth of dominant, charismatic leaders. Even in Egypt, none of al-Banna's successors have exerted the same degree of control and some have presided over fairly raucous internal debates (the recently retired leader Mahdi 'Akif is often described by members as having encouraged freer expression within the movement). Most movements have shown a growing inclination toward collective decision making and consensus politics. With some exceptions, leaders retire after serving fixed terms. (The Egyptian mother movement was one of the last to display this characteristic when 'Akif stepped down after one term in 2010.) Each country-based movement is headed by a "general supervisor"; the more august title "general guide" is reserved for the

10. Not all the established procedures are public. But on 5 November 2009, the Egyptian opposition daily *al-Dustur* published a series of internal bylaws and organizational documents. These were brought to my attention by the weblog of a young Brotherhood activist, 'Abd al-Mun'im Mahmud, http://ana-ikhwan.blogspot.com/2009/11/blog-post.html.

11. This is a major theme in Lia, *Society of the Muslim Brothers in Egypt*; it is also stressed in Masoud, "Why Islam Wins."

figure who doubles as head of the Egyptian movement and of the international organization. Such features may not seem remarkable, but they are unusual in the Arab world, a region where most organizations tend to be loosely structured around specific individuals and very few outlive their founders.

Engagement

A second organizational feature of the movements is their dedication to social and political engagement. There is, of course, a considerable commitment to personal improvement that is expected of all members. And movement members often speak of *da'wa*, loosely translated as "missionary work." But it encompasses more: indeed, it is often far less focused on bringing new converts to Islam than on, quite literally, preaching to the faithful; it can also mean serving as an example of rectitude and fostering belief and appropriate behavior in all kinds of ways.

The goal is not to build an isolated community of saints, however; it is to change the broader society and foster the development of social practices that follow Islamic teachings—by example, advocacy, activism, teaching, organizing, and preaching. As Quintan Wiktorowicz has observed, "the Brotherhood's method of change is not the erection of a new system of politics; it is a reformist strategy of working through the current system to imbue it with more Islamic tones."[12]

From its very beginning, the Brotherhood has managed to build an organization that emphasizes tight personal bonds while seeking to avoid turning inward on itself. When permitted (and that is not always the case), members of movements modeled on the Brotherhood strive to use their organization to better the society. On a 2010 trip to Kuwait, I asked a prominent Brotherhood activist about the Brotherhood's own activities in Kuwait, especially because it had accorded considerable autonomy to a nongovernmental organization (NGO) it inspired (the Social Reform Society) and a political party it backs (Hadas). He replied that one of its major tasks left to the Brotherhood itself was "*tarbiya*," a word that implies that the movement educates or fosters the development of its members. He went on to say that the word took on a specific meaning in the Brotherhood context: it refers to a group of activities that train and improve members in various ways. One of the most popular, for instance, was training in public speaking.

This engagement can lead to a measure of cautiousness and gradualism rather than impatience and insistence on immediate perfection. The ambitiousness of

---

12. Quintan Wiktorowicz, *The Management of Islamic Activism: Salafis, the Muslim Brotherhood, and State Power in Jordan* (Albany: State University of New York Press, 2001), p. 94.

the Brotherhood's long-term agenda should not be overlooked, but it seeks to move toward a more Islamic society step by step, reforming current institutions and practices rather than upending them.

Flexibility

Third, movements based on the Muslim Brotherhood model show great responsiveness to the political context and the legal environment in which they operate. With a broad focus and a wide range of possible activities to pursue, Muslim Brotherhood–type movements can often squeeze themselves into any opening that conditions allow. This can take the form of registering as a charitable association, chartering a political party, or opening an orphanage. Movements resist grabbing such opportunities only if they restrict or threaten other activities. In other words, a party or an NGO drawing on the movement may register and operate under the relevant law and regulatory oversight, but the entire movement will not operate under the rubric of that registered body. Movements tend to be reluctant to pursue one activity to the exclusion of all others, although they clearly choose to emphasize some aspects of their missions over others in response to the opportunities and costs that are externally imposed.

This responsiveness and flexibility can take another form as well: not only do the movements form their own panoply of organizations, they also sometimes enter others. In many countries, individuals with a background in Islamist movements have been active in the field of Islamic finance. Student and professional associations or local charitable organizations have sometimes provided inviting fields for Islamist activists to pursue their reform agenda. In Kuwait, for instance, the student union has been an Islamist bastion since the 1980s; in Egypt, Islamists moved into professional associations in the 1980s (provoking a set of hostile countermeasures by the regime); in 2010, the Jordanian minister of education was so frustrated by the prevalence of Islamist teachers in an ongoing attempt to form a teachers union that he suggested their time would be better spent shaving off their beards.

This third feature can be put differently in a quite succinct manner: Islamist movements are opportunistic. When all legal (or tolerated if not fully legal) avenues are closed, they can move underground and even spawn armed apparatuses. This happened with Islamist movements in Palestine (Hamas since the late 1980s), Syria (since the 1970s), and Kuwait (briefly under the Iraqi occupation). Islamist leaders' record on this score is not fully one of reaction and necessity: the formation of the "special apparatus" in Egypt in the 1940s came under somewhat repressive circumstances, but the movement had not yet lost its ability to operate openly. Most Islamist movements insist that they eschew such measures (their attitude toward political violence is considered more fully in the next section), but they often take a defensive tone when discussing the exceptional instances of armed wings and minimize their significance.

Tubular and Ambiguous Movements

Formally organized and often tightly knit, socially and politically engaged, and flexible and opportunistic: taken together, these features describe movements that can survive and pursue their agenda in a broad variety of settings. And they also suggest why some regimes find that Islamist movements based on the Muslim Brotherhood act something like a sealed toothpaste tube: squeezing the movement in one place simply leads it to be directed elsewhere. Closing a political party results in a redirection of energy into the remaining open political spaces in professional associations or university campuses; restrictions there lead to a focus on social work.

Further, these organizational characteristics also explain why regimes sometimes have difficulty determining where an Islamist movement begins and ends. Where a movement is formally recognized and licensed—or even merely tolerated, as in Egypt—it will quickly establish a headquarters and a public leadership. But other organs—a political party, for instance, or a charitable society—may have no formal relationship with the movement. Some offshoots may be fully independent but informally allied; others might be more tightly controlled by an interlocking leadership (such as Jordan's Muslim Brotherhood, the associated Islamic Action Front, and the closely aligned Islamic Center—all formally independent of one another and yet closely and openly linked).[13] And still other organizations might have some vague overlap in terms of membership or orientation with the formal movement but still be fully independent of it.

To make relationships even more difficult to discern, the last few decades have seen a flourishing Islamic sector in most Arab societies, with a wide range of formally established and informal charitable societies, clinics, schools, and study circles. Most have no relationship at all with any Islamist movement; others may have some involvement by individual Islamist activists but not be closely controlled by the movement; and others may be virtual wings of the formally organized movement. This diverse sector reaches large parts of the society, forming a supportive subculture in which the movement can operate (and at election time, expect a sympathetic hearing to appeals for votes). Still, much (and generally

---

13. For useful in-depth portraits of the relationship between the Muslim Brotherhood and Islamic NGOs, see Wiktorowicz, *Management of Islamic Activism,* and Janine A. Clark, *Islam, Charity, and Activism: Middle-Class Networks and Social Welfare in Egypt, Jordan, and Yemen* (Bloomington: Indiana University Press, 2004).

most) of the sector can operate independently of the formally organized movement. In Turkey, where a similar Islamist sector arose, along with a political party that launched Islamist appeals, one scholar quotes a social activist as simply stating: "If they close the party, then a few politicians lose their job; that's all. It has no effect on us. We're a social movement, not a party."[14] Similarly, a leading study of the Islamic sector in Egypt provides an account of its origins in which the Muslim Brotherhood played a limited role at first.[15] Many current Egyptian Brotherhood leaders recall spending early days as activists completely independent of the Brotherhood; only in the 1980s did the Brotherhood make a concerted effort to recruit such activists.[16]

Yet the broadly based social trend, even if it includes many unaffiliated organizations and projects, still has significance for any movement attempting to organize more formally on an Islamist agenda. One study of Islamic social institutions in several Arab countries found that their significance "lies not in the actual services they provide—many NGOs do the same—or in some form of Islamic 'framework' within which they provide the services, for by and large there is none. Rather it lies in the intangible accumulation of social capital—trust, solidarity—that develops among the providers of charity."[17]

If the organizational forms of Brotherhood-type movements show most of their consistency in their plasticity and flexibility, then the same can be said about their ideological and policy positions. There are, to be sure, strong overall themes that most movements emphasize, but those themes are sufficiently general to be applied in a myriad of ways, making the movements appear either nimble or slippery, depending on how favorably they are viewed.

Ideology and Themes

When we refer to "ideology" in this book, we are moving between two different levels of abstraction (always attempting to be explicit as we do so). At its more general, we use the term to refer to the world view of the groups; at its

14. Jenny B. White, *Islamist Mobilization in Turkey: A Study in Vernacular Politics* (Seattle: University of Washington Press, 2002), p. 5.

15. Wickham, *Mobilizing Islam*.

16. 'Abd al-Mun'im Abu al-Futuh, a prominent former Brotherhood leader—and perhaps the most prominent member of the generation that joined the movement after its reemergence in the 1970s—has written a useful set of recollections, *Shahid 'ala ta'rikh al-haraka al-islamiyya fi misr*, available at http://www.abolfotoh.net/%D8%A3%D8%A8%D9%88%D8%A7%D9%84%D9%81 D8%AA%D9%88%D8%AD%D9%81%D9%89%D8%A7%D9%84%D8%B5%D8%AD%D8%A7 %D9%81%D8%A9/tabid/67/ctl/Details/mid/396/ItemID/148/Default.aspx.

17. Clark, *Islam, Charity, and Activism*, p. 151.

more specific, ideology refers to programmatic commitments and statements. We will often combine these seemingly distinct levels—the first abstract and per-haps more steady; the second concrete, practical, and perhaps more ephemeral—because that is what the groups themselves do. Islamist movements modeled on the Brotherhood certainly have a distinctive world view that informs their po-litical programs. And they speak politically, sometimes with extraordinary ver-bosity, through programs, statements, and platforms. But if their world view is distinctive, it is hardly codified: movements based on the Muslim Brotherhood model have only vague ideological texts, and their leaders are generally highly practical people rather than ideologues or intellectuals. Indeed, the movements pride themselves on their practical natures.

More than a defined ideology, the leaders and movements display a strong sense of mission: reforming the individual and the society along Islamic lines. They are guided, their leaders insist, on fixed principles, but they talk far less about ideology or even codified principles than about their movement's *manhaj* (method or model) and its *marja'iyya* (reference point, a concept we will explore later). And indeed, it might be more precise to conceive of the Brotherhood not just as an ideological organization but even more as a "mission-driven" one. Its members constantly reiterate that they are dedicated to reforming the individual and the society along Islamic lines, but they rarely articulate what that means outside a particular application.

This is not to say that their ideology is only an effect of their political practice. In subsequent chapters, we will pay close attention to the way Islamist ideology evolves with political involvement; our understanding of such movements is that ideas do influence their behavior. As we made clear in the previous chapter, we view ideology as explaining the stickiness of movement behavior. The relation-ship between ideology and behavior is a complicated one because—especially for practical movements like those under study here—they influence each other so deeply. This mutual influence is often missed. On the one hand, many political scientists find ideology so malleable that they believe it cannot be used fruit-fully to explain much of anything. Stathis Kalyvas, for instance (a scholar whose work on Christian Democracy has deeply influenced my own work on Islamists), quickly dismisses religious doctrine as a useful explanation of behavior.[18] But on the other hand, many of the writings on Islamist movements in politics not written by political scientists betray the equally unhelpful opposite assump-tion: not only that they are highly ideological movements but that their actions,

18. See Kalyvas, "Commitment Problems in Emerging Democracies: The Case of Religious Par-ties," *Comparative Politics* 32, no. 4 (2000), 379–399.

decisions, strategies, and tactics can best be understood largely by reference to their ideologies (leading these writers to overlook how context shapes action and how ideological commitments evolve in response to conditions). This explains the enormous interest in policy discussions in Western capitals concerning the democratic credentials of Islamist movements.

Islamist movements modeled on the Brotherhood are indeed highly ideological. And their ideologies do inform their actions. But their ideologies are also fairly general and allow considerable flexibility not merely on tactics but also on strategy and especially on the question of elections and even on democracy.[19] In order to understand the choices they make, therefore, we will need to probe not merely the nature, ideas, and motives of the movements but also, in subsequent chapters, the way that other political forces treat them and the choices that are presented to them by the political systems in which they operate.

Four themes in particular are deployed consistently over both time and place: a commitment to reform, a stress on Islamic values and especially Islamic law, a long-term focus, and a fear of partisanship and division.

Reform

The first theme, reform, has been present in Brotherhood-type movements since the first one was founded in Egypt in 1928. But as was suggested in the discussion of the history of the "mother movement" above, the conception of reform is extremely broad, encompassing various dimensions and allowing for a range of emphases to satisfy whatever internal impulses or external incentives and sanctions are presented. The reform that such movements seek is personal, religious, educational, political, economic, and social. And, they insist, one dimension does not take logical precedence over another. Muhammad Habib, a former deputy guide of the Egyptian Muslim Brotherhood, stated: "The society has three tasks that must be balanced and harmonized—these are educational [tarbawiyya], missionary [da'wiyya], and political. None of these tasks should dominate the others."[20] Leaders insist that these various dimensions are not simply of equal

---

19. For an example of flexibility combined with an insistence on principles, see the July 2010 interview by the Jordanian Islamist paper al-Sabil of Khalid Mish'al, chairman of the political bureau of Hamas. Mish'al posits flexibility and holding to fixed principles (thawabit) as distinct virtues, each with its own contribution. But he provides only the vaguest guidance on when each virtue is called for. The text of the interview concerning flexibility is available at http://www.alzaytouna.net/arabic/print.php?a=121572.

20. "Dr. Muhammad Habib, the Resigned Deputy General Guide of the 'Brotherhood' in a Heated Interview with Al-misri al-yawm," Al-misri al-yawm, 5 January 2010. Remarkably, in the same interview, Habib claimed he had no doubt that the Brotherhood would some day rule Egypt, but that it would compete for authority based only on popular means.

importance but also linked and not fully distinguishable. Specific circumstances might call for emphasizing one kind of reform over another, but that is neither a call for postponing the other area indefinitely nor a calculation that one area of reform is a precondition for another. All are mutually dependent. When I asked one Egyptian Muslim Brotherhood leader how he responded to younger activists who are frustrated with the futility of the struggle for democratic reform, he described a reply that directly linked the personal and the political: "What kind of democracy do you practice at home? Do you use violence or impose your will? Do you listen to the opinion of others? Do not talk to me about democracy in Egypt if you still need to learn to practice it in your family." By this he did not mean to delay work for political reform (though in extremely unpromising conditions some Brotherhood movements have felt forced to take such a path, and indeed, shortly before the Egyptian revolution of January 25, 2011, this particular leader admitted to me that at that moment the political path seemed almost completely blocked for the organization) but only to insist that there were other areas of reform at particular times when the political path might be unpromising.[21]

Sometimes Islamist activists will describe the areas of reform as the personal and the societal; sometimes they will speak of political and organizational dimensions (the first looking out toward political participation and the second turning in toward building up the organization); sometimes politics and da'wa (missionary work); and sometimes slightly more elaborate combinations of agendas. Whichever categories are used, the field for reform seems boundless. But what kind of reform? How are individual, society, and polity to be improved?

Islam as a Reference

It is the second theme that specifies the kind of change: Islam provides the source and reference points for reform efforts. Yet if Islam is a constant reference, it does not seem to be a narrowly determinative one. Claiming, as the movements do, that Islamic teachings are to serve as the basis for a better person, society, and political system gives little guidance on how those teachings are to be understood and applied. The slogan that has come to be associated with the Muslim Brotherhood over the past two decades—"Islam is the solution"—perhaps best captures both the centrality of Islam and the extreme generality of the commitment.

---

21. Personal interview, Gamal Hishmat, Cairo, July 2009 and December 2010.

Here Islamist movements often show comfort with general themes and even pluralism (not always explicitly acknowledged as such). Part of this is undoubtedly because the leadership of most movements is dominated by those with educational backgrounds and professional specializations in fields other than religious studies (though religious scholars in some countries have lent support and even shown a level of leadership in the movements, and some movement leaders with other backgrounds have sought supplemental religious education, both formal and informal). With a leadership that consists largely of pious amateurs and autodidacts in religious matters, an organizational insistence on the duties of individual Muslims to find the right path, and an emphasis on practice rather than doctrine, movement leaders show diversity in their interpretations of Islam. Indeed, it is quite common for movement members to distinguish between their own positions and those of the movement (especially on those issues on which the movement has taken no position).

But the Islam pursued by the movements, while general, is neither vacuous nor vapid. Certain themes arise consistently over time and place. First is a generally conservative set of values regarding public life: a concern that religious values be reflected in sexual modesty in dress, public discourse, education, and media; an aversion to gambling and consumption of alcohol; a general support for gender segregation;[22] and an insistence on a state duty to foster moral rectitude. Second, movements show suspicion of political movements that eschew a religious reference point and at times a marked hostility to secular, leftist, or Marxist forces and ideologies.

Most important, perhaps, the movements show an unwavering commitment to the Islamic shari'a—presented both as a source for legislation and as divine guidance on what behavior is required and what is prohibited.[23] As it is widely

---

22. The Islamist movements under study here do not seek to block all participation by women in public life. In Egypt, Jordan, and Palestine, the Islamist movement in question has run female candidates for parliament, and in Kuwait some leaders are prepared to do so. Women play a subordinate role in the organizations, however (see Omayma Abdel-Latif, *In the Shadow of the Brothers: The Women of the Egyptian Muslim Brotherhood* [Carnegie Papers, Carnegie Endowment for International Peace, October 2008]). And in general, the movements act as a conservative force wary of changes in existing practices. In a prominent case in which a movement took a position against full political rights for women (such as Kuwait), movement leaders managed to hammer out a tortured position that sought to resolve internal differences by arguing that the opposition was based not fully on religious grounds but also on conservative social practices; that women's suffrage was far less problematic than women serving in specific public offices (such as minister); and that the outcome of the constitutional process would be respected even if it violated the movement's own positions.

23. I have explored some of the implications of the legal, moral, and behavioral conceptions of the Islamic shari'a in "Shari'a and State in the Modern Muslim Middle East," *International Journal of Middle East Studies* 29, no. 3 (1997), 359–376; see also my "Debating the Islamic Shari'a in the 21st Century: Consensus and Cacophony," in *Shari'a Politics: Islamic Law and Society in the Muslim World*, ed. Robert Hefner (Bloomington: Indiana University Press, 2011).

understood in much of the Arab world today, the shari'a provides both binding rules and general principles; it can be used to guide political authorities but
also individual Muslims and general social behavior. With this combination of
a specifically legal and a general moral commitment to the Islamic shari'a, an
Islamist movement's ideological orientation can thus take many different forms:
an insistence on implementing specific provisions based on the Brotherhood's
understanding of shari'a (such as a ban on alcohol sales); pressure for incorporating shari'a into the constitutional order (requiring the head of state to be Muslim or that the Islamic shari'a be a, or even the, primary source of legislation);
general exhortation for Muslims to follow shari'a-enjoined practice (such as
regular prayer and fasting during Ramadan); and even modification of personal
comportment (speaking gently and calmly with interlocutors) in accordance
with the movement's understanding of shari'a-based norms. When developing
interpretations of the Islamic shari'a, the movements take clear positions only on
matters that seem to them unambiguous, regularly resorting to external authorities whom they trust in order to receive guidance on specific issues and insisting
that no Muslim (and certainly no state structure) has the authority to impose a
specific interpretation as binding as a matter of doctrine (the state may impose
some interpretations as the law to be enforced at a particular time, but no Muslim
can be compelled to drop belief in an alternative).[24]

Time Horizon

A third theme characteristic of the Islamic movements under study here is a
long time horizon. Such a long-term focus is dictated by both religious and
practical considerations. In religious terms, the movements present patience as
a divinely enjoined virtue and stress that fellow Muslims need to be gently persuaded and won over to following a fully Islamic path. In practical terms, the
movements' agendas are so broad, their political circumstances subject to such
vicissitudes, and the periods of repression experienced by many so extended
and trying that an extended time horizon is the only way to forestall frustration,

---

24. States have the authority in their view to impose specific interpretations as legally binding,
but such a decision, while enforceable, does not require those who disagree to accept the interpretation as binding in creedal terms. Formal organizations associated with these movements generally
have internal committees for determining interpretations of the shari'a to guide the movement, but
they regularly resort as well to outside authorities whom they respect. Many have an ambivalent attitude toward official religious authorities: on the one hand, they strongly favor state support for religious institutions of various kinds; on the other, they view many official organs suspiciously, worried
that they have been co-opted by rulers. In Egypt, for instance, the Muslim Brotherhood regards Dar
al-Ifta'—the State Mufti's office—as overly deferential to the regime; some scholars within al-Azhar
are accorded greater respect even though it is a state institution.

anger, and despair. Movement leaders are striking in their constant insistence that any apparently crippling setback can be survived and that whatever the current tribulations, in the long run the movement's objectives are in line with divine guidance.

In 2005, I interviewed 'Isam al-'Iryan, a leading Brotherhood figure, about the movement's strategies and priorities. While he was clearly a talented political tactician, the goals that he articulated—for instance, the lifting of Egypt's state of emergency—seemed to me far out of the movement's reach. When I pressed him on what the movement would do if it failed in its objectives, he merely smiled and invoked the movement's long-range view of matters: "If we fail in this—we have survived two kings and several presidents. We will continue." And we were both right. The state of emergency remained very much in effect. And al-'Iryan, arrested several times over the next few years, appeared in every photograph that I saw of him in his prison jumpsuit smiling broadly, perhaps eyeing the distant future rather than his dreary immediate surroundings. And when that future arrived in 2011 with the fall of the regime that had deployed its emergency powers directly against him, al-'Iryan undoubtedly felt deeply vindicated.

The long-term outlook of the movements guides not only their tolerance of hardship but also their willingness to grasp current opportunities that do not flatly contradict their general vision. Put more simply, the insistence on the importance of distant goals does little to dictate short-term decisions. Instead, it allows movements to choose among a variety of immediate steps and measures so long as they fit within a plausible path to the realization of ultimate objectives. The result of this orientation is perhaps to accentuate both the tactical flexibility and toothpaste-tube nature of the movements. As Shaul Mishal and Avraham Sela note, the movements "have moved away from dogmatic positions in a quest for innovative and pliable modes of conduct, the opposite of doctrinaire rigidity, ready to respond or adjust to fluid conditions without losing sight of their ultimate objectives."[25]

Unity

Fifth and finally, the movements show great fear of division, both within the broader Muslim society and among their own ranks. The general fear of dividing the society has been a strong theme since the original Muslim Brotherhood was founded and expresses itself in a variety of ways: general calls for intra-Muslim

---

25. Shaul Mishal and Avraham Sela, *The Palestinian Hamas: Vision, Violence, and Coexistence* (New York: Columbia University Press, 2000), p. 7.

understanding, even sometimes across the Sunni-Shiʻi divide; a denunciation of partisan politics; a stress on Muslim unity; and an insistence on using gentler rhetoric in community matters (exemplified best, perhaps, by Egyptian Muslim Brotherhood general guide Muhammad Mahdi ʻAkif's famous scolding of the brash Egyptian Kifaya movement—a broad coalition formed to oppose the election of President Husni Mubarak to a fourth term—that its public discourse was "impolite"). There are, of course, exceptions to all these tendencies—Sunni Islamist movements are quite capable, for instance, of referring to Shi'a Muslims in disparaging terms or using shrill and divisive rhetoric.

But for all the movements' interest in engaging in political activity, they show a marked hesitancy on the issue of forming a political party. The complicated evolution of Islamist movements' attitude toward political parties and party politics is of particular interest in the context of this book, since one of our major points of concern is the organizational forms that the movements take. For that reason, a brief excursus into the topic will be helpful in illuminating subsequent discussion.[26]

Islamist movements have participated in political campaigns, run candidates for office, and composed platforms; in some countries, they appear to be the most organized parties (without even the exception of the governing political parties). But they have been traditionally suspicious of party politics and most eschew the label "party," preferring such terms as "movement," "front," or "list." What set of attitudes motivates this ambivalent behavior?

The fear of party politics is not insurmountable, but it runs deep and flows from three different sources, one ideological and two organizational. First, the general ideological disinclination toward dividing the community extends to suspicion of political parties. While that suspicion is ultimately of religious provenance, it generally expresses itself in tones that echo earlier generations of Western republican thinkers who saw political parties as vehicles for placing group, class, regional, or individual interests above those of the entire community. The early Muslim Brotherhood's denunciation of "party politics" (*hizbiyya*) strikes precisely this pose and still resonates in more recent positions taken by some Islamist leaders. More abstractly, as I wrote with two colleagues,

> At the philosophical level, Islamists have trouble accepting the unfettered freedom of individuals to choose for themselves because they believe that the community has a common interest that overrides that of individuals. Islamists concede that there can be disagreement about what the interest of the community is but find it difficult to accept that

---

26. For a recent discussion of the issue by a prominent Hamas figure, see Mushir ʻUmar al-Misri, *Al-hayah al-siyasiyya fi zill anzi-at al-hukm al-muʻasira* (Mansura, Egypt: Dar al-Kalima, 2006).

every individual is entitled to his separate version of the good. Fear of dividing the community also leads Islamists to reject partisanship, at least in principle.[27]

Second, parties have sparked nervousness not only because of the risk of dividing the community of Muslims but also because they can divide Islamist movements. Movements that plunge into daily political debates, alliances, and maneuvering often see their internal deliberations grow into discordant internal struggles. Indeed, as explored more fully in Chapter 6, it is precisely the entrance into party politics that leads to the few schisms that such movements experience.

Third, Islamist leaders view parties warily because they risk confining the movement in rigid frameworks and positions. Political parties often operate under restrictive legal frameworks in the Arab world; they also expose movements to pressures to take specific positions on difficult issues. Since the organizational model of these movements offers fluidity and adaptability, taking steps to form alliances with existing political parties—or taking the bolder step of forming a new party—comes with some cost.

The Alternatives

In both ideological and organizational terms, our portrait of Islamist movements has stressed elements that are both paradoxical (fixed formal organizations with fluidity and adaptability) and general (wide-ranging ideologies and diverse organizational forms). It might seem that the movements studied here are so indeterminate that they could encompass virtually any vaguely religious organization or movement in the Muslim world. This is emphatically not the case, however. The best evidence that, for all its generality, the model of an Islamist movement has a definitive shape and content is a review of the alternatives: a host of organizations and movements that share a religious orientation but have sharply different characteristics than (and often a contemptuous or patronizing attitude toward) the Brotherhood model.

One of the most prominent alternatives to the Brotherhood model in recent years has been the salafi trend.[28] Salafi movements show three marked differ-

---

27. Nathan J. Brown, Marina Ottaway, and Amr Hamzawy, "Islamist Movements and the Democratic Process in the Arab World: Exploring the Gray Zones," Carnegie Paper 67, Carnegie Endowment for International Peace, March 2006, p. 14.

28. See Marc Lynch, "Islam Divided between Salafi-jihad and the Ikhwan," *Studies in Conflict and Terrorism* 33, no. 6 (2010), 467–487; Wiktorowicz, *Management of Islamic Activism;* and Roel Meijer, *Global Salafism: Islam's New Religious Movement* (New York: Columbia University Press, 2009).

ences from the Islamist movements considered here. First, their interest in correct interpretation of texts and following appropriate practice trumps all other concerns. (I have sometimes heard "textualist"—*nususi*—used as a synonym for salafi.) In contrast to the more freewheeling approach of Islamists, with their willingness to admit many interpretations as plausible, salafis strive to find the best possible (and therefore correct) reading and apply it to personal behavior. Second, salafi movements tend to be far less formally organized as a matter of choice.[29] Third, they tend to be much less committed to involvement with the broader society.

These characteristics taken together lead to a tendency to form small, informal groups clustered around particular experts. Some salafi movements focus mostly on correct practice for their own members; their social involvement outside their own circles might extend at most to hectoring others. Their political involvement might consist only of offering unsolicited advice to rulers about the correct path. Others are more involved in society and politics but no more conciliatory—most dramatically, there is a jihadist strain of salafism that has attracted great global attention. Whatever strain of salafism is involved, one would expect the Islamist movements studied here to appear to salafis as overly loose in their approach to religion and insufficiently focused on correct practice. And indeed, that is precisely the criticism that is directed by salafis toward Islamist movements: one can hear over and over from salafis the patronizing and disdainful refrain that "the Muslim Brotherhood is less about religion than it is about politics."[30]

A second set of movements that differ sharply from Islamist movements are Islamic political parties that are not connected to broader movements. In both Egypt and Jordan, for instance, a "Center Party" (Hizb al-Wasat) has formed. These rare splinter groups have attracted a small group of former Brotherhood members. While such parties gain attention primarily for their ideological positions (the Center Parties of Jordan and Egypt or the Khalas Party that briefly formed among Palestinians offered softer versions of the ideology of the parent movement), what is just as striking is their exclusively political focus. Unconnected to any broader movement, they have generally performed unimpressively at the polls; Islamist movements tend to regard them as overly willing to compromise on core principles in order to attain a legal status that offers few benefits.

---

29. Wiktorowicz, *Management of Islamic Activism.*
30. Some salafi movements have followed the Brotherhood movements into political participation in parliaments and elections. On salafis in parliament in Kuwait and Bahrain, see Steve Monroe, "Salafis in Parliament: Party Politics and Democratic Attitudes in the Gulf" (B.A. honors thesis, Stanford University, 2010).

A third set of organizations shares the broad focus of the Islamist movements studied here but eschews existing politics—not based on a principled renunciation of the political sphere, much less any secularist inclinations, but out of a deep distrust of the existing political system. The goal of the Hizb al-Tahrir, for instance, whose followers are found most notably among Jordanians and Palestinians in the Arab world as well as in several non-Arab Muslim communities, is the re-creation of the caliphate. In the absence of the caliphate, the party rejects existing governments but views any collective violent action as premature. The result is a radical political ideology that denounces all existing rulers as non-Islamic but also renders the followers unwilling to do more than call for a change of leader. The grassroots focus and societal involvement of Islamist movements based on the Brotherhood model is viewed by Hizb al-Tahrir members as diluted and overly compromising. Less radically, the Moroccan al-'Adl wa-l-Ihsan movement rejects the Moroccan political order but does not rule out the possibility of participation in different circumstances.[31] Its followers may have provided vital electoral support at times to the Party of Justice and Development (not associated with the Muslim Brotherhood but closely resembling its model), but in general the movement leaders view the Party as overly opportunistic and compromised. As with the Hizb al-Tahrir, the result is a potentially more radical but practically quiescent alternative.

Finally, there is a group of movements that focus almost exclusively on the social, religious, and cultural aspects of religion, largely staying away from formal politics. Turkey's Gulan movement,[32] Sufi brotherhoods, and a large and diffuse "pietist" trend[33] have a significant social presence but are politically far less involved—and generally much more reluctant to spark opposition from existing regimes than Islamist movements that follow the Brotherhood model. Some Sufi movements in particular have shown an inclination to have far more cooperative relationships with officials than the Islamist movements considered here.

Thus the model followed by the Brotherhood movements is flexible and general but not infinitely so. It is flexible enough to edge into some of the categories just mentioned—as Hasan al-Banna famously described, the Brotherhood model shares characteristics with salafism, Sufi orders, political parties, and other movements and organizations. Some movement members are viewed as having salafi tendencies, and indeed, one leading specialist in the Egyptian Brotherhood

---

31. For an explanation of the stance of the movement, see Francesco Cavatorta, "Neither Participation nor Revolution: The Strategy of the Moroccan *Jamiat al-Adl wal-Ihsan*," *Mediterranean Politics* 12, no. 3 (2007), 381–397.

32. Berna Turam, *Between Islam and the State: The Politics of Engagement* (Stanford, Calif.: Stanford University Press, 2007).

33. Saba Mahmood, *The Politics of Piety: The Islamic Revival and the Feminist Subject* (Princeton, N.J.: Princeton University Press, 2005).

has written in some detail about what he views as the "salafization" of the movement there.[34] A prominent member of the Jordanian Brotherhood (Muhammad Abu Faris) has adopted ideas close to those of Hizb al-Tahrir (by denouncing the Jordanian government as apostate but counseling the righteous that patience is the proper response); others have advocated not simply forming political parties but granting them some autonomy from the mother movements. But such overlap, while notable in some instances, is hardly complete: the advocates of the alternatives sometimes harshly criticize the broad Islamist movements for not hewing to their favored narrower path. The alternatives to the general model thus exist not merely in theory but very much in practice and indeed often form the chief competition for the Islamist movements under study here.

In this chapter, we have edged implicitly toward understanding how and why Islamist movements on the Brotherhood model can function under semiauthoritarian conditions. Their organizational structure and ideological flexibility allow them to adapt and continuously reconfigure themselves and their efforts, to tinker with their appeals as needed without losing sight of their distinctive mission, to weather harsh periods of repression, and to draw on reservoirs and networks of support in more open times. In the next chapter, we will make their experience more explicit by examining the implementation of this model through the evolution of Brotherhood-type movements in four semiauthoritarian settings in the Arab world.

---

34. Husam Tamam, *Tasalluf al-ikhwan: ta'akkul al-atruha al-ikhwaniyya wa-su'ud al-salafiyya fi jama'at al-ikhwan al-muslimin* (Alexandria: Biblioteca Alexandrina, 2010).

THE MODEL IN PRACTICE IN FOUR SEMIAUTHORITARIAN SETTINGS

In presenting itself to Palestinian voters in January 2006, Hamas regularly referred to its relationship with the "mother movement," Egypt's Muslim Brotherhood. Why would a group running for national office for the first time introduce itself to the electorate in terms of its foreign affiliation? Part of the message was precisely the international aspect of the relationship: Hamas leaders had an interest in countering any image of their movement as a global pariah. But they also sent a subtle message not to the broad electorate but to their committed foot soldiers: Hamas, the movement with "resistance" as its middle name, held true to its Brotherhood roots by participating in elections. Palestinian Islamists were following the path already blazed by their Egyptian mentors when they set aside deep misgivings and fielded candidates in an election. Hamas leaders were implicitly arguing that there was a Brotherhood approach to politics, one that was leading them to plunge into electoral politics just as they had earlier taken up the cause of resistance. Their shifting behavior was very much in keeping with the ethos of a movement dedicated to broad social and political reform.

Brotherhood movements pride themselves on being practical: they take general principles very seriously but do not allow the quest for ideological purity prevent them from political and social engagement. They work within existing social and political arrangements even as they seek to reform them. For movements following the Brotherhood model, neither the vision of personal improvement nor the dedication to building an organization of righteous Muslims leads them to cut themselves off from the broader society.

The generality of the reform goal can lead in many different directions, however. It has generally (but not always) avoided the extremes of quietism and violent resistance, but the movements can move back and forth between these two poles. The regimes under which the movements operate have varied as well, gravitating between full authoritarianism and semiauthoritarianism. How does the establishment and operation of a reliably semiauthoritarian set of political structures affect the movements?

In this chapter, we will trace the ways that the various movements reacted to semiauthoritarianism. We will be attentive to the emergence of semiauthoritarianism but even more to how movements adapt to semiauthoritarianism's shifting nature. We have selected four cases for detailed consideration: Egypt, Jordan, Kuwait, and Palestine. In all four cases, we are interested in variation within the same country over time—how both the emergence and operation of semiauthoritarianism affected the movements.

All four movements are based on a Brotherhood model and have clear historical links with the "mother movement" described in the previous chapter, but each has followed a distinct organizational path. In Egypt, the Muslim Brotherhood reemerged in the 1970s and 1980s, though its revived form differed in some ways from the movement that existed in earlier decades. It remained without any legal recognition as either a movement or a party throughout the Sadat and Mubarak presidencies; only the overthrow of the Egyptian regime in 2011 offered the prospect of regaining legal status. In Jordan, the Muslim Brotherhood has existed continuously since the 1940s, but it also formed a legally recognized and technically independent political party, the Islamic Action Front, in 1992. In Kuwait, the Muslim Brotherhood formally broke its links with the international organization in the aftermath of the Iraqi occupation of 1990 and formed a party the next year, but its leaders quietly acknowledge that they follow the model (*manhaj*) and thought (*fikr*) of al-Banna and his Brotherhood. The movement operates quietly and unofficially; the party has no legal status, but it is open and fully tolerated. And in Palestine, Hamas was formed out of the local Muslim Brotherhood (as an attempt by movement activists to overcome an overly quietist attitude they saw as a deviation from the Brotherhood model). Hamas is currently treated informally as the Palestinian affiliate of the Brotherhood. Without legal existence except as an electoral list (called "Change and Reform"), Hamas is at the same time the governing party in Gaza.

We will probe each of the four cases in turn, paying particular attention to the effects of the emergence of semiauthoritarianism (and thus the moment at which the Islamists were, in a sense, invited into politics) and the continued operation of semiauthoritarianism (in which Islamist movements learned and were forced to react to the shifting rules, limits, and red lines). Proceeding in this manner emphasizes the change within each case more than the variation among them. Nevertheless, in examining the reaction of these movements to the creation and operation of semiauthoritarianism, we will see two clear patterns repeat themselves.

First, as the regimes become more consistently semiauthoritarian—and to the extent that they do—the movements devote more attention to politics. But they resist full conversion to a political agenda. Their oppositional stances generally become more clearly defined as well, though also within limits. In other words, they become more political and more oppositional but not unreservedly so.

Second, the process is characterized by friction and unevenness, occurring by trial and error rather than careful design. The movements react gradually and cautiously, deliberating and debating each step. And they make miscalculations, learn their lessons, and adapt. They gradually gain political experience, sophistication, and skills—and they also learn the harsh limits semiauthoritarianism places even on politically skillful opposition movements. The movements are not the only ones that will be shown to learn by trial and error. The same constant readjustment and improvisations are evident among regimes. The debate and internal jockeying in the halls of power are less obvious, since regime decision making can be more opaque than that of many opposition movements.

Overall, then, we will see what happens when the sort of regime described in Chapter 2—one that combines constant tinkering with rules with fixed ultimate results—emerges and operates. The political pattern between regime and opposition that results will be something of a cat-and-mouse game. In this chapter, we will see the game emerge with the rise of semiauthoritarianism; at the end of the next chapter, we will examine the contours of the game in more detail.

We used a toothpaste-tube metaphor in the previous chapter to describe how Islamist movements react to constraints and opportunities in general, across all sorts of regimes and spheres of affairs. The cat-and-mouse metaphor refers more specifically to the relationship in the political sphere between semiauthoritarian regimes and Islamist movements. The metaphor is fairly capacious: it suggests little more than an ongoing game between a powerful party and a weak but clever one; the cat plays to dominate but not to kill, while the mouse has no hope of dominating but scrambles to survive. The most likely outcome is simply a continued game. That continuity is obscured by the constant motion of both parties. Islamist movements are often a bit more lumbering in their behavior than the nimble mouse image implies, and regimes perhaps a bit more clever in their own way than the metaphor requires.

In this chapter, we will examine each of the four movements and trace the way it reacted to and was shaped by the emergence and operation of semiauthoritarianism. In Chapters 6 and 7, we will examine particular issues in more detail (the effects of semiauthoritarianism on organizations in Chapter 6 and

Islamist ideological development in Chapter 7), proceeding thematically in those chapters rather than historically and geographically. And we will leave aside the possibility of the change from a semiauthoritarian regime to a fully democratic one until Chapter 8.

Egypt

In the 1970s, Egypt gradually shifted from a fully authoritarian to a semiauthoritarian system, one that survived until 2011. The nature of Egyptian semiauthoritarianism was never constant, and its development was anything but linear. It began by opening to a slightly more pluralist party system in the 1970s and then unevenly loosened up in some other areas as well (professional associations in the 1970s and 1980s; the press in the first decade of the 2000s). Indeed, it varied from one area to another (in the 1980s, for instance, parties were given freer rein, but in the first decade of the 2000s, the most liberal area was the press). The harshest tools of authoritarianism were not so much abolished as held partly in abeyance, still trotted out on occasion. In this shifting environment, the Muslim Brotherhood slowly reemerged and stepped gingerly into politics, gradually accumulating greater interest and experience but also running the risk of provoking a harsh regime response if it pushed too far.

In this section we will see how Egyptian semiauthoritarianism allowed the Islamist movement to reemerge in various spheres; how a new generation of Brotherhood activists sought to take advantage of opportunities to coax the movement into a greater political focus; how the Brotherhood thus emerged as the leading opposition movement in the country but also the leading target of the regime's repression; and how this led the movement to decrease its political involvement and retreat into more cautious behavior.

The Emergence of Semiauthoritarianism and the Reemergence of the Brotherhood

In writing his 1969 book on the Egyptian Muslim Brotherhood, still one of the best and most level-headed scholarly works on the subject, Richard Mitchell explained that he did not take the trouble to use diacritical marks because "the subject of this study has had its moment in history" and "for very few of its leaders will historians reserve a place larger than a footnote."[1] He had buried them

---

1. Richard Mitchell, *The Society of the Muslim Brothers* (Oxford: Oxford University Press, 1993), p. xxxi (originally published 1969).

at the bottom of the page prematurely. In the 1970s, the leaders reemerged from prisons (and the footnotes) to revive the organization that had been so harshly suppressed in the 1950s and 1960s.[2]

The limited political liberalization initiated by the Egyptian regime in the 1970s was circumscribed in many ways (and neither then nor in the years since has it progressed to the point that the Brotherhood has regained its legal status). But four aspects of the regime's political readjustments of the 1970s allowed the Brotherhood to return to Egyptian political life in a different, more muted, but also perhaps more sustainable and sophisticated form.[3]

First, the wave of political arrests and extended detentions (and some of the apparatus of special tribunals and harsh security measures) characteristic of the fully authoritarian period was gradually reversed. Brotherhood leaders in prison were released; some of those who had moved overseas felt secure enough to return. Not only did individuals feel freer, but the organization as a whole found

---

2. The leading works on the reemergence of the Muslim Brotherhood include Carrie Rosefsky Wickham, *Mobilizing Islam: Religion, Activism, and Political Change in Egypt* (New York: Columbia University Press, 2002); Hesham al-Awadi, *In Pursuit of Legitimacy: The Muslim Brothers and Mubarak, 1982–2000* (London: Tauris Academic Studies, 2004); Tarek El-Miselhy Masoud, "Why Islam Wins: Electoral Ecologies and Economies of Political Islam in Contemporary Egypt" (PhD diss., Yale University, 2008); Husam Tamam, *Tahawwulat al-ikwhwan al-muslimin* (Cairo: Maktabat Madbuli, 2006); and Khalil al-'Anani, *Al-ikhwan al-muslimun fi misr: shaykhukha tusari' al-zaman* (Cairo: Maktabat al-Shuruq al-Duwaliyya, 2007).

A very useful article is Mona El-Ghobashy, "The Metamorphosis of the Egyptian Muslim Brothers," *International Journal of Middle East Studies* 37, no. 3 (2005), 391. On the construction of a capable parliamentary bloc, see Samer Shehata and Joshua Stacher, "The Brotherhood Goes to Parliament," *Middle East Report* 240 (Fall 2006), 32–40. Other helpful articles, especially on the Brotherhood's recent activity, include Bruce Rutherford, "What Do Egypt's Islamists Want? Moderate Islam and the Rise of Islamic Constitutionalism," *Middle East Journal* 60, no. 4 (2006), 707–731; Marc Lynch, "The Brotherhood's Dilemma," Middle East Brief 25, Crown Center for Middle East Studies, Brandeis University, January 2008; and Chris Harnisch and Quinn Mecham, "Democratic Ideology in Islamist Opposition? The Muslim Brotherhood's 'Civil State,'" *Middle Eastern Studies* 45, no. 2 (2009), 189–205. The work of Nabil 'Abd al-Fattah on religion-state issues in Egypt is also useful; see, for instance, *Al-mashaf wa-l-sayf* (Cairo: Maktabat Madbuli, 1984). Also of interest is Salwa Ismail, *Rethinking Islamist Politics: Culture, the State and Islamism* (London: I. B. Tauris, 2006).

In addition to these sources, I have relied on daily press coverage of the Brotherhood and its activities (especially *Al-misri al-yawm* and more recently *Al-shuruq*) and the Brotherhood's own extensive web presence (in particular http://www.ikhwanonline.com). And I have conducted a series of interviews since 2006 with Sa'd al-Katatni, Muhammad Mursi, Ibrahim al-Hudaybi, 'Isam al-'Iryan, Gamal Sultan, Abu al-'Ila Madi, 'Abd al-Mun'im Abu al-Futuh, Hamdi Hasan, Rashad al-Bayumi, Khayrat al-Shatir, Akram al-Sha'ir, Muhammad Habib, Khalid Hamza, Zahra al-Shatir, Sherif Ayman, Ahmed Akil, Ahmed Osman and Gamal Hishmat.

3. 'Abd al-Mun'im Abu al-Futuh, a prominent former Brotherhood leader—and perhaps the most prominent member of the generation that joined the movement after its reemergence in the 1970s—has written a useful set of recollections, *Shahid 'ala ta'rikh al-haraka al-islamiyya fi misr* (http://www.abolfotoh.net/%D8%A3%D8%A8%D9%88%D8%A7%D9%84%D9%81%D8%AA %D9%88%D8%AD%D9%81%D9%89%D8%A7%D9%84%D8%B5%D8%AD%D8%A7%D9%8 1%D8%A9/tabid/67/ctl/Details/mid/396/ItemID/148/Default.aspx); other Brotherhood members have contested some of the details, but the basic outline of events seems sound.

that it could resume some activities, such as meeting and even some publishing, despite its lack of legal status.

Second, at the same time as the general liberalization, the atmosphere on college campuses throughout the country proved friendlier than it had been earlier. Student protest on nationalist and leftist grounds punctuated the late 1960s and early 1970s. The Egyptian regime seemed to find Islamist student activists by contrast less threatening and therefore displayed more tolerance toward an emerging Islamist trend.[4]

Third, the upsurge on campuses was matched by an upsurge in activism and organization in Egyptian society. Related in part to the declining abilities of the Nasserist welfare state to provide social services, jobs, and cheap food and consumer goods, Egyptians in the 1970s and 1980s began organizing at the grass roots to provide medical care, education, and other goods and services for themselves; a wave of charitable organizations started as well. Many of these organizations had a religious coloration (both Muslim and Christian). While most Islamic organizations were not associated with the Brotherhood, the Brotherhood profited from this trend. Its members could operate through legally recognized nongovernmental organizations at a time when the movement as a whole still lacked legal recognition (indeed, Brotherhood leaders at the time felt the regime was steering them into becoming a purely social movement). In addition, the emergence of an Islamic social sector helped provide a supportive subculture for the reemerging Brotherhood.

Fourth, the regime's mild political liberalization was coupled with gradual but striking ideological adjustment friendlier to the Brotherhood. Pan-Arabism, already in decline, was largely jettisoned; socialism was gradually abandoned as well. In their place, the regime sought to enhance its religious basis of legitimacy.

As the Brotherhood found a friendlier environment, it reemerged and rebuilt itself slowly, stepping cautiously into the political realm. The regime was slowly dismantling its sole political party, the Arab Socialist Union, in favor of a multiparty system (with a dominant governing party, eventually the National Democratic Party). The Brotherhood briefly flirted with the idea of affiliating with one of the constituent parts of the dissolving Arab Socialist Union but eventually shied away from any formal political affiliations. Some members ran as independents in the parliamentary elections that took place in the mildly liberalized

---

4. Wickham, *Mobilizing Islam*, provides the most thorough analysis of this trend as well as the later move into the professional associations. Patrick D. Gaffney, *The Prophet's Pulpit: Islamic Preaching in Contemporary Egypt* (Berkeley: University of California Press, 1994), chap. 4, provides an early account of the emergence of an Islamist student movement in Minya, one in which the Brotherhood played a marginal role.

climate, but in this way they were only returning to the historic Brotherhood pattern of dabbling in political activity.

In the 1980s, however, the Brotherhood moved more ambitiously—or perhaps it might be more accurate to say that it was pulled along by its more youthful energetic members. By attracting a new generation of student activists (who graduated and entered the professions), the Brotherhood had folded into its ranks politically skilled and ambitious cadres, fully prepared for moving beyond a superficial presence in the political sphere. Their efforts took shape in three arenas.

First, the Brotherhood took a major plunge into parliamentary elections in 1984. The system put in place for those elections allowed only candidates with a party affiliation to run, so the Brotherhood formed an electoral alliance with the Wafd party (a largely liberal party from the pre-1952 era that, like the Brotherhood, was exploiting the semiauthoritarian opening to reenter the political scene). Clearly an alliance of convenience for both sides (the Wafd sought to ensure that its list won the 8 percent of the national vote required to gain parliamentary representation, and the Brotherhood needed a legal umbrella for its candidates), the tactical alignment did not survive far past the election. But it catapulted a group of Brotherhood leaders (eight won seats) into a national political role, affording them a platform but also confronting them with a series of difficult political questions: Would they run again and if so, how? Would they attempt to form their own political party? Would they pursue a narrow religious agenda or a broadly reform-oriented one? And how would they react when President Mubarak's term expired in 1987? (The constitutional task of the parliament at that time was to nominate a single candidate to present to a popular referendum.)

Second, the Brotherhood moved ambitiously into Egypt's professional associations.[5] With a growing basis of support among professionals in most fields (such as engineering, law, and medicine), the new generation of Brotherhood activists found professional associations an inviting field. The association elections operated in comparative freedom, thus rewarding the same kinds of skills younger activists had learned in university politics and student association elections. Voting was characterized by low turnout (an ideal context for a well-organized movement able to mobilize highly motivated and loyal constituencies). And the results were hardly inconsequential: professional associations provided a host

5. On the Brotherhood in the professional associations, see Wickham, *Mobilizing Islam*. Also of interest are Geneive Abdo, *No God but God: Egypt and the Triumph of Islam* (Oxford: Oxford University Press, 2000), chap. 4; and Ninette S. Fahmy, "The Performance of the Muslim Brotherhood in the Egyptian Syndicates: An Alternative Formula for Reform?" *Middle East Journal* 52, no. 4 (1998), 551–562.

of benefits for their members and offered access to public debates (not only on matters of professional concern but sometimes on issues of wider public debate). By the late 1980s, Brotherhood slates dominated most of Egypt's leading professional associations.

Third, the Brotherhood moved into the economic sphere. It must be stressed, however, that the precise nature of the Brotherhood's economic activities is difficult to describe: they have drawn less attention, and the subject is complex.[6] Further, since the Brotherhood has no legal existence, it operates no enterprises under its own name. But individuals associated with the Brotherhood have been quite active; they work in a variety of fields, sometimes in areas with a religious coloration (such as Islamic finance or production of religious articles or publications) and sometimes not. Whether they are standing in for the Brotherhood as an organization or pursuing purely private activities (donating a share of their earnings to the organization, to be sure) is not always clear. And alongside the economic activity of Brotherhood members lies a whole range of religiously themed economic enterprises (most visibly in Islamic finance but in other fields as well) that, like the Islamic social service sector, often have no connection with the Brotherhood whatsoever but might provide a protective subculture for the Brotherhood's activities.

The increased political and social role of the Brotherhood set off discussions within both the movement and the regime about the movement's political role. And it led many leaders to develop a more ambitious agenda and a sharper oppositional focus. In 1987, the Brotherhood switched electoral alliances to run candidates under the banner of the more ideologically congenial Socialist Labor Party (a party then metamorphosing from a socialist and nationalist orientation into a more Islamist one), increasing its share to thirty-eight seats. The movement's deputies voted in favor of a second term for President Mubarak that same year. But three years later the Brotherhood struck a more confrontational pose, joining with almost all other opposition forces to boycott parliamentary elections in a protest over the lack of guarantees for free and fair procedures.

A group of younger Brotherhood activists, led by those who had grown up in student and then professional associations, worked to concretize the Brotherhood's new political focus by forming a political party. In 1995, some members of this group finally took the initiative to form one themselves (the Hizb al-Wasat,

---

6. While the general field of Islamic finance has drawn considerable attention, much less work has been done on the economic activities of the Brotherhood. Perhaps the most useful general work is Bjorn Olav Utvik, *Islamist Economics in Egypt: The Pious Road to Development* (Boulder, Colo.: Lynne Rienner, 2006). A rich study, Utvik's book is concerned more with program, thought, and ideology than with actual business activities, and his focus extends far beyond the Brotherhood.

or Center Party). Initially, they had limited support from some Brotherhood figures, but ultimately the movement distanced itself from the party, opening an
angry rift between the two.

Egyptian Semiauthoritarianism in Practice: Coping with Capriciousness

If the Brotherhood was becoming more comfortable and skilled at participation,
Egypt's political and security leaders were growing more hostile to the movement's political role. A shift away from liberalization that began toward the close
of the 1980s was unannounced but still quite clear. Leading regime figures and
their mouthpieces began to assert that the Brotherhood and violent groups were
simply two aspects of the same movement. And when a violent upsurge from radical Islamist groups—in some areas close to an insurgency—erupted in Egypt during the early 1990s, the Muslim Brotherhood was caught in the crossfire. Various
forums where the Brotherhood had made some strides (such as in student associations and university elections) were gradually restricted. A new law governing
professional association elections was clearly aimed (and succeeded to a significant degree) at prying the leadership of those bodies out of Brotherhood hands.

Perhaps the regime's most intimidating tool in the crackdown was the use of
military courts. When President Mubarak took office in 1981, he prided himself
on avoiding the panoply of exceptional courts constructed by his predecessors
and on honoring judgments issued by the regular courts. But facing an upsurge
in violence from radical Islamists in the 1990s, he began transferring cases to the
military courts. (These were technically regular rather than exceptional courts,
but their jurisdiction over civilians would seem to have been barred by the text
of the 1971 constitution until its amendment in 2007. Despite the constitutional
prohibition, the 1966 law governing the military courts allowed the president to
transfer crimes to them for trial; when he did so, those courts responded with
ruthless efficiency.) By the middle of the decade, this tool was directed at dozens
of Brotherhood leaders themselves, most of whom received multiyear sentences.

Yet in keeping with the reliably unreliable rules of semiauthoritarian politics,
not all gates to political activity were closed. Indeed, some new ones opened,
especially in the first decade of the 2000s. The Brotherhood continued to operate
openly, and Egypt's rulers left the Supreme Guide himself unmolested. Further,
the regime found that its ability to manipulate elections was restricted by a series of Supreme Constitutional Court rulings (asserting the rights of independents to run for election and mandating fuller judicial supervision of voting).
This made it more difficult to prevent the Brotherhood from running and led
to a voting process that was less susceptible to manipulation. The result allowed

Brotherhood candidates to run and forced manipulative regime countermeasures outside the polling place (sometimes by merely a few feet as Brotherhood campaign workers were harassed and beaten). In 1995, the Brotherhood secured a single seat, but in 2000 the movement's share increased to seventeen.

The combination of repression in some areas and opening in others marked the full operation of the cat-and-mouse game. But in the middle of the first decade of the twenty-first century, the possibility of a qualitative shift in Brotherhood political activity seemed briefly possible. The 2005 parliamentary elections—held in three stages in order to allow a stretched Egyptian judiciary to supervise balloting in all polling places—occurred in an unprecedented international spotlight.

By this time, the younger generation of leaders had risen to positions of influence in the movement. Many strove to seize the moment by recasting the Brotherhood's political message in more general terms to appeal to a wider group of voters. They realized some success in internal debates, and by the middle of the decade, political reform and freedom had become the Brotherhood's most consistent themes. Mahdi 'Akif, the movement's general guide, attracted attention in 2005 when he substituted the Brotherhood's older "Islam is the solution" slogan with "Reform is the solution"; he went on to say: "Freedom is a basic part of the Islamic order. If it is absent then the slogan 'Islam is the solution' has no value. It becomes the problem, not the solution."[7] And 'Abd al-Mun'im Abu al-Futuh, the most outspoken of the new generation of leaders (and the highest ranking at the time, since he served on the sixteen-member Guidance Bureau) went even further, declaring publicly that he found the slogan outdated and overly emotional. (Some Brotherhood leaders regarded Abu al-Futuh as having gone too far; Muhammad Mursi, his less pliable colleague on the Guidance Bureau, defended "Islam is the solution" as the "permanent" slogan of the movement.)[8]

The new stress on political reform was a clear response to a perceived political opening. The Brotherhood nominated candidates for about one-third of the parliamentary seats, ultimately winning eighty-eight (about one-fifth of the body). But those numbers obscure how impressive the Brotherhood's performance was. In head-to-head competition between Brotherhood candidates and those from the ruling National Democratic Party, Brothers won two-thirds of the races. Now the leader of the largest opposition bloc in any post-1952 Egyptian parliament, Brotherhood deputies sketched out an ambitious reform agenda. The movement as a whole also responded by devoting more resources to political activity, sup-

---

7. Muhammad 'Abd al-Quddus, "The General Guide of the Muslim Brotherhood Affirms to al-Dustur: Now . . . Freedom Is the Solution!" *Al-dustur,* 15 June 2005, p. 8.

8. For Mursi's comment, see the website for the 2005 parliamentary campaign in his district, http://www.dayra23.com/asp/solution.asp.

porting the parliamentary bloc, and working on a comprehensive program for a political party (a preliminary draft of which was issued in 2007).

But the Brotherhood's political success prompted a harsh regime response. In 2007, Egypt's rulers pushed through a series of constitutional amendments, many of which (such as a ban on parties with a religious reference) were clearly aimed directly at the Brotherhood.[9] Brotherhood activists were rounded up in ways to make continued participation difficult. (In a 2009 conversation with a Brotherhood parliamentarian, I asked how he and his colleagues ran their offices in their districts. He explained that they could not do so anymore, since many of their staff members had been arrested.) Wealthy individuals associated with the Brotherhood were singled out for harassment in an evident effort to dry up the movement's financial base. The Brotherhood was harassed sufficiently to make participation in elections for the upper house of the Egyptian parliament and local councils impossible. By 2010, one-third of the movement's top body, the Guidance Bureau, was held in prison.

Advocates of a political approach—many of the same leaders who had argued for a more general and less religious rhetoric earlier—now pressed for a confrontational attitude. They sought not to leave the political field but to step up coordination with other opposition actors and to boycott the 2010 elections. But such voices were no longer heeded by the movement as a whole. In internal elections, advocates of a more cautious approach won the day. A new general guide, Muhammad Badi', was elected; Badi''s more bashful style bespoke an emphasis on internal organizational health over strident political engagement. Somewhat paradoxically, the less politically minded viewed an election boycott at first as excessively confrontational; thus the movement maintained its verbal criticism but held back from coordinating a boycott with other opposition groups. In the 2010 parliamentary elections, however, the movement was dealt such a severe blow in the first round of voting that it pulled out of the subsequent runoff round.

It was this slightly withdrawn and politically shy leadership that was confronted with the revolutionary situation of January 2011. But by this time a new group of youthful activists (generally drawing from university students and recent graduates) pushed the movement as a whole to align itself with the emerging revolutionary coalition. The leadership as a whole demurred, ultimately giving members permission to demonstrate as individuals. But as the political confrontation between the regime and the demonstrators escalated in the last days of

---

9. I analyzed these amendments with some colleagues; see Nathan J. Brown, Michele Dunne, and Amr Hamzawy, "Egypt's Controversial Constitutional Amendments," Carnegie Web Commentary, 23 March 2007, http://www.carnegieendowment.org/files/egypt_constitution_webcommentary01.pdf.

January 2011, the leadership felt pressured to take sides. It still sought a compromise stand—fully endorsing the demonstrations but also showing up to meet with Egypt's vice president, a security figure hastily brought in to manage the crisis. It proved impossible to straddle for long, and the Brotherhood eventually embraced the revolution, but its hesitation showed that the movement's leadership had lost the seemingly sure political footing it had shown a few years earlier.

The political pattern of the reemerged Brotherhood is clear: greater openness leads eventually to greater politicization; greater politicization is often more confrontational rather than less (though it always stops far short of violence); greater politicization and more confrontational tactics provoke harsh regime responses; harsh responses eventually generate partial retreat. But the clarity of this general pattern does not obscure the contentious nature of each step within the movement and the trial-and-error nature of decision making.

Jordan

Jordan's Islamists have never experienced the extreme bouts of repression that their counterparts have in Egypt; for much of its history, the Jordanian Brotherhood's relationship with the regime has been far less hostile.[10] But the emergence of semiauthoritarianism in Jordan had a similar effect. It led to an increase in the Brotherhood's politicization and a slow but definite move to grasp at the opportunities presented by casting itself as the country's most viable opposition political force. While the general contours of the Jordanian cat-and-mouse game are similar to the Egyptian (in which initial moves toward politicization have been tolerated but later moves have sparked regime countermeasures), the Jordanian regime has been a bit steadier and less capricious.

In this section, we will first consider the Jordanian Brotherhood's history before the emergence of semiauthoritarianism—a period in which the Brotherhood invested less in politics, reacted more uncertainly to the possibility of change

---

10. There is a significant body of writing on the history of the Jordanian Muslim Brotherhood, but there is not so much as to overwhelm the reader. I have relied most heavily on the helpful work of Ibrahim Ghurayba, notably *Jama'at al-ikhwan al-muslimin fi al-urdun* (Amman: Al-Urdun Al-Jadid Research Center, 1997). Ghurayba, a Jordanian journalist and former Brotherhood member, is seen by some within the movement as a partisan source (especially because of his view that the Brotherhood should primarily operate as a Jordanian organization and therefore maintain some distance from Hamas), but his work is careful and well documented, and indeed forms the major source for many other writings on the movement. Other useful Arabic-language sources include Husayn Abu Rumman, ed., *Al-harakat wa-l-tanzimat al-islamiyya fi al-urdun* (Amman: Dar Sindbad li-l-nashr, 1997); *Hizb jabhat al-'amal al-islami,* Guide to Party Life in Jordan, series no. 1 (Amman: Al-Urdun al-Jadid Research Center, 1993); and Musa Zayd al-Kilani, *Al-harakat al-islamiyya fi al-urdun wa filastin, dirasa wa taqyim* (Dar al-Bashir, 1995).

(and was more likely to side with the regime than the opposition at critical moments), and focused much of its energy on nonpolitical activities, where it had
a much freer hand. We will then turn to the emergence of semiauthoritarianism
in the late 1980s and its operation since that time. Shedding its initial diffidence
toward and hesitation about involvement in politics, the Jordanian movement
has seized on the opportunities offered over the past two decades by semiauthoritarianism by founding a political party, developing detailed political programs,
and entering elections with enthusiasm. But as a direct result, the movement has
provoked a regime response and has found itself caught in a gentler version of
a cat-and-mouse game. It has also increasingly been afflicted by divisive debates
over political positions, strategies, and tactics.

A Politically Aloof Movement

The Jordanian Muslim Brotherhood, like many of its counterpart organizations in the Arab world, traces its origin to an inspirational meeting between the
founder of its chapter, 'Abd al-Latif Abu Qura, and Hasan al-Banna in 1945. Abu
Qura was able to register the organization as a religious society and secure some
support from the king. Partly because of this origin and the movement's early
political stances, it is common in English-language scholarship on the Jordanian

---

Two active participants in the movement have written comprehensive histories. From the radical wing, Muhammad 'Abd al-Qadir Abu Faris stresses the movement's steady oppositional role in
Safahat min al-tarikh al-siyasi li-l-ikhwan al-muslimin fi al-urdun (Amman: Dar al-Qur'an, 2000).
And Bassam 'Ali al-'Umush, a former member, has written an account explicitly dedicated to better
movement-regime relations, *Mahattat fi ta'rikh jama'at al-ikhwan al-muslimin fi al-urdun* (Amman:
Academic for Publishing and Distribution, 2008). Also of interest on specific questions are Khalid Sulayman, "Al-mumarisa al-dimuqratiyya dakhil hizb jabhat al-'amal al-islami," *Al-mustaqbal al-'arabi*
296 (October 2003), 52–81 (on democracy), and Muhammad Abu Rumman, *Al-siyasa al-urduniyya
wa tahaddi hamas* (Amman: Friedrich Ebert Stiftung, 2009) (on the relationship with Hamas).
   In English, the most recent works of interest are Jillian Schwedler, *Faith in Moderation: Islamist
Parties in Jordan and Yemen* (Cambridge: Cambridge University Press, 2006); Quintan Wiktorow-
icz, *The Management of Islamic Activism: Salafis, the Muslim Brotherhood, and State Power in Jordan*
(Albany: State University of New York Press, 2001); and a rich variety of writings by Janine Clark:
"Threats, Goals, and Resources: Islamist Coalition-Building in Jordan" (paper presented at the annual
meeting of the American Political Science Association, Boston, August 2008); "The Conditions of
Islamist Moderation: Unpacking Cross-Ideological Cooperation in Jordan," *International Journal of
Middle East Studies* 38 (2006), 539–560; *Islam, Charity, and Activism: Middle-Class Networks and So-
cial Welfare in Egypt, Jordan, and Yemen* (Bloomington: Indiana University Press, 2004); "Islamist and
Family Law Reform in Morocco and Jordan," *Mediterranean Politics* 13, no. 3 (2008), 333–352 (with
Amy E. Young); and "Who Opened the Window? Women's Activism in Islamic Parties," *Comparative
Politics* 25, no. 3 (2003), 293–312 (with Jillian Schwedler).
   For the history of the movement, two English-language books are useful: Amnon Cohen, *Political Parties on the West Bank under the Jordanian Regime, 1949–1967* (Ithaca: Cornell University Press,
1982); and Marioun Boulby, *The Muslim Brotherhood and the Kings of Jordan* (Atlanta: Scholars Press,
1999). A more specialized work is Anne Sofie Roald, *Tarbiya: Education and Politics in Islamic Movements in Jordan and Malaysia* (Stockholm: Almqvist & Wiksell, 1994).

Muslim Brotherhood to describe its relationship with the Jordanian monarchy as friendly and the movement as a political ally of the regime for several decades. But this picture is misleading: the relationship was more tense and guarded than the standard rosier portrait allows. It might be better to describe the movement as tolerated by—and tolerant of—the regime for many years.

The movement's first dozen years were tumultuous ones for the country: Jordan became fully independent; adopted a constitution that provided for a potentially uneasy mix of parliamentarism and monarchy; fought in a war over the creation of the state of Israel; annexed the West Bank; saw the assassination of its founding king and the deposition of its second; and witnessed the rise of Arab nationalism (and the enthusiastic support of some Jordanians for Nasserism and other nationalist movements). Throughout these events, the Brotherhood's basic attitude was clear: it was generally supportive both of the monarchy and of the Palestinian cause (sending volunteers to fight in the 1948 war); it also harbored deep suspicions of nationalist and leftist forces. But such general stances did not lead to any consistent involvement in politics. The movement sometimes made clear its opposition to government policies (focusing on the religious and cultural realms but also delving into the regime's close alliance with Western powers). Its leaders debated about running in parliamentary elections (and its first change of leadership occurred in a dispute over the subject in 1953).[11] Some members ran as independents, and the movement moved as far as advancing candidates under its own banner by the middle of the decade. It scored some modest successes, securing four seats out of a forty-member parliament in two elections in the mid-1950s.

Throughout the period, as the fault lines in Jordanian politics became increasingly sharp, the Brotherhood stood largely aloof. The movement showed a willingness to criticize the regime in the 1950s—with the movement's publication suspended at one point and its leader arrested at another—but it straddled the fence when a broad coalition formed in the 1950s to push for parliamentary democracy and alignment with Arab nationalism. Initially offering guarded support to the opposition, the Brotherhood tilted back toward the monarchy in a showdown between the king and the opposition in 1957. But leaders criticized the king's willingness to rely on Western forces and claim to have rejected an invitation to join the cabinet, preferring to remain outside positions of authority.[12]

---

11. See the chapters by 'Ali 'Abd al-Kazim and Ibrahim Ghurayba in Abu Rumman, *Al-harakat.* The new head of the movement, 'Abd al-Rahman Khalifa, continued in his position for four decades until he retired amid a new dispute over the formation of a party and electoral participation.

12. According to some accounts, the king offered the Brotherhood leader the chance to form a cabinet, but he declined, offering only his support rather than full participation. See Bassam al-'Amush, *Mahattat fi tarikh: jama'at al-ikhwan al-muslimin fi al-urdun* (Amman: Dar Zahran, 2008), p. 270.

In the wake of the crisis, a more fully authoritarian order settled in. Not seen as an opposition movement, the Brotherhood was able to run candidates in the (now much more constrained and less competitive) elections, securing a small number of seats. When the movement ventured too far into the political field or seemed to edge into overt opposition, the regime responded by pressuring leaders or suspending movement publications. When Palestinian movements began organizing in the second half of the 1960s, the Muslim Brotherhood lent them some support but again stood aloof in 1969 and 1970s as the regime suppressed them. In the 1970s, a movement leader, Ishaq al-Farhan, served as minister of education. His acceptance of the post was controversial within the Brotherhood, forcing him to freeze his membership as he served.

The Brotherhood's political straddling did not mean it was inert; the movement shifted its attention to nonpolitical spheres. Since the Brotherhood was registered as a religious rather than a political organization and one that had proved useful to the king, it escaped the full effects of Jordanian authoritarianism. In 1965, its leading members formed the Islamic Center, a legally independent nongovernmental organization that became the hub of many of the movement's social activities. The Islamic Center set up branches throughout the country, established one of Jordan's leading hospitals, and inspired a steady growth in Islamically oriented nongovernmental organizations.[13] Many of the new organizations were closely associated with the Brotherhood or its leading members, but others had a more attenuated relationship and still others had no ties at all other than sharing a general religious coloration. Also during the 1960s and the 1970s, Islamists slowly began working in student and professional associations, competing when those bodies held internal elections.

Positioned for Semiauthoritarianism

By the 1980s, the Brotherhood and associated organizations had established a significant presence in Jordanian society. Thus, when Jordan moved back to a semiauthoritarian system at the end of the 1980s, the Islamists found themselves in a strong position, one that allowed them to seize the initiative and plunge (however contentiously) fully back into a Jordanian political scene they had never completely abandoned.

Jordan's limited political liberalization came in the midst of a series of events that had little to do with the Muslim Brotherhood. In 1988, the king abandoned

---

13. See the chapter by Walid Hammad, "Islamists and Charitable Work," in Abu Rumman, *Al-harakat,* for the most detailed presentation of this sector; also of interest are Clark, *Islam, Charity, and Activism,* and Wiktorowicz, *Management of Islamic Activism.*

most of Jordan's claim to the territory of the West Bank (making new parliamentary elections possible without confronting the vexatious question of whether and how the West Bank would be represented); the following year, rioting broke out over economic grievances in some Jordanian cities. The regime's response—a political liberalization consisting of more open elections, relaxation on restrictions on organization and expression, and appointment of a royal commission to draft a "National Charter" outlining a comprehensive and consensual reform program—allowed openings for the Brotherhood on many fronts. The pockets of more democratic practice in student and professional associations were expanded. A more liberal official attitude toward NGOs allowed the Brotherhood to build on its success with founding such bodies for a variety of educational, medical, charitable, and other social work.[14] Al-Farhan, the former minister of education, had gone on to head the University of Jordan. He rejoined the movement and was able to work with others with Islamist inclinations to form Al-Zarqa Private University, a new institution with a heavy emphasis on religious subjects.

The most dramatic opportunities came in the political sphere. More open parliamentary elections in 1989 led to an astonishing accomplishment for the Muslim Brotherhood: twenty-two of its twenty-nine candidates gained seats (in a parliament now expanded to eighty members). Showing that it could convert its organizational successes in other spheres into fielding an impressive electoral machine, the Brotherhood emerged as the most successful (and perhaps arguably the only viable, at least in electoral terms) political party in Jordanian history. But this success confronted both the movement and the regime with many questions. Brotherhood leaders, of course, viewed their movement as much more than a political party and had to concern themselves with how to balance and integrate the movement's political activities with the remainder of their broad agenda. They also had to face the need to devise a full political program, communicate accomplishments to constituents, plan a parliamentary strategy, and contemplate the possibility of accepting a role in government. The regime was forced to confront the reality that a formidable movement—one with a largely oppositional coloration—had shown itself to have a real constituency.

Both regime and opposition were uncertain about how to play the game of semiauthoritarian politics. At first, the regime seemed to vacillate between attempts to co-opt and to contain the Islamists.[15] And the Islamists were equally

---

14. See Wiktorowicz, *Management of Islamic Activism*, especially chaps. 1 and 3.

15. In his book on the history of the Brotherhood, former IAF MP Bassam al-'Amush reprints a brief 2007 exchange with prominent journalist and economist Fahd al-Fanik which includes the latter's observation that after the elections of 1989, "the Brotherhood was transformed in the view of the regime from a supporting to a threatening element. And they are now the strongest challenge to the regime." Al-'Amush, *Mahattat fi tarikh*, p. 404.

unsure of how to use their new position. In the wake of the 1989 elections, the Brotherhood was able to place its candidate in the speaker's chair, but its deputies seemed unprepared to take a leading parliamentary role; the organization had a general program supporting political reform and Islamization of public life, but the content remained vague and there was no clear prioritization or ability to translate general principles into specific legislative initiatives. Faced immediately after taking their seats with the question of whether to support the cabinet, Brotherhood parliamentarians reacted uncertainly: they decided to support a confidence motion but then attached a lengthy list of conditions for their support. Soon the press of politics became even more intense: the Brotherhood was invited to join the cabinet in a minority capacity. The resulting dispute within the movement was sufficiently severe that the matter was referred to the international Muslim Brotherhood, which delivered a predictably ambiguous (as well as tardy) response. In the end, after considerable internal wrangling, the supporters of participating in the cabinet won out, though the experience was not a particularly happy one. While they were able to introduce some changes in the ministries they controlled, the five Brotherhood ministers found that they had little influence on the broad outlines of government policy; their critics were therefore able to portray them as focused only on trivial and symbolic issues. And Jordan's growing involvement in the effort to find a negotiated settlement to the Israeli-Palestinian conflict threatened to place the movement in a difficult position should it remain in government. The Brotherhood ministers were dropped when a new prime minister was appointed in 1991. Brotherhood deputies joined the ranks of the opposition, where they seemed more comfortable, denouncing the cabinet's shortcomings in political reform, Islamization, and foreign policy.

Coping with Evolving Semiauthoritarianism

Since the emergence of semiauthoritarianism in the late 1980s, the Jordanian regime has tinkered with the degree of openness and worked to contain the challenge of the Islamist opposition. The Brotherhood has reacted by operating within the rules imposed while trying to push for more political openness. Internally, it has quarreled incessantly about whether and how to participate in elections and how harsh an opposition pose to strike. Indeed, the internal dispute set off by the movement's 1989 success steadily worsened over the next two decades.

The cat-and-mouse game between regime and opposition is best seen through the lens of a series of parliamentary elections in 1992, 1997, 2003, 2007, and 2010. Neither the rules of semiauthoritarian politics nor the terms of the movement's politicization have remained consistent from one election to the next.

The 1993 elections were preceded by two legal changes, one of which (a 1992 law on political parties) offered the Islamists better terms than the previous authoritarian system provided but the other of which (an amended electoral system) was clearly aimed against them. Both changes prompted debates within the movement on how to respond.

The 1992 change allowed political parties to form. A movement that had been able to paper over most ideological differences in the past suddenly found itself in the middle of a bitter debate: should the Muslim Brotherhood transform itself into a political party? The disagreements were both principled (whether the movement should participate in a system that was not based on Islamic teachings) and practical (whether transformation to a political party would undercut the broad agenda of the movement). In the end, the Brotherhood opted for a compromise solution: it would endorse the effort to create a new political party, the Islamic Action Front (IAF). The Brotherhood movement would continue to operate as it had; the new IAF would be open to those Brotherhood members who wished to join, but it would also serve to attract independent Islamists.

The IAF was the first party to register under the new parties law. But while the Front might be viewed as a success (it has remained Jordan's largest and most significant political party), it has never served as the autonomous party that its founders envisaged. Its leaders now refer to it as the "legitimate son" of the Brotherhood and sometimes as the Brotherhood's "political wing." Critical decisions about the party, its platforms, and its actions continue to be made by the Muslim Brotherhood and then forwarded to the IAF for implementation (and sometimes ratification, such as the selection of the party leader). Further, its success as a party has led to criticism among sympathetic observers that the Brotherhood has become focused on politics at the expense of the other parts of its mission: that social activity, organization among students, recruitment of new members, missionary activity, charitable works, and education have all come to seem less glamorous, and that political maneuverings and internal rivalries now dominate the attention of most leaders.

The second change preceding the 1993 parliamentary elections was a new electoral law issued by decree that aimed to counteract Islamist strength by favoring tribal over party loyalties.[16] The move came among a series of indications

---

16. Referred to in Jordan as the "one vote" system, and more technically as the "single non-transferrable vote," the new law allowed voters to name only a single candidate in each of Jordan's multimember districts. The previous system had allowed voters to select as many candidates as there were deputies for the district. The regime was apparently convinced that voters, when given only a single vote, would generally opt for a candidate with whom they had a family or tribal connection. Ideological candidates would fare less well. And in fact the law seemed to have that effect. It should

that the pendulum was swinging against political liberalization.[17] The IAF, which had already prepared for the election based on the old law, complained vociferously but decided against pulling out. It saw its share of deputies fall from twenty-two to sixteen, despite the fact that it ran more candidates (thirty-six in an eighty-member parliament). For all its bitterness over the course of Jordanian politics (the regime's abandonment of the program of further political reform promised at the beginning of the decade and its negotiation of a peace treaty with Israel), the IAF did not completely reverse its accommodationist tendencies at first. When the Jordanian-Israeli peace treaty was presented to the Jordanian parliament in 1994, the movement maintained its shrill rhetoric and principled rejection of any settlement with Israel, but IAF deputies decided to absent themselves from the chamber rather than vote against the clear wishes of the king.

Still split on the issue of participation by the time of the 1997 elections, the Brotherhood polled its own members, the majority of whom opted for a boycott.[18] When some members decided to run as independents, they were drummed out of the movement. Yet leaders insisted that the boycott was not a strategic decision against political participation but only a political move designed to back the demand for a fairer law. Some opposition parties joined with the IAF in sitting out the elections.

The experience of sitting outside parliament was not pleasant for a movement that had taken firm steps toward politicization. A six-year hiatus before the next elections in 2003 accordingly gave the IAF time to study its options more thoroughly; while there was still sentiment among some leaders to continue the

---

be noted that the "one vote" system joined another element of the Jordanian electoral machinery to discriminate against Islamists: districts are gerrymandered to privilege areas populated by those with East Bank roots; Palestinian areas (where Islamists have polled more successfully) are underrepresented in the parliament.

17. Even the use of a "decree law" to bring about the change in electoral system was part of the deliberalization: the Jordanian constitution allows for laws to be issued by decree when parliament is not in session, but only for matters that admit of no delay. Dissolving the parliament and then suddenly discovering the need for a new election was an implausible (and almost certainly unconstitutional) device for forcing electoral reform, but it has since become standard operating procedure for Jordanian elections.

Besides the electoral law change, there were moves toward a tighter press law, also issued by decree. When the country's High Court found this decree law unconstitutional, the king publicly denounced the ruling and the chief justice was forced into early retirement; the law was then pressed on a reluctant but ultimately obedient parliament. In subsequent years, the regime pursued two restrictions that were particularly irksome to the Islamists: greater regulation of mosque preachers and limitations on unlicensed fatwas.

18. For the more recent history of the Brotherhood and IAF, I rely in part on personal interviews between 2006 and 2009 with movement leaders ʿAbd al-Latif ʿArabiyyat, Muhammad al-Buzur, Naʾil Musalha, Muhammad al-ʿAql, Ruhayl Ghurayba, Zaki Bani Arshid, ʿAzzam al-Hunaydi, Jamil Abu Bakr, Nabil al-Kufahi, and Nimr al-ʿAssaf. Some observers of the movement, including Muhammad Abu Rumman, Ibrahim Ghurayba, Samih al-Muʿayta, ʿUrayyib al-Rantawi, and Khalid Walid, also contributed valuable information.

boycott, the movement as a whole decided that it would participate in a limited fashion. In 2003, the IAF ran fewer candidates (thirty for an expanded 110-member parliament), winning seventeen seats.

By now a melodramatic pattern had been established: the IAF would threaten a boycott, leaders would debate among themselves, and a decision one way or the other would be made, sometimes at the last minute. Internal debates over participation grew increasingly acrimonious. The movement's uncertain politicization was not simply the product of internal division. It was also a result of growing tension with the regime and a clear (though by Egyptian standards gentle) attempt to rein the Islamists in. Already in the 1990s there were signs that the Jordanian regime was growing quite wary of the Islamist movement. When King Hussein, who had a complicated but not entirely hostile track record with the movement, died, he was succeeded by a son who had no such credentials (and appeared less interested in cultivating them). In 2006, for instance, the regime seized the Islamic Center, charging financial irregularities and corruption; it also moved to curtail student associations and developed plans to restrict professional associations from taking political stances. In 2007, the leadership of Al-Zarqa Private University was pressured to dismiss sixteen faculty members, including some IAF leaders.

By the time of the 2007 elections, regime pressure had aggravated internal disputes to an unprecedented extent. IAF members bickered over participation and even more over the composition of the slate of candidates. After a bitter internal struggle, those within the movement most interested in emphasizing domestic issues and signaling some willingness to work with the government managed to seize control of the campaign, placing their leaders on the ballot (and running a smaller number of candidates than usual in order to signal clearly that they did not wish to govern). Other wings within the party reacted unenthusiastically to the slate. When the IAF secretary-general largely absented himself, his opponents brought him before a Muslim Brotherhood disciplinary board. With a divided movement and, leaders charged, an upsurge in official manipulation, only six members of the IAF's reduced slate of twenty-two candidates won.[19]

The 2007 election made clear how polarized the internal debate had become. Within the movement, observers (and, in their franker moments, leaders) had often spoken of different tendencies. For a long time, the split over participation reflected a deeper ideological division between "hawks" (less willing to compromise on Islamic issues, generally more skeptical of participation, and more willing to use strident language and toss out terms like nonbeliever [*kafir*] or idolatry

---

19. A research institute close to the IAF issued a report attempting to document the irregularities. See Markaz al-umma li-l-dirasat wa-l-abhath, *Al-intikhabat al-urduniyya li-'amm 2007 bayn riwayatayn* (Amman, n.d.)

[*taghut*])[20] and "doves" (more conciliatory in both style and substance and more interested in reaching an accommodation with the government). But a second area of division had grown in the 1990s with the signing of the Israeli-Jordanian peace treaty, the rise of Hamas among Palestinians, the periodic moves by the Jordanian government against Hamas, and the growing tilt in the movement's base toward those from a Palestinian background. A camp arguing for a greater stress on Jordanian politics began to square off against enthusiastic supporters of Hamas.

In the wake of the 2007 elections, these two divisions became increasingly connected, and hawks and Hamas supporters began to dominate the movement's rank and file. Not only did the movement seem to be splitting among polarized camps, but internal comity began to break down. By 2010, the rivalry was at once public and byzantine. Hawks accused doves of fraud in an internal IAF election, and doves publicly threatened a mass resignation from the movement—a virtually unprecedented public escalation of the rivalry. In 2010, the two sides managed to paper over their differences sufficiently to demand electoral law reform; when their demands were not met, the IAF decided to boycott the parliamentary balloting that year. By the end of the year, the two camps managed to patch over divisions sufficiently to develop a program of political reform that they prepared to press on the regime, but even then, the centerpiece of the effort for some members (a proposal to move toward a constitutional monarchy) was not embraced by all leaders.

While the details of the Jordanian experience differ, the cat-and-mouse game between regime and opposition and the constant internal wrangling over politicization mirror the Egyptian experience. There is another odd parallel as well: as the internal conflict escalated, those more committed to politicization began to strike a stronger oppositional pose, and those who regarded the regime with more disdain began to show reservations about a confrontational approach. Late in the first decade of the 2000s, for instance, the dovish/Jordanian camp began to develop calls for comprehensive constitutional reform and for transition to a constitutional monarchy; it was the hawkish/Palestinian camp that refused to back the proposal (perhaps preferring to focus less on Jordanian politics and more on the Palestinian cause).

Kuwait

The Kuwaiti experience with semiauthoritarianism is perhaps the mildest in the region. From independence up to the Iraqi invasion of 1990, Kuwait gravitated

---

20. For a sample of such language, see Abu Faris, *Safahat min al-tarikh.*

between a semiauthoritarian and a fully authoritarian system; in this environment the Islamist movement was able to establish itself and develop some political experience, but it held back from any ambitious political strategy. With semiauthoritarianism firmly cemented in the period after the liberation of the country from Iraq, the Kuwaiti system now allows for an open press, a vociferous parliament, and a growing degree of parliamentary influence over key decisions. The basic rule of semiauthoritarian politics—the opposition can run but cannot win—is enforced not through heavy-handed repression but through more subtle manipulation of elections and a divide-and-rule strategy. The reliance on dividing the opposition is generally effective in preventing the opposition from governing, but it allows some limited possibilities for concerted opposition action and even occasional legislative victories.

The posture of the Kuwaiti Islamist movement resembled that of its Jordanian counterpart before the 1980s. In this section we will review how the early limited opportunities of the 1960s and 1970s led to an Islamist movement that, as in Jordan, dabbled in politics but stayed aloof from opposition coalitions and instead focused on other spheres. But beginning in the 1980s, it began to participate in an effort to pry the political system open; in the 1990s and first decade of the 2000s, real opportunities—greater than those in Egypt and Jordan—to affect public policy opened. As Kuwait's political system veered toward the more liberalized end of the semiauthoritarian spectrum, the Islamist movement gravitated between two choices: working to cash in its current position for policy influence or taking the risk of forging a broader opposition coalition to press for fuller liberalization and even the possibility of a constitutional monarchy.

The Kuwaiti Brotherhood in a Monarchical Order

The Islamist movement in Kuwait, like the Jordanian, traces its origin to personal contact between its founder, 'Abd al-'Aziz al-Mutawwa', and Hasan al-Banna.[21] Al-Mutawwa' apparently joined the Egyptian organization before traveling to

---

21. The best source by far on various Islamic movements in Kuwait is a dissertation by Ali Fahed Al-Zumai, "The Intellectual and Historical Development of the Islamic Movement in Kuwait, 1950–1981" (PhD diss., University of Exeter, 1988). Al-Zumai has been an active participant in the movement in several ways: it was he who established the Public Foundation, discussed below, and he has also been very active in Islamic finance. His political role has diminished in recent years. His colleagues in the movement were aware of his dissertation and expressed great curiosity about its contents, but very few had read it, and indeed he seems to have avoided having it circulated in Kuwait. Other useful general sources on the movement are Falah 'Abd Allah al-Mudayris, *Jama'at al-ikhwan al-muslimin fi al-kuwayt* (Kuwait: Dar Qirtas li-l-nashr wa-l-tawzi', 1994); Sami Nasir al-Khalidi, *Al-ahzab al-siyasiyya al-islamiyya fi al-kuwayt* (Kuwait: Dar al-naba' li-l-nashr wa-l-tawzi', 1999); and Baqir Salman al-Najjar, *Al-harakat al-diniyya fi al-khalij al-'arabi* (Beirut: Dar al-saqi, 2007).

visit al-Banna in 1945. He then founded an autonomous Kuwaiti branch in 1952, naming it the Islamic Guidance Society.[22]

From its beginning and through the 1980s, the Kuwaiti group was often directly influenced by the parent Egyptian organization. Formal organizational ties existed, but more important were the personal contacts: Egyptian teachers and some other officials came to work in Kuwait as the country developed economically, and many Egyptian Muslim Brotherhood leaders found the Gulf states friendlier places than Nasserist Egypt to live when the Nasserist regime moved against the organization after 1954. Over the years (in the late 1940s and early 1950s and then much more significantly in the 1970s and 1980s), Kuwaiti students in Egypt were shaped by the ideology and example of the Egyptian movement. Some Palestinian Islamists (including some of the founders of Fatah with Brotherhood inclinations, among them Khalil al-Wazir) were present in Kuwait during the movement's early days and played a role in sustaining Brotherhood activities.

The Islamic Guidance Society, as the Brotherhood's initial Kuwaiti branch, undertook a broad social, missionary, and educational agenda in its first years before declining at the end of the 1950s.[23] For most of the period that it remained viable, its stance brought it some official support; the mufti of Kuwait served as the honorary head, and the amir was perhaps relieved to deal with a fairly conservative and socially oriented group at a time when he was challenged by leading merchant families and by nationalists influenced by pan-Arabist currents in the Arab world. But there was little room for participatory politics during this period, for Kuwait had no parliament.

After a short hiatus following the Islamic Guidance Society's disappearance, the Brotherhood revived itself and formed a new organization, the Social Reform Society. The new body had a largely social, educational, and charitable focus. The Social Reform Society, dominated by but legally distinct and autonomous from the Brotherhood, remains perhaps the most active and visible legal expression of the Islamist movement in Kuwait. While widely regarded in Kuwait as the social arm of the Brotherhood, the Society and its members have always insisted that there is no organizational link and that many Society members are not members of the Brotherhood. And indeed, the Brotherhood itself, as much as it is the umbrella organization for the movement as a whole, has almost always had a loose

---

22. The movement eschewed the name "Brotherhood" because a militant Wahhabi group by that name and associated with the Saudi family had invaded Kuwait in 1921.

23. These are best described in Al-Zumai, "Islamic Movement in Kuwait," chap. 2. He even mentions an unsuccessful attempt to found a women's school. Al-Zumai emphasizes internal divisions in the decline of the Islamic Guidance Society, although other accounts lay a greater stress on a general political clampdown preceding independence—a clampdown that, like the Jordanian one that slightly preceded it, specifically exempted the Islamists since theirs was deemed a religious group.

and opaque structure; it has also tended to act quietly, leaving most social, political, and other activity to the organizations it has spawned.

The early 1960s witnessed the election of a constituent assembly for the newly independent country; that assembly approved a constitution that provided for an elected parliament. Under the new Kuwaiti constitutional order, the ruler selected a prime minister (traditionally a leading member of the ruling family and, for four decades, also the crown prince). That prime minister then assembled a cabinet. The cabinet did not need to receive an initial vote of confidence from the parliament, but deputies could question individual ministers and remove confidence from them (in the case of the prime minister, the parliament could declare its inability to cooperate with him, necessitating either a new election or a new prime minister). Early Kuwaiti parliaments were sometimes diffident about using their authority, and on two occasions when they struck out more boldly against ministers (in 1976 and 1985), the amir reacted by suspending the parliament for several years.

The Kuwaiti Brotherhood, again like most of its counterpart movements early in their lives, dabbled in electoral activity when the opportunity was originally presented in the 1960s, focusing most of its political energies on religious and moral issues (such as banning the sale of alcohol) and hardly striking a strong oppositional stance. The inexperienced movement unsuccessfully backed some candidates in the 1961 elections for a constituent assembly. In the first parliamentary elections of 1963, however, six candidates backed by the movement entered the fifty-member body.[24]

The Brotherhood did not pursue a sustained political role in this period, however, and its organizational status (as well as the distinction between the Brotherhood and the Social Reform Society) remained murky. The chief political struggle pitted the government against a group of nationalist and leftist leaders and movements; the Islamists were not very active participants but tilted toward the government. In an attempt to dilute the electoral support of its opponents, the government extended the franchise to areas farther out from central Kuwait populated by poorer (and often quite literally second-class) citizens; the Islamist movement made some headway recruiting supporters among those new voters because of its conservative social message.

During the 1970s and 1980s, the parliament was twice suspended, but that hardly impeded an Islamist movement that focused on other spheres. In the social, charitable, and intellectual realms, the Brotherhood was able to expand the

---

24. The most useful comprehensive source of information on Kuwaiti parliamentary elections is a website maintained by Michael Herb: http://www2.gsu.edu/~polmfh/database/database.htm.

scope and scale of its activities considerably. Members founded a new magazine, *al-Mujtamaʿ*, which was technically the journal of the Social Reform Society but quickly established itself as one of the leading outlets for Islamist writings in the Arab world and a key publication for Brotherhood members in Kuwait.[25] Brotherhood activists began to increase their role in various Kuwaiti organizations that had internal elections, ranging from neighborhood cooperative societies to student associations. By the 1980s, an Islamist coalition dominated by young Brotherhood activists won elections for the leadership of most branches of the Kuwaiti student association, a set of positions they have dominated ever since.[26] The teachers union became a similar movement preserve. After an initial foray, the Islamists decided to concede control of the Graduates Society (an organization for those with college degrees that had proved to be a bastion for nationalists and leftists) to its ideological rivals.

The activity of Islamists in social, educational, and charitable fields also grew. In the 1990s, a movement member served as minister of religious affairs and established a new body (termed the Public Foundation), partly autonomous within his ministry, to attract new money to the charitable sector, manage it professionally, and advance beyond charity to development and other long-term projects. While it is a governmental body attached to a ministry, the Public Foundation is widely regarded in Kuwait as a Brotherhood stronghold. Finally, movement leaders were enthusiastic in their support for the establishment of Kuwait Finance House, a successful financial institution dedicated to operating in accordance with Islamic law. Movement members insist that from an early date, Kuwait Finance House has been more a creature of the government (because of substantial deposits of public funds) than of the movement itself, and they claim that movement leaders, acting only as individuals, were more involved in founding the body than in its continuing operation. This is probably true, but Kuwait Finance House has never lost its reputation, however exaggerated, as a movement bastion and even as a frequent employer for movement followers with university degrees.[27]

By the end of the 1980s, the Brotherhood-inspired Islamist movement had not simply greatly increased its scope and scale of activities; it had also cultivated

---

25. The movement took great pride in the central role played by its journal, but the journal also caused them some headaches: two former editors of *al-Mujtamaʿ* broke with party discipline and accepted ministerial posts without party approval (Ismaʿil al-Shatti in 2006 and Muhammad al-Busayri in 2009).

26. Humud ʿAqaluh al-ʿAnazi, *Al-haraka al-tulabiyya al-kuwaytiyya* (Kuwait: Ittihad al-watani li-talabat al-kuwayt, 1999).

27. On the Kuwaiti Finance House and the nature of its Islamic project, see Kristin Andrea Smith, "From Petrodollars to Islamic Dollars: The Strategic Construction of Islamic Banking in the Arab Gulf" (PhD diss., Harvard University, 2006).

a cadre of energetic and youthful leaders, schooled in electoral politics (in student association elections, for instance), coalition building (especially with other Islamists), and political maneuvering against rivals. Their success was such that they even attracted the envy of salafi movements, some of which bucked their suspicions of democratic politics and entered the electoral sphere.

But if there was brewing interest and emerging talent in the political realm during the 1970s and 1980s, opportunities were uncertain, especially because Kuwait seemed to be lurching in a fully authoritarian direction. The parliament created by the 1963 constitution proved to be difficult at times for the rulers to manage. The inclusion of new voters (whose votes for a long time could be attracted by the provision of government services) did not completely tame the body. The Brotherhood, which had participated in elections, backed the continuation of the electoral process. But when the amir of Kuwait closed down parliament in 1976, the movement equivocated; one of its leaders served as a minister after the suspension, and some figures cooperated with an attempt by the amir to amend the constitution as a condition of restoring it. These actions earned the movement a permanent reputation for being too quick to curry favor with the government; the suspicions created by its actions during the first suspension of parliament continue to this day.

Securing Semiauthoritarianism

Parliamentary life returned in 1981, and the Muslim Brotherhood again won a few seats. These deputies struck a more confrontational pose toward the government than their predecessors had done. The restored parliament proved no more cooperative than its predecessor, however, resulting in a second suspension of parliamentary life beginning in 1986. This time the Brotherhood made its stand clearer, participating in (though hardly leading) efforts to call for the restoration of parliament.

It was the 1990 Iraqi invasion and occupation of Kuwait that permanently changed the Brotherhood's political role, resulting in the creation of a movement political party, the Islamic Constitutional Movement (al-Haraka al-Dusturiyya al-Islamiyya, also known by its Arabic initials, Hadas). During the occupation, the Brotherhood helped organize resistance among those who remained in Kuwait. The formation of this resistance led to a shift in the leadership of the movement: younger activists, many of whom remained in Kuwait during the occupation, gained stature at the expense of the older generation and those who had fled. Immediately after the Iraqi withdrawal, younger Brotherhood elements who had led the resistance formed Hadas. At the same time, the Kuwaiti Brotherhood broke its international links with the Muslim Brotherhood, which the

Kuwaiti movement felt had not given sufficient support to the cause of Kuwaiti liberation.

The younger generation attempted to develop political language that had broader appeal. One of the founders of the party explains that when members of the Muslim Brotherhood spoke among themselves, they could argue primarily in religious terms. But when Hadas began attempting to persuade and mobilize voters, it had to find language that demonstrated it could address popular material as well as moral concerns.[28]

While other Islamist movements have dithered about the formation of a political party (and some, like Egypt's Muslim Brotherhood, continue to waver, at least about timing), there appears to have been little controversy among Kuwaiti Islamists about the matter. Criticisms of the move from what might be viewed as the Islamic right—based on rejection of democratic politics or participation in a non-Islamic system—were made gently and then dropped, perhaps partly because salafi groups (traditionally aloof from regular politics) themselves had followed the Brotherhood into participation in parliamentary elections in the 1980s.

While the creation of Hadas sparked little opposition, it marked a significant step in several ways.[29] First, the leaders of Hadas tended to be younger. Most came out of the student movement that older activists had cultivated in the 1970s and 1980s; the new leaders therefore did not represent a repudiation of the movement's path, but they tended to be far more accustomed to political activity and electoral politics. Second, Hadas sought to have a comprehensive political agenda and hardly restricted itself to religious and cultural issues. Indeed, it showed an early willingness to tackle sensitive topics, including corruption, accountability in the use of public funds, and the level of political freedoms.

Just as striking was the self-consciously oppositional pose struck by the new party. While the movement before 1990 had been seen by its critics as having overly cozy relations with the government, Hadas pressed Kuwaiti rulers for the full restoration of the constitution and parliament. Indeed, by placing "Constitutional" in the title of their new party at a time when critical parts of the constitution were suspended, the leaders signaled that they were fully determined to push

---

28. Isa Shahin, personal interview, Kuwait, October 2006.

29. My presentation of Hadas's history is based on periodic trips to Kuwait (beginning in 1994), press coverage, and interviews with Hadas and Islamist leaders (including Badr al-Nashi, Muhammad Dallal, Nasir al-Saniʿ, Usama Shahin, Mubarak al-Duwayla, Isa Shahin, Jasim Mihalhal, Khudayr al-ʿAnazi, ʿAws Shahin, ʿAbd al-ʿAziz al-Gharabali, Muhammad Busayri, Khalid Sultan, Salim al-Nashi, ʿAbd al-Razzaq al-Shayji, and Wafaʾ al-Ansari. I have also been able to compare notes with other observers of Kuwaiti politics, including on several occasions Maryann Tetreault, Michael Herb, Edward Gnehm, Muhammad al-Ghanim, Khalid Bishara, Fahad al-Radi, and Lindsey Stephenson. Also useful is Hadas's website: http://www.icmkw.org.

Kuwait in the direction of faithful observance of the 1963 constitutional text and to stress the elements in that document that suggested a constitutional monarchy.

Hadas also struck out in a new direction by showing a willingness to work with non-Islamist groups, including some of the movement's traditional nationalist and liberal rivals, in pursuit of political reform. The ground had been set for such cooperation when Kuwaiti political figures across the spectrum met with leaders from the ruling family in Jidda, Saudi Arabia. In 1991, a wide range of political leaders—with Hadas's founders spearheading the effort—issued a comprehensive reform document titled "The Future Vision for Building Kuwait," which called for application of the shari'a and full observance of the constitution.

When parliament was restored in 1992, Hadas secured four seats. Other opposition groups also did well, leading the ruling family to form a diverse cabinet with representatives from various political blocs. Hadas entered the cabinet, securing the portfolios for commerce and religious affairs.

Navigating Semiauthoritarian Politics

The cooperative spirit of the opposition soon dissipated, however, partly because of the deep divisions among its members and partly because the ruling family found ways to aggravate those divisions and prevent a cohesive opposition majority from forming. The ideological division between liberals and Islamists in particular became more marked over the 1990s, and the two sides scuffled over a series of cultural and educational issues (especially the Islamist push for gender segregation in the universities and against the liberal reforms of Minister of Education Abmad al-Rub'i). Hadas deputies were active participants in these struggles, though the most vociferous Islamists were generally salafis or independents. Led by Hadas, Islamists secured parliamentary approval of a constitutional amendment to make the Islamic shari'a the (rather than merely a) principal source of legislation, a politically popular cause that forced some skeptics to take a public stand in favor of Islamization. But that paper victory had no effect when the amir successfully forestalled the amendment.

Hadas lost its cabinet posts in 1994, when the prime minister reshuffled his cabinet to make it less divisive; the party was therefore freer to move into fuller opposition. In electoral terms, it performed at a steady clip, equaling or exceeding its 1992 performance at the polls. Given Kuwait's fragmented electorate and parliament (with fifty seats sprinkled among tribal, ideological, progovernment, and other orientations), Hadas's four to six deputies were hardly able to dominate the body and could score only isolated successes by assembling ad hoc majorities. Sometimes Hadas seemed more focused on general reform (pressing for a more liberal press law, for instance), and sometimes it hewed closer to a specifically religious agenda by joining with other Islamists in cultural tussles with liberals.

In 2003, however, this period of prolonged stasis was disturbed when Hadas secured only two seats in parliamentary balloting. At the same time, the amir's illness and the atmosphere of an impending transition highlighted rivalries within the Kuwaiti ruling Al Sabah family (which held the amir's position, the premiership, and some key ministries and other institutions), leading to a political system characterized by not only a fragmented parliament but also a fragmented ruling family.

The lackluster electoral performance and the sense of political change prompted Hadas to reorganize itself in a significant way. Some of the founders of the party were gracefully shunted out of a public role; instead of relying primarily on its most dynamic and prominent parliamentarians, Hadas brought in new, still younger leaders to run the party itself. The new secretary-general, for instance, was a reserved figure without discernible personal ambition. The party leadership embarked on an effort to revive and professionalize its operations, hiring, for instance, an outside communications and marketing firm to help fine-tune its message to Kuwaiti voters.

The new Hadas leadership also worked hard to revive the party's early efforts at spearheading reform calls, even coordinating when possible with ideological rivals. In 2005 and 2006, Hadas joined with other forces across the political spectrum to support a reform in the country's electoral law to reduce the number of districts from twenty-five to five. (Indeed, Hadas has also signaled support for making Kuwait a single electoral district. This would necessitate proportional representation and a party list system and perhaps force the issue of a political party law—another reform the party called for—onto the country's political agenda.) As it became clear that a parliamentary majority favored the five-district reform, the ruling family, worried perhaps that the larger districts would diminish its ability to intervene in local races, began to dawdle.[30] A cabinet reshuffle brought a Hadas leader back into the cabinet, and the party allowed him to accept the post. But when the new minister broke party discipline by voting to delay electoral reform, the now invigorated party cut its ties with him.

In 2006, Hadas threw in its lot fully with the coalition pursuing a confrontational strategy toward the government, uniting with erstwhile rivals to press

---

30. The government (or sometimes members of the ruling family) was often accused of intervening in elections by showering "service deputies" with benefits to pass on to their constituents or by funding campaigns it supported. Larger electoral districts, it was anticipated, would render such interventions much more expensive and encourage campaigns based more on ideology than on personality.

hard for the electoral reform. When the government reacted by escalating the confrontation, dissolving parliament, and calling for new elections, Hadas and its partners scored an impressive victory. The new party leaders appeared to be vindicated in their tougher approach. After the election, Kuwaiti political observers proclaimed that the opposition was now the majority—an untenable situation in any parliamentary democracy, because an opposition movement winning an electoral majority would cease to be an opposition and instead form the government. Hadas hoped that such an anomalous situation would prove the basis for further political reform. But while the opposition was able to secure a victory on electoral reform, it had not broken the barrier of semiauthoritarian politics, though Hadas pushed in that direction.

Indeed, Hadas now banked on one of two possible democratizing changes to the Kuwaiti political order. One possibility was the beginning of party politics. The various ideological orientations in the parliament coalesced into loose blocs: one Islamist (including Hadas), one liberal, and one populist. The blocs not only strove to maintain internal coherence; they also worked to form what they called a "bloc of blocs," turning their combined numbers into a working majority that could pursue a consensual agenda. After months of wrangling, the bloc of blocs developed a list of laws that they would pass. But after successfully forcing the government to accept the proposed electoral reform (and also passing a new law mandating corporate alms contributions, an Islamist demand), the bloc of blocs began to come apart. The ideological divisions among the blocs became an obstacle to cooperation, and internal cohesion within each bloc began to dissolve. Hadas managed to maintain its own party discipline, but other members of the Islamist bloc showed a decreasing interest in cooperation and the other blocs experienced a similar decline in coherence.

The second possible change that Hadas hoped for entailed a move to party politics through a different route. Instead of having the opposition in parliament coordinate across ideological cleavages, Hadas leaders suggested to the ruling family that the prime minister assemble a government with a clear parliamentary majority by selecting one of the parliamentary blocs to lead the government (allowing the others to either join or form a loyal opposition). Such a development might help the evolution toward what Kuwaitis termed "popular government," meaning a prime minister who was not from the ruling family. Such a step might even be seen as a way station in a process of transforming Kuwait into a constitutional monarchy.

When the bloc of blocs dissolved and the ruling family rejected the idea of party politics and popular government, Hadas found both paths to political reform stymied. In 2007, Hadas leaders realized that neither coordinating a united opposition nor directly governing as part of an Islamist-dominated cabinet was an option. Accordingly, the party accepted a ministerial post when offered, making its peace with Kuwaiti semiauthoritarianism. The result was to move Hadas back to an ambiguous political position, suspended between government and opposition.

Hadas received a further jolt in 2008 when, in an election called after a standoff between the government and the parliament, the new electoral law worked very much to Hadas's disadvantage. Much to its surprise, the vaunted move toward ideological politics and against vote buying did not occur. Tribes in outlying districts held primaries (an illegal but long-followed practice), and their candidates dominated returns in two of the five new districts. In the remaining three districts, new, more expensive campaigns allowed some wealthy individuals to gain seats, but Hadas found its own representation dropping from six to four. Hadas retained a cabinet post but began to feel that its participation in the government allowed it little influence while still forcing it to support official policy. It withdrew from the cabinet and launched an attempt to bring the prime minister in for questioning before parliament. Rather than allow the prime minister to be publicly questioned by commoners, the amir (after considering a suspension of the constitution) called for yet another election. In 2009, Hadas found itself reduced to two seats, a performance as dismal as the 2003 setback. The movement's leadership resigned—a step that certainly indicated their failure but in an odd sense also showed one sign of organizational health: in this region, most parties are really clusters of individual leaders, and those leaders cling to posts no matter how they perform.

The electoral setbacks of 2008 and 2009 forced some soul-searching in both the movement and the party. Older movement leaders worried that Hadas had led the Brotherhood too far down a political path; they feared that the party had dragged them into an excessively confrontational relationship with Kuwait's ruling family. Some party activists and advocates of deeper politicization came to a very different conclusion—that the party should distance itself more from the movement in order to form a broader (and more successful) electoral coalition of religious and conservative forces. Unlike the situation in Jordan, where movement disputes proved polarizing and increasingly public, the muted tones of the Kuwaiti debate are striking (indeed, there was little public echo of the internal discussions; movement leaders were willing to discuss the matter in detail only in private). But if more polite, the debate has been no more decisive; the movement and the party pulled gently in different direction without going their separate ways. Offered far more freedom and opportunity than their counterparts in Egypt and Jordan, Kuwaiti Islamists pursued politicization with more determination and skill, but they had limited gains to show for their efforts. And the resulting situation—in which advocates of politicization were sometimes the more strident voices of political opposition—paralleled Egypt and Jordan.

Palestine

At first glance, Palestine would not seem to fit in the category of semiauthoritarian regimes—it is not, after all, even a state. The differences between Palestine and the other three political systems (Egypt, Jordan, and Kuwait) are quite real. But there are some remarkable parallels in the evolution of the Palestinian political system, and in critical ways the environment in which it has operated has been semiauthoritarian.[31]

First Religion, Then Resistance—But Not Yet Politics

Egypt's Muslim Brotherhood showed an interest in the Palestine cause from the 1930s, and the new chapters established in neighboring countries shared this concern. A Palestinian branch was founded as the British Mandate in Palestine

---

31. Writings on Hamas show more convergence than one might expect, given the movement's partly underground status, its involvement in the Israeli-Palestinian dispute, and its use of violence. Accounts and analyses often differ in their emphasis and details, but there is surprising consensus on the basic features of the organization's history, structure, development, ideology, and positions. The most reliable comprehensive academic works are Jeroen Gunning, *Hamas in Politics: Democracy, Religion, Violence* (New York: Columbia University Press, 2008); Shaul Mishal and Avraham Sela, *The Palestinian Hamas: Vision, Violence, and Coexistence* (New York: Columbia University Press, 2006); Khaled Hroub, *Hamas: A Beginner's Guide* (London: Pluto Press, 2006); and Khalid Nimr al-'Umrayn, *Hamas: harakat al-muqawima al-islamiyya; juzuruha-nasha'tuha-fikruha al-siyasi* (Cairo: Markaz al-hadara al-'arabiyya, 2001). Two very recent works are also quite useful: Paola Caride, *Hamas: From Resistance to Government* (Jerusalem: PASSIA, 2010); and Beverley Milton-Edwards and Stephen Farrell, *Hamas* (Cambridge: Polity Press, 2010).

Three works by journalists are also interesting: Paul McGeough, *Kill Khalid: The Failed Mossad Assassination of Khalid Mishal and the Rise of Hamas* (New York: New Press, 2009), focuses on Hamas's external origins and history; Azzam Tamimi, *Hamas: A History from Within* (Northampton, Mass.: Olive Branch Press, 2007), comes from a figure closely associated with the movement; and Zaki Chehab, *Inside Hamas: The Untold Story of the Militant Islamic Movement* (New York: Nation Books, 2007), is less reliable but provides a useful focus on Gaza. Sara Roy, *Failing Peace: Gaza and the Palestinian-Israeli Conflict* (London: Pluto Press, 2006), is a collection of writings by a scholar knowledgeable about both Hamas and Gaza.

Some older works remain very useful. Nasir al-Din al-Sha'ir, *'Amaliyyat al-salam al-filastiniya-al-isra'iliyya: wijhat nazar Islamiyya* (Nablus: Markaz al-Buhuth wa-al-Dirasat al-Filastiniyah, 1999), is an analysis of Hamas's stance toward the Oslo process written by an academic who later served as deputy prime minister in the 2006 Hamas-led cabinet; Beverley Milton-Edwards, *Islamic Politics in Palestine* (London: I. B. Tauris, 1996), is particularly rich in the early history; Andrea Nusse, *Muslim Palestine: The Ideology of Hamas* (Amsterdam: Harwood, 1998), also provides an analysis written during the Oslo process; and Ziad Abu-Amr, *Islamic Fundamentalism in the West Bank and Gaza: Muslim Brotherhood and Islamic Jihad* (Bloomington: Indiana University Press, 1994), is strong on the rivalry between Islamists and non-Islamists in the 1980s.

came to an end and war broke out between Arabs and Jews over control of the territory. Volunteers from various neighboring Muslim Brotherhood organizations joined the fray, cementing a firm ideological and programmatic link between the Brotherhood and the Palestinian cause that continues to this day. But if the various Brotherhood chapters took enormous pride in their participation, they felt only despair at the result: after the fighting ended, there was no Palestine (as a political entity) left standing. The Palestinian population was divided among Gaza (administered by Egypt with a population enormously swollen by refugees); Israel (with a significant Palestinian minority living for close to two decades under martial law); the West Bank (annexed by Transjordan with the Palestinian inhabitants now becoming citizens of the renamed Hashimite Kingdom of Jordan); and a diaspora (beginning in neighboring Arab states but eventually fanning out around the world).

The various remnants of the Muslim Brotherhood generally followed the paths of the territory they inhabited. Gaza's organization remained independent but was closely associated with the Egyptian movement; after the Nasserist regime came to power in 1952, the Gaza movement found itself operating under the watchful eye of Egyptian authorities. Those Brotherhood activists who became Israeli citizens went into extended hibernation. Eventually, an Islamist movement based in part on the memory of the organization revived in the 1980s and 1990s, though it soon split over the issue of participation in Israeli national elections.[32] West Bank Brotherhood members joined the Jordanian Brotherhood, and the Jordanian and Palestinian movements have remained difficult to disentangle up to the present day. And in the diaspora, Palestinian Brotherhood activists sometimes gravitated toward the movement in the country where they were

---

More specialized works include Loren D. Lybarger, *Identity and Religion in Palestine: The Struggle between Islamism and Secularism in the Occupied Territories* (Princeton, N.J.: Princeton University Press, 2007); and Muhsin Muhammad Salih, ed., *Qira'at naqdiyya fi tajribat hamas wa-hukumatiha, 2006–2007* (Beirut: Markaz al-zaytuna li-l-dirasat wa-l-istisharat, 2007). Particularly useful articles include Glenn E. Robinson, "Hamas as a Social Movement," in *Islamic Activism: A Social Movement Theory Approach*, edited by Quintan Wiktorowicz (Bloomington: Indiana University Press, 2003); Menachem Klein, "Hamas in Power," *Middle East Journal* 61, no. 3 (2007), 442–459; and Klein, "Against the Consensus: Oppositionist Voices in Hamas," *Middle Eastern Studies* 45, no. 6 (2009), 881–892.

In addition, I have relied on writings appearing on websites close to the movement, including the Palestine Information Center (http://www.palestine-info.info), the newspaper *Filastin* (http://www.felesteen.net), the newspaper *al-Risala* (http://www.resalah.info), and the journal *Filastin al-muslima* (http://www.fm-m.com). The Al-Zaytouna Center for Studies and Consultation in Beirut is independent and draws on diverse perspectives, but its work clearly reflects an Islamist viewpoint (http://www.alzaytouna.net). Finally, I interviewed a variety of individuals close to the movement, among them Nasir al-Din al-Sha'ir, Muhammad al-Barghuti, 'Aziz al-Duwayk, 'Umar 'Abd al-Raziq, Khalid Sulayman, Usama Hamdan, and Hamid al-Bitawi.

32. The Islamic movement in Israel has recently drawn some scholarly attention. One current work is *Al-haraka al-islamiyya fi isra'il* (Dubai: Markaz al-Misbar, 2009).

living. They were influential, for instance, in helping the Kuwaiti Brotherhood establish itself in its early days (though that movement soon began to assert its particular Kuwaiti nature and Palestinians resident in the country were drawn instead toward Fatah or the Jordanian Brotherhood, though later toward Hamas); Palestinians with Brotherhood sympathies in Egypt came under the ideological sway of the Brotherhood there (particularly when it revived among Egyptian youth in the 1970s and 1980s).

None of these various remnants distinguished itself in the political sphere. Indeed, many Palestinian Brotherhood leaders worked to make a virtue out of the necessarily bleak political situation: recalling that Hasan al-Banna had founded an organization dedicated to reform the individual as a step toward reforming the society, the Palestinian Brotherhood retreated into personal and religious affairs. The 1967 war, in which Gaza and the West Bank fell under Israeli control, did not shake the tendency toward patience, religious work, and short-term political passivity; neither did the rising criticisms from other Palestinian political forces that such patience amounted to resignation and defeatism. As new Palestinian groups arose in the West Bank, Gaza, and the diaspora, the Muslim Brotherhood's remnants remained largely aloof from the struggle and disdained the new movements and the umbrella organization that sought to unite them, the Palestinian Liberation Organization (PLO). Islamists criticized the ideologies and practices of the alphabet soup of nationalists, Marxists, and radical groups dominating the Palestinian political scene for their inattention to—and even betrayal of—deeply embedded social and religious values.

In the 1970s and 1980s, however, a new generation of leaders arose within the Brotherhood that wished to have the movement enter what Palestinians referred to variously as the "resistance" or the "revolution" (and with their antileftist stance, Islamists greatly preferred the former term) as well as heighten their own levels of social and political engagement. Although they were bucking the trend of the previous generation, they saw themselves as returning to the original Brotherhood path by pursuing a broad reform agenda rather than focusing simply on the religious and personal spheres. The new leaders arose most visibly in Gaza, where they first worked on constructing a new group of Islamic institutions in the educational, charitable, and social realms. The most prominent sign of their effort was the Islamic Complex (al-Mujamma‘ al-Islami), which quickly established itself as a leading nongovernmental organization in Gaza (resembling—probably consciously—the Islamic Center in Jordan). A new Islamic University also quickly became friendly territory for Gaza Islamists.

Analogous but less ambitious or centralized efforts took place in the West Bank.[33] Far less publicly, Palestinian Islamists abroad—most notably in Jordan but also in Kuwait and Egypt—launched their own efforts to support a new (or revived) social and political movement. The external group focused on building a diplomatic and political apparatus as well as giving the group an ability to sustain itself in areas not controlled by Israel.

Given the Brotherhood's historical quiescence—sullen as it may have been— Israel's initial attitude toward the newly emerging Islamist movement was permissive. And in the 1980s, the slowly rising Islamist trend was far more visible in the way it challenged nationalists and leftist groups than in any resistance to the Israeli occupation. Not only did the younger generation of leaders build their own structures apart from the nationalist movement, they also began to seek a presence in older Palestinian organizations (such as student groups and professional associations) that had been the preserve of other groups. Violent clashes on campuses (and most notoriously, a 1980 raid by younger Islamists on the Red Crescent Society in Gaza City) marked the trend's emergence as an alternative to the other forms of Palestinian nationalism.

Yet it was precisely the rivalries with other groups that led the Islamist tendency to take up arms against Israel. Indeed, the pattern of the Palestinian national movement in general has been that rivalries and divisions increase the likelihood, though not the effectiveness, of armed action against external adversaries; the rise of Hamas has certainly accentuated that trend.[34] Continuously taunted by its leftist and nationalist rivals, and threatened by a new Islamist movement (Islamic Jihad, which, inspired in part by the Iranian Revolution, advocated immediate action against Israel and showed much less interest in the traditionally broad Islamist agenda), the more active Brotherhood elements began to prepare for direct participation in "resistance." Such resistance meant attacks on the Israeli occupation and, eventually in some circumstances, Israeli targets more generally, including civilians. Some early mistakes and arrests failed to abort that effort but provoked leaders of the new group into making a far-reaching organizational decision: they created a separate armed wing with considerable autonomy and a

---

33. The rise of Hamas in the West Bank has been less well documented. One peculiar work of interest is Mossab Hassan Yousef, *Son of Hamas* (Carol Stream, Ill.: Tyndale House, 2010). Yousef, son of one of the most prominent Hamas leaders in the West Bank, became an Israeli informant and converted to Christianity. His account seems honest (though it is strongly self-exculpatory and bears some marks of unhelpful ghost writing); it is still quite unreliable because of the limited nature of the author's perspective (he saw most key developments through his father's activities).

34. Wendy Pearlman, *Violence, Nonviolence, and the Palestinian National Movement* (New York: Cambridge University Press, 2011).

cell structure to ensure that detection or arrest of one leader would not unravel the entire group.

In 1987, when Palestinians in the West Bank and Gaza launched an uprising against the Israeli occupation, the new Islamist group was poised to leap into the fray. When it did so, the leaders adopted the name Movement of Islamic Resistance and the acronym Hamas. Hamas opened its doors to any Palestinians who were sympathetic to its agenda of blending Islamism and resistance; new affiliates did not have to pass through the more rigorous requirements for membership in the Muslim Brotherhood. The new movement was so successful that it quickly eclipsed the Brotherhood from which it had emerged; within a short time, the Brotherhood continued in existence largely through its association with Hamas. Yet Hamas, for all its attempts to appeal to a large public audience, remained partly underground.

The result is that the movement's membership and organization remain cloudy to this day; it is not uncommon to have a figure closely associated with Hamas in public discussions deny formal membership in the movement. Similarly, the results of internal elections and the occupants of leadership positions are widely rumored but only infrequently formally announced.

From its beginning, Hamas dealt with the dispersion of its organization across several fields of activity and geographical areas in three ways, all very much in keeping with broader Brotherhood patterns. First, it allowed for specialization: certain cadres and branches focused on politics while others organized for armed action; those overseas devoted energies to politics, diplomacy, and linkages with sympathizers.

Second, Hamas evinced considerable flexibility within a few very general "fixed principles" (*thawabit*). Priding itself on its "practical" nature, Hamas insisted only on the centrality of resistance and rejection of the legitimacy of the state of Israel. And even on those two issues, its position evolved in tantalizing but hardly definitive ways.[35] Resistance gradually shifted from being the movement's raison d'être to being a tool that it would suspend for long periods but not disavow; the position on Israel shifted over time from a religious opposition to a political one, and the movement offered a variety of ambiguous hints and half steps toward a less rigid position. But the flexibility reached beyond ideology and was indeed more notable in the organizational realm. Hamas could, according to its calculation of the demands of the political and social context, variously emphasize resistance, politics, or social work.

---

35. This evolutions is explored by Hroub, *Hamas;* al-Sha'ir, *'Amaliyyat al-salam;* and Gunning, *Hamas in Politics.* The most analytical account is Mishal and Sela, *Palestinian Hamas.*

Third, Hamas was not only flexible; it was ambiguous. Its leaders showed a remarkable ability to feint in different directions without fully committing to any of them. This was most obviously the case in its political positions. It rejected peace with Israel but was open to an armistice. It rejected the Oslo Accords but would consider running in the elections they made possible. It accepted the PLO as an umbrella authority but only if it was reformed. The movement was committed to resistance but might suspend its activities, even unilaterally, for the national good. Remarkably, ambiguity extended to organizational questions as well, including who made decisions within the organization and how. Given the organization's rapid growth, the diversity in its membership, the clandestine nature of some of its parts, its far-flung reach, and difficulties in communicating among different branches, it should not be surprising that Hamas would work to find formulas that could unite all its disparate cadres. Ambiguity stemmed not only from organizational challenges but also from organizational culture: as part of a self-styled "practical" organization, Hamas leaders tended to define themselves and their movement by action. Individuals did not necessarily know what the movement would do—and perhaps would not even know their own position—until a question was forced by events. On a few critical occasions (especially as their political involvement increased), leaders gave the impression of not having decided until after they had acted. (An example was the 2006 victory in parliamentary elections: while the decision to enter the elections was deliberate and painstakingly made, the decision to pursue victory seems never to have been made.)[36]

Indeed, as much as these three features—specialization, flexibility, and ambiguity—served the organizational needs of Hamas in most ways, they presented a particular problem in one sort of situation: when Hamas had to make a clear decision. And as the organization rose in prominence, extended in reach, and found the environment rapidly changing, the need for it to develop clearer positions and paths of action was sometimes acute. The desire to maintain organizational cohesion and loyalty within the ranks militated in most situations for a prolonged process of internal consultation and debate. Hamas members—and especially leaders—deliberated so endlessly and argued so incessantly that external observers forever proclaimed them on the brink of a schism. Remarkably, however, the movement not only held together but managed to sustain itself

---

36. Usama Hamdan, Hamas representative in Lebanon, told me in a personal interview in December 2010 that Hamas decided to enter elections in 2005 but never discussed the "participation, not domination" strategy because its leaders did not think a victory would be allowed. However, he also claimed that victory seemed within reach by late in 2005, but nobody in the movement argued for pulling back.

even as many of its leaders (including a large proportion of the founders) were arrested or assassinated. And while the internal debates were intense, and at times even broke out into public view, members at all levels generally accepted both the process and the outcome of the decision-making apparatus.[37] On occasion, some Hamas leaders took advantage of the organization's tendency to act first and make decisions later by moving before internally ponderous structures had decided what to do; the seizure of power in Gaza in June 2007, for instance, seemed to be an effort by some within the organization to present the movement as a whole with a fait accompli.

The Birth of a Palestinian Semiauthoritarian Order

In short, what Hamas's founders managed to design was an organization that was by turns supple and sluggish. Such a structure seemed to serve it well in a series of tumultuous changes the organization faced in the Palestinian political environment: Hamas was forced to react to the creation of the Palestinian Authority (PA), the second intifada, the resumption of domestic Palestinian political debates as that intifada waned, and electoral victory. Each of these developments posed a severe challenge to Hamas; it weathered all (with the possible exception of the last) in a manner that left the organization stronger over the long term.

The first development, the creation of the Palestinian Authority, was the most difficult. Hamas was founded to resist Israeli occupation, but this commitment gave little guidance on how to react to the creation of a set of Palestinian governmental institutions. The issue pressed itself on Hamas immediately, even as the Oslo Accords were being negotiated: the inauguration of the PA in Gaza was followed quickly by violent clashes between newly established PA security forces and Hamas supporters. Was Hamas to continue resistance or suspend its struggle? Was it to enter the PA, fight it, ignore it, or negotiate an understanding with it? What stance was most in keeping with the group's ideology and strategy? And what was most promising in light of the rapidly shifting political environment? Different elements in Hamas favored different paths, and the organization as a whole experimented with each of them.

Hamas's eventual preferred option—to continue resistance against Israel but eschew intra-Palestinian fighting—provoked sometimes harsh PA countermeasures and undercut the organization's popular standing at a time when hope for negotiations still existed. Thus, while it never disavowed continued armed action

---

37. Gunning in particular found the rank-and-file acceptance of leadership decisions as legitimately representing the collective will of the organization despite internal disagreements.

(and indeed launched a horrific campaign against Israeli civilian targets in 1995), Hamas held back for most of the second half of the 1990s. It attended talks with other Palestinian factions and debated entering elections—but it also rejected disarmament, abandonment of resistance, or acceptance of the legitimacy of the Oslo Accords. Hamas chose ultimately to sit out the 1996 parliamentary elections, but only after considerable debate and an effort on the part of some leaders to compose their own electoral list outside formal movement support. (The boycott was not total; Hamas leaders steered their supporters to some candidates, and a few activists actively ran outside the rubric of the movement.)

While keeping every door open and all spheres of activity viable, Hamas shifted the focus and relative weight of its efforts from resistance, politics, and diplomacy to the social sphere.[38] Squeezed by public opinion, domestic repression, and international pressure, Hamas recalibrated its attention and priorities. External observers often spoke of Hamas as having earned the loyalty of the Palestinian population through the provision of social services, but such a claim is misleading. The resources of Hamas could not compete with those of the PA (the recipient of a tremendous amount of international aid); leftist, secular, and nonpolitical NGOs were also the beneficiaries of generous amounts of international funding. If a monthly stipend or a job was enough to buy political loyalties, then Hamas's rival Fatah, which controlled the Ministry of Social Affairs, should have received enthusiastic popular support. What Hamas's social activities earned the organization was something less tangible but ultimately more sustainable: a reputation for being public-spirited, clean, and competent. The emerging PA and certainly the Fatah movement were lacking in all three areas.

After the creation of the PA, the next development challenging Hamas's ability to adapt was the eruption of the second intifada in September 2000. As the peace process frayed in the late 1990s and then collapsed in a paroxysm of violence, Hamas was well positioned to pivot quickly. Its maintenance of an armed wing, its arms-length relationship with the PA (a body that began to decay under severe internal and external pressures), and its cultivation of a strong popular basis and reputation in Palestinian society led it to take a leading role as "resistance" sprang again to the fore of the Palestinian political agenda. Hamas engaged in a combination of active collaboration and coordination with other groups (through an umbrella consultative group called Nationalist and Islamic Forces) and competition with them (especially in the escalation of violence).

The return to a full focus on resistance provoked a devastating Israeli response, including the assassination of top leaders (several of Hamas's founders

---

38. This shift was noted by several observers of Hamas but is probably most fully explored by Roy, *Failing Peace*.

were killed) and local cadres as well as widespread arrests; this was coupled with an international effort to disrupt the movement's finances, led by the United States with cooperation from Europe. Yet what was deadly for the organization's leaders left far fewer scars on the organization as a whole: because Hamas had successfully built a structure that did not depend on particular personalities, it weathered the storm of the intifada more effectively than any other Palestinian organization. And its reputation for self-sacrifice, however grotesquely earned during the intifada, was enhanced by its actions.

Thus Hamas was well poised to reap the benefits of the third challenge: the resumption of Palestinian domestic politics. Beginning in 2003, as the intifada slowly waned and the decayed PA passed through a succession crisis with Yasser Arafat's marginalization and death, Palestinian political attention shifted back from resistance to internal matters. The PA leadership attempted to coax Hamas into its structures (and implicitly into international diplomacy). Because this development came slowly and was carefully negotiated, Hamas was able to deliberate fully internally before choosing its course. After protracted internal debate, it chose the path of political participation. In doing so, it did not abandon any of its past positions in principle: Hamas maintained its commitment to resistance, rejected participation in diplomatic negotiations with Israel, and insisted that involvement with the PA was based on the irrelevance rather than the acceptance of the Oslo Accords. Yet Hamas leaders, for all their insistence that they had not changed, still accepted a unilateral cease-fire, committed themselves to participation in the PA, and showed a willingness to work as partners with those who did negotiate with Israel. They did so out of what verged on a sense of civic responsibility.

Quite confident of their popular standing, imbued with the conviction that they entered the election with what they called "clean hands," and convinced that the Fatah leadership had failed through a combination of venality, cravenness in the face of Palestine's adversaries, and incompetence, Hamas leaders felt a duty to their own followers to take up the political challenge, whatever that might be. By embarking on the process of "politicizing" the organization—as Palestinians themselves sometimes termed the process—Hamas leaders were not only positioning themselves to take advantage of new opportunities but also subjecting their organization to strong pressures, the nature of which was difficult to know in advance. The decision to invest in politics was ambivalent and incremental—Hamas had decided not to participate in the 1996 elections only after considerable deliberation; it had then moved on to participate (and perform well) in the 2005 municipal elections. By the time of the 2006 parliamentary elections, Hamas was swayed in part by the experience of its counterpart organizations elsewhere in the Arab world, all of which strove to participate in the political system. Most of all, however, the move toward politicization was limited. The decision was made simply to run candidates; all other questions were postponed.

And then Hamas won.

Coping with Success

The parliamentary majority for the Hamas-sponsored "Change and Reform" electoral list constituted an unexpected challenge for the organization. Hamas could easily have avoided the problem—as its counterpart organizations advised it to do[39]—by running fewer candidates than it did. But as the possibility of victory (which became quite clear in the month before the election) loomed larger, either pride or sluggish decision making prevented Hamas from pulling back. Having decided to enter politics, Hamas suddenly found itself pressed to govern.

Its leaders at first demurred, working to assemble a broad coalition government. Failing in the effort to coax in other parties, Hamas then worked to produce a cabinet that featured technical expertise and maintained a distinction between movement leadership and cabinet office. But that government was unable to perform. The PA was fiscally dependent on Israel (for a portion of its tax collection) and international donors; those funds were cut off.[40] Fatah activists, still strong at all levels in the PA, launched strikes; the presidency (still under Fatah control) kept a firm hand on some PA institutions; the president himself threatened to dismiss the cabinet and hinted that a combination of constitutional and unconstitutional devices might be used to bring it down; and Fatah and Hamas activists clashed in the streets. Hamas reacted alternately by joining the fight and by attempting to strike a more conciliatory pose. When Fatah and Hamas supporters hammered out a compromise set of principles in an Israel prison, Hamas appeared divided; finally, under considerable Arab diplomatic pressure, Hamas and Fatah leaders built on that agreement to form a national unity government. Argument about the agreement within Hamas spilled out into public view, and one prominent movement leader denounced it as paving the way for embroiling Hamas in a negotiated settlement with Israel; other Hamas leaders worked to fend off this criticism by insisting that the agreement contained no concessions. These

---

39. In Egypt, the general guide of the Muslim Brotherhood was reported at the time in Arab press to have advised Hamas to follow the "participation, not domination" path ; in Jordan, a Muslim Brotherhood leader told me in a private conversation that leaders there had advised Hamas to run candidates if it felt the need but not to try to win. However, Usama Hamdan denied that the movement received such advice in a personal interview in December 2010.

40. The international funds were suspended until the new government recognized Israel, disavowed violence, and accepted past PLO agreements.

signals not only confused Hamas followers; they also failed to break the international isolation of the Palestinian government. And Hamas-Fatah clashes only increased, especially in Gaza. Charging that Fatah's international supporters were preparing to oust the Hamas government by force, Hamas seized power in Gaza in June 2007. The PA president retaliated by seizing control of the West Bank.[41]

Having insisted that it had clear legal and constitutional prerogatives, that the PA (even when headed by officials from Hamas) was distinct in its programs and authority from Hamas as a movement, and that it did not seek political power but exercised it only reluctantly, Hamas after June 2007 departed from its proclaimed principles by building a governing authority in Gaza that elided the distinction between movement and government and showed an increasingly cavalier attitude toward constitutional procedures. In short, Hamas built a party-state in Gaza after 2007 that differed from the party-state Fatah worked to build between 1994 and 2006 only in its efficiency.[42]

Conclusion: Probing and Profiting from Semiauthoritarianism

In Egypt, Jordan, Kuwait, and Palestine, semiauthoritarian regimes have come slowly into being in the past few decades. The political system has opened up to opposition forces, allowing freer speech and organization as well as some pluralism in national elections. But those openings have often shifted according to the regime's needs of the moment, and they have stopped short of allowing the opposition any opportunity for electoral victory (the one exception, the case of Hamas, provoked a half-successful effort to remove it from power long before the next scheduled elections).

---

41. The accounts of the various parties—domestic and international—vary greatly and determine whether the Palestinian split was viewed as a Hamas coup or a preemptive action or counter-coup. It is clear that international actors led by the United States advocated a dismissal of the Hamas government and gave material support to forces under presidential command, and that at least two U.S. officials (the consul general in Jerusalem and the secretary of state) were untruthful in describing the Palestinian president's constitutional powers. Also clear is that Hamas's actions in seizing control of Gaza displayed violence and vindictiveness. I have written of the constitutional issues in "What Can Abu Mazin Do?" Carnegie Web Commentary, 15 June 2007, available at http://www.carnegieen dowment.org/files/abumazinupdatejune1507.pdf. and of the political issues in "The Peace Process Has No Clothes," Carnegie Web Commentary, 15 June 2007, available at http://www.carnegieendowment. org/files/BrownCommentaryjune072.pdf.

42. For a useful analysis, see Yezid Sayigh, "Hamas Rule in Gaza: Three Years On," Middle East Brief 41, Crown Center for Middle East Studies, Brandeis University, March 2010; and International Crisis Group, "Ruling Palestine I: Gaza under Hamas," Middle East Report 73 (March 2008).

The four movements examined so far show the common features described in the earlier chapters. They are flexible, adaptable, and resilient. Their ideologies are strongly developed but so vaguely defined that they allow leaders considerable tactical and even strategic flexibility. They operate on the basis of consensus and build strong organizations that can survive and even flourish with leadership change.

In response to the rise of semiauthoritarianism, all four movements have shown an increased interest in politics. As Islamist movements gain the ability to organize more freely and compete in unfair elections, they generally take it. And they generally invest more as the opportunities increase. But their responses are slow, sometimes uncertain, almost always uneven, and often cantankerous. Movement leaders act more like cagey (and caged) political actors than grateful recipients of freedom. And those who are most in favor of emphasizing the political path are not always the softest in their rhetoric and positions; in recent years, they have tended to be more confrontational.

What we have narrated in four cases has been a cat-and-mouse game: Islamist leaders are allowed some freedom in the political realm, but the nature and extent of that freedom is unreliable and the rules are written and rewritten to deny the possibility of governing. Using an inductive and historical approach, we have seen in the four cases how the movements respond.

We will now switch the focus slightly. Instead of asking simply how movements respond, we will ask what happens to them when they decide to participate in a game that allows them to play but denies them the chance of winning. How does it affect their organization and ideology? We will shift not only the focus but also the approach: we will examine organizational and ideological changes thematically, asking how the movements are changed in a variety of areas. Chapter 6 will focus on organizational changes, and Chapter 7 will turn to ideology.

CAN ISLAMISTS PARTY?

Political Participation and
Organizational Change

We have seen that our existing knowledge about political parties operating on the edge of political systems suggests that in general and over time, given a political process that offers substantial rewards for participation and substantial risks for other strategies, parties on the edge of a system will indeed become politicized within it.

We have also tried hard to change the subject—or at least move our attention in a different direction—by insisting that we focus more on the hedges and qualifications ("over time," "substantial rewards," "substantial risks," and the meaning of "politicization") than on the "moderation" of such movements. In a system in which participation is unlikely to lead (at least over the short to medium term) to an opportunity to govern, how do rewards and risks operate? How much and how far do they operate—that is, how much politicization is likely in a system that is built to solicit participation but deny meaningful contestation? In the previous chapter, we examined Islamist movements and saw them willing to play semiauthoritarianism's cat-and-mouse game. They respond cautiously, unevenly, and slowly. And they complain. But they still position themselves to take advantage of the limited opportunities presented by semiauthoritarianism. In general, the clearer, more significant, and more sustained those opportunities, the more they respond. If systems move toward closure, movements respond as well by scaling back on politicization.

In this chapter, we will probe the details of how Islamist movements respond organizationally. Our purpose will be to move beyond the general description of the cat-and-mouse game analyzed in the previous chapter to exploring how the game affects the organization of Islamist movements. How, when, and how much do leaders reshape movements in order to participate? How do they evaluate the rewards and risks of organizational change? How much time does it take for noticeable effects on a movement's organization to occur? And when do they move beyond making tactical adjustments to committing to deeper and more permanent organizational changes?

We will begin with an organizational puzzle: Islamist movements modeled on the Brotherhood take their ideology very seriously, argue incessantly, but almost never split; on the few occasions they do fissure, it is because of concrete decisions and organizational questions, not ideas. From a discussion of this puzzle, we will begin to understand the centrality and nature of organizational questions for Islamist movements.

Second, using these insights to probe what sorts of organizational steps are particularly difficult for the movements, we will discover five (and sometimes six): deciding on how much to invest in elections, whether to form a party, whether to forge alliances with other political actors, how to use parliamentary seats, and whether to accept cabinet posts, as well as (for some movements) whether to forswear violence. We will see that the organizational ramifications of each of these decisions loom far larger for the movements than the ideological implications. By studying these decisions, we will see that politicization affects Islamist movements by rewarding and strengthening some members (those most active and skilled in the political realm) and weakening or bypassing others (who are less enthusiastic about politics).

Third, we will turn to each of these five issues in turn, selecting for detailed consideration one of the four movements that has dealt with the question so that we can best capture the effects and changes wrought by semiauthoritarianism over time. We will find that under semiauthoritarian conditions, Islamist movements accept the idea of participation, seek to take advantage of whatever opening they find (but sometimes quite slowly), leave a line of retreat to protect their nonpolitical activities, pursue a broad legislative agenda, and disavow violence.

A Puzzle: So Much Bickering, So Few Divorces

We begin with two personal notes that will at first seem tangential at best. The first involves family lore, according to which a relative of mine served as a member of a small organization that, while it still soldiers on today, has not left much of a significant historical trace: the Communist Party of Indiana. My relative served, that is, until his comrades purged him from the Party sometime in the late 1930s for ideological deviations (which nobody remembers) from the cause of communism in Indiana. The family account rings true, not so much because of my relative's person (I met him only a few times and never had the opportunity to probe his Marxist-Leninist credentials) but because of the famously fissiparous nature of Marxist groups more generally. Ideological schisms and purges among a small group of Indiana Communists would surprise few people.

Of course, Marxists hardly have a monopoly on intense ideological debates, schisms, purges, and rigid enforcement of core creeds and beliefs. The early Christian Church famously split quite literally over an iota. Organizations that are founded on ideological principles often work to maintain unity, coherence, and control by rigidly policing doctrine and thus are prone to schisms and purges. Yet not all behave this way, and Islamist movements sometimes seem to be impervious to schisms.

That brings me to my second personal note. The purge of my relative came to my mind in May 2007 when I managed to secure an interview with a group of top leaders of Jordan's Islamic Action Front. I had wanted to meet with each leader separately, but they decided to honor my interest in their party by organizing a single joint session for me at the Front's headquarters. The discussion was useful for my purposes only in the opportunity to discover the formal position of the movement on political issues; my attempts to uncover internal debates were parried with recitations of standard party positions and general statements that reflected the collective view of the leadership. With a few exceptions, the results were either predictable or anodyne. Two members stayed behind when the others had left, however, and they chatted briefly in hushed tones, seemingly oblivious to my presence. One of them referred to (but did not name) a rival faction in the party, and the other responded, "We will soon be finished with them." Unsurprisingly, the comity I had witnessed was shallower than any leader would openly admit to me at the time (later some became more comfortable with discussing such internal divisions in private): as brutally frank as they might sometimes be with each other, the leadership preferred to present a unified front to outsiders.

The hushed comment stayed with me, not because it gave me any certain information, but because it was one of the first times I had heard a direct reference to factionalism by movement leaders. While I had hunches, I did not know for sure what the other faction was or what divided the movement's leaders. My suspicions were confirmed a few months later, however, when the Front's splits came into public view, breaking out because of a severe dispute over participation in the November 2007 parliamentary elections. The contest polarized what had been a complex factional game inside the movement into two camps. It culminated in a protracted battle fought over several years—one involving a collective resignation of one faction in September 2009 (over organizational issues, some of them related to the relationship between the Jordanian movement and

Hamas), a rejection of that resignation, a closely fought internal election in 2010 (in which the defeated faction alleged that the results had been manipulated), another threatened group resignation, and a collection of public charges and accusations. Jordanian Islamists were acting like Indiana Communists, but only up to a point. There was a critical difference: each escalation also brought its own mediation attempts, and with each turn in the struggle the defeated faction restricted its reaction to sulking and maneuvering. Angry factions remained in the movement. The hushed comment by the leaders that one faction would be "finished with" the other did not indicate an impending night of long knives. It was a far tamer suggestion that internal maneuvers and procedures would result in a clear victory for their faction in the matter of forming an electoral list. That prediction was accurate, but the momentary internal triumph in 2007 did not resolve the battle. Neither did the battle itself lead to a split. In December 2009, a movement leader (no longer able to disguise the divisions) simply acknowledged to me that a formal rupture had been avoided but none of the underlying issues had been resolved. By the summer of 2010, an ad hoc group of movement elders was called in to paper over differences, which they did without addressing them. In a December 2010 visit to Jordan, I found all the leaders inaccessible, locked in a weekend conclave to knit the movement back together. In a visit two months later, after the attempts to heal the rifts had made some progress, I still heard traces of the earlier disputes and contrasting versions of what the movement as a whole had decided. Jordanian Islamists have been as fractious as any other similar movement in the region, but they have avoided the fractiousness of many other ideological movements. Islamist movements seldom fissure.

They do argue, however. Indeed, probing the reactions of the movements to political openings is complicated since the leaders themselves are usually uncertain and often divided about how to respond. Political participation over the past two decades has exposed the movements to enormous pressures, not all of which they negotiate in an easy or consensual fashion. Jordan's Islamic Action Front has exhibited some deep divisions over whether to run candidates, how many to run, and which candidates should run; its political involvement has also led it to argue over how to respond to security crackdowns, answer speeches from the throne, and structure relations with Hamas. Hamas's leadership has argued publicly over how to negotiate with Fatah, whether to reach a cease-fire agreement with Israel and on what terms, and whether to run for elections. Egypt's Muslim Brotherhood leaders pride themselves—as do leaders of most counterpart movements—on sorting out differing opinions through collegial and calm discussion and are especially averse to airing their quarrels in front of nonmembers. But they have increasingly publicly squabbled over internal elections and procedures, how many candidates to run for parliament, whether to develop a political party platform, and what to put in it. Their leaders confess that the enhanced public role has placed a spotlight on internal deliberations that used to be carried out in private; the effect is disorienting. Kuwait's Islamic Constitutional Movement has passed through some comprehensive leadership changes, generally in reaction to poor electoral performance. In a 2006 meeting, one party leader rolled his eyes when I remarked that I found Hadas members less strident and suspicious in their discourse than Islamists in some other countries. "Really? How many of us have you met?" he asked with an embarrassed smile, implicitly deriding some of his fellow Kuwaiti Islamists as unsophisticated conspiracy theorists.

In all these cases in which divisive debates became undeniable, outside observers rushed to speculate about possible splits in the movement. But the splits did not occur. The organizational pattern exemplified by the Communist Party of Indiana—an ideological movement that policed orthodoxy through expulsions and often suffered schisms—is common to all kinds of movements; it is shared by a variety of ideological or religious organizations that are based on fidelity to core principles. But the Islamist movements considered here rarely follow it. In stark contrast to many movements, the Islamist movements studied here stand out for their relatively cohesive organizational forms. Their followers and leaders can quarrel endlessly, to be sure. But it is usually short-term tactical and organizational questions, not ideological or religious questions, that occasion the bitterest debates. And these debates rarely lead to splits. More succinctly, Islamists rarely split, and when they do, it is over how to organize or act, not over what to think or say.

The same is true with expulsions. It remains difficult to be tossed out of an Islamist movement, and almost impossible to be evicted for a belief or a statement. The ties among members are deep and personal and are generally sundered only if a member clearly acts in violation of an unambiguous movement decision. Members have deeply different opinions on a range of ideological and religious issues—their attitudes toward salafism, Shi'ism, shari'a, and sufism vary greatly without causing schisms. But it is generally only actions or violations of an authoritative decision (running in an election boycotted by the movement, accepting a government appointment without movement sanction) that lead to suspension or expulsion. In short, the organization's health or mission can be imperiled—in the eyes of Islamist leaders—by what members do, not by what they say or think.

These tendencies need to be explained. Not only are they interesting in themselves, but they also provide a fruitful entry point for understanding the organizational effects of electoral participation, the subject of this chapter.

What is so puzzling about Islamist movements here? Cohesiveness is not in itself unusual. While highly ideological organizations are often fissiparous and quarrelsome, there are different kinds of organizations that find unity less challenging. Broad and diffuse social movements, for instance, may carry along more diverse coalitions but simply cannot enforce rigid creeds and ideologies. Similarly, large catchall parties, assembling diverse coalitions for the purpose of attaining electoral majorities, also often avoid splits by means of ideological and organizational looseness, especially if the electoral rules encourage them to stick together to improve the chances of victory.

The puzzle is thus that Islamist movements seem to combine apparently irreconcilable characteristics. They retain hierarchical organizations and ideological focus without losing the pluralism and freewheeling spirit of informally broad social movements and catchall parties.[1]

The reasons for their relative success in avoiding schisms can be traced back to many of the features of the Muslim Brotherhood model discussed in Chapter 4: with core programs and texts often more Delphic than definitive, the secret of the movements' successes has been tight organizational and personal bonds more than ideological ones. Their leaders have been practical people who take the movements' ideas (and the strictures of their faith) quite seriously but also preserve great elasticity in applying basic beliefs. Strong personal ties connect movement members to each other; they are underscored by fidelity to a general vision and approach but not to a detailed creed. The broad and diffuse reformist agenda of the movements allows followers to pursue their individual inclinations and preferences, whether it is in education, charity, or politics. The prospect of electoral victory is often too distant to force movements to worry about adulterating or diluting their central ideological claims. And the movements' ideologies take the form of long-term visions of a society based on Islamic principles while allowing considerable flexibility in specific beliefs or detailed programmatic objectives. The result is a set of movements that have sustained themselves under difficult conditions and have adapted to a variety of circumstances.

But here we come to the challenge of semiauthoritarian politics: political participation can complicate matters as its attractions grow. As will become clear, flexible movements must sometimes make hard organizational choices when they enter politics, and they can become more rigid in the process. The Islamist movements under study here claim that they are part of the society and have no principled objection to political participation. Indeed, they embrace it under the right circumstances. But in what ways? How much? How do they configure their organizations to do so? And what are the right circumstances? These are

---

1. The Brotherhood's distinctive stress on formal organization is a major theme of Quintan Wiktorowicz, *The Management of Islamic Activism: Salafis, the Muslim Brotherhood, and State Power in Jordan* (Albany: State University of New York Press, 2001).

vexing and sometimes divisive questions because they demand answers that can imply organizational commitments. Some movements have dithered interminably about whether to run in particular elections, what kinds of platforms to write, whether to form distinct political parties, and how many candidates to field.

Weighing Participation

The general benefits of participation are clear and have already been discussed in Chapter 2. Even in a semiauthoritarian environment, participation in elections allows opposition leaders greater freedom to organize, more channels for proclaiming their message, opportunities to develop a new set of political skills, and increased access to the media and to public spaces. This would seem to make the choice of participation an easy one. And indeed, it would be, if the movements were primarily political in nature and if there were no costs to participation. But the movements have broad agendas that extend far from the political field, and participation has real costs.

We can understand the issues much better if we cast them in organizational terms. What happens to an Islamist organization when it invests more in politics?

Islamists who run in elections, like the Christian Democrats and Social Democrats discussed in Chapter 3, have their roots in complex larger social movements—and those movements have broad religious, educational, social, charitable, and missionary agendas. The relationship between the electoral organization and the broader social movement can take many forms. In Egypt, the Muslim Brotherhood is both a broad movement and a proto-party (and neither organizational aspect was recognized by law when Egypt was governed by semiauthoritarian systems). In Jordan, there is also overlapping leadership between party and movement, and the distance between the two is minimal and shrinking. In Kuwait, the movement and the party are linked but largely defer to each other in their respective realms (social activity and politics). In Palestine, Hamas is a broad movement that established a separate electoral list under which it ran both its own members and some allies; a brief crack in 2006 and 2007 in which the electoral list seemed to be pulling one way and movement leadership another was closed when the movement seized power in Gaza, marginalizing the emerging party structure.

Why is there so much organizational variation? Constructing an electoral organization with separate leadership and autonomy from the movement carries significant but varying costs and benefits. First, a political party operates under a specific (and, in the Arab world, often quite restrictive) legal framework. Parties find their finances, internal governance, and platforms regulated and inspected by a semiauthoritarian regime, often in ways that are intentionally hostile to Islamist parties. And sometimes legal recognition is simply not a possibility, as in Sadat's and Mubarak's Egypt, where no Islamist parties were licensed and where their illegality was finally constitutionally entrenched at the end, or Kuwait, where the law does not provide for political parties, which prevents the Islamist Constitutional Movement from even opening a bank account or signing a contract with a consultant in its own name.

Second, establishment of a political party generally entails the emergence of a new leadership group within the movement. Leaders feel a strong ambivalence here. On the one hand, they wish to show that their movement can develop new skills and that its mission is comprehensive. The emergence of skilled Islamist politicians is a good thing. On the other hand, it leads to some tensions. Party officials and members of parliament now speak for the group and develop a distinct voice and agenda—an occasional problem for Islamist movements that strive, for all their internal arguments, for unity of ranks. Further, forming a distinct party forces an organization to make hard choices about who speaks for the movement politically. Islamist movements are often not merely pluralistic but fractious. They overcome strategic and ideological differences by developing unifying but vague slogans and platforms. When developing an electoral list and nominating candidates, a party is forced to signal the internal balance of forces.

Third, creation of a party not only calls forth new leaders; it also creates new followers. Islamist movements organized on the model of the Muslim Brotherhood form tightly organized groups of members in small units; membership is graduated and requires considerable commitment and time. Political parties seeking to operate effectively in elections will generally have different (and lower) membership requirements; in many cases, it is necessary on both legal and political grounds to recruit regardless of religious affiliation.

Fourth, establishment of a party requires resources that could be devoted to other movement goals, such as educational or charitable work. The emergence of an eighty-eight-member Muslim Brotherhood bloc in the Egyptian parliament— even though it was not formally recognized as a party—led the movement to divert significant expertise and resources to support the deputies so they could play an active legislative role.[2]

Fifth, electoral organizations often force the movement to make calculations based on a different time horizon than the one they claim to prefer. Islamist leaders insist that they think in decades or generations; they count patience as a divinely enjoined virtue. But electorally oriented parties calculate time in electoral cycles. Maximizing votes does not always require ideological or programmatic

---

2. See Samer Shehata and Joshua Stacher, "The Brotherhood Goes to Parliament," *Middle East Report* 240, (Fall 2006), 32–40.

moderation in the short term—sometimes, for instance, pugnacious stands are popular—but it does involve placing a primacy on electoral politics and likely dilutes a party's message over the long term. In the Palestinian case, Hamas's entry into the electoral process necessitated a stress on the political at the expense of the religious, a shift that led to criticisms from radical groups that Hamas had abandoned an Islamic agenda. In interviews with Hamas parliamentarians in 2006, I was repeatedly told that the movement had decided to postpone any religious agenda. In Kuwait, a founding member of the Islamic Constitutional Movement explained to me that the entry into electoral politics required members to learn to speak a new political (rather than religious) language.[3]

Sixth, movement leaders who ask their supporters to organize, campaign, contribute, and turn out at the polls (often at some personal risk) may find themselves under some internal pressure to show real benefits to their followers. Participation that brings neither material benefits nor policy changes may demoralize the rank and file. And it may also put the movement at risk in competition for supporters: it exposes Islamist leaders to criticism that they have forgotten religion for politics. Indeed, that is precisely the patronizing refrain Brotherhood leaders throughout the Arab world hear from their salafi rivals (the salafi trend emphasizes close fidelity to foundational texts).

Finally, participation can generate fear among a movement's adversaries. Other opposition groups sometimes show great apprehension at Islamists' strength (often even allying with regimes against them). And regimes themselves have often reacted with alarm at Islamist movements that seemed to wish to push the boundaries of participation too far. Those boundaries are rarely constant within a political system over time. For example, what the Egyptian regime regarded as acceptable in 2005 was far more than it was willing to countenance a decade earlier; in subsequent years, that tolerant spirit declined. Boundaries vary considerably over space as well; some countries are much friendlier to the idea of participation by Islamists than others. A movement that enters politics risks exposing itself to a variety of repressive tools wielded by regimes that seek to have movements learn the hard way where the limits are at any particular time. And more profoundly, the decision to participate has fundamentally altered rulers' perception of Islamist movements, often turning them in official eyes from potential partners or harmless fulminators into active security threats.

Armed with this body of concerns, how do Islamist leaders regard the decision to enter the political arena? Or, more precisely, when and how do they position their movements to enter it, and when and how do they hold back or hedge their organization's bets?

---

3. 'Isa Shahin, personal interview, Kuwait, October 2006.

Two aspects of Islamist participation should be immediately clear. First, occasional dabbling in elections is usually an easy choice for the movements. Running a few candidates reaps some of the benefits of participation but requires little organizational cost; such activity is easily seen as reinforcing the broad movement agenda. Second, an increasingly open electoral environment—one that offers more freedom to campaign, the possibility of winning more seats, and better opportunities to enter and steer public debates—can entice even a recalcitrant movement into reconfiguring itself organizationally to emphasize its political role.

Thus participation might vary from a little to a lot, depending on conditions. But moving beyond this generalization requires us to uncover how movement leaders balance the enticing features of political participation against the possible organizational costs. Given the fluid nature of the rules of the political game in many semiauthoritarian systems, when will Islamic movements go beyond dabbling in politics, how much, and in what ways? When will they make ongoing organizational commitments to political participation, even those that incur the organizational costs just described? When leaders debate among themselves over whether and how much to participate, how are the arguments likely to be framed, and how are they likely to be resolved? It is precisely because such questions are both momentous and difficult that—as noted at the opening of this chapter—they can lead to deep divisions in movements that negotiate their ideological differences with relative ease. The analysis presented thus far suggests that six decisions are likely to be particularly difficult precisely because their organizational costs are high and because some of the steps are difficult to reverse: how hard to run (whether to participate in any particular election and how many candidates to put forward); whether to form a party and how much freedom to give it; how and whether to form alliances; how to manage a parliamentary bloc; and whether to enter the cabinet. For some movements, the question of disarming also poses a difficult organizational challenge.

We will examine each of these organizational decisions in turn, highlighting the experience of specific movements. For the first decision, how hard to run, we will examine the experience of the Egyptian movement, since none of the other movements (with the possible exception of the Jordanian) have deliberated so long, under so many different conditions, or so openly. For the second decision, formation of a party, we will focus on the Jordanian experience as the most sustained, but we will also consider Egypt and Kuwait briefly. On the third issue, alliances, we will examine Kuwait since the potential benefits of such alliances have been greatest there; we will understand how the matter is challenging even under favorable circumstances. For a similar reason, on the matter of the parliamentary bloc, we will focus on Egypt since the eighty-eight deputies who served in the 2005 parliament represented the most significant and sustained opportunity for an Islamist movement in the Arab world (Hamas, it is true, obtained a majority in the 2006 elections, but the parliament was unable to function after just a few months). In order to understand the issue of participation in a cabinet, we will turn to the Jordanian movement, the one that has debated it most intensely and for the longest period. Finally, on the matter of violence and an armed wing, we will focus on the two movements that have confronted the issue most squarely: Egypt's Muslim Brotherhood and Hamas.

After considering each decision, we will be able to discern a general pattern—that semiauthoritarian systems induce Islamist movements to make significant investments but discourage deep commitments to electoral politics. The results will illuminate much of the cat-and-mouse game between regimes and oppositions.

Arguing over How Hard to Run

In conducting research on Islamist movements in various countries, I have asked in many interviews what the movement's plans are for any upcoming elections. I have almost invariably been told that the decision to participate in principle has been resolved and is no longer widely debated. But when I move the discussion from principle to practice, my interlocutors make clear that they cannot speak for the movement as a whole because such a decision has not been made. Most leaders speculate that the movement will indeed run candidates in an upcoming election, usually speaking in terms of an upper limit (such as "we will not compete for more than one-third of the seats"). But they try hard to change the subject from their calculations to the regime's misdeeds, complaining that the rules governing the elections are unfair, as is their administration. The image is of a movement that is carefully calculating about how to participate in a rigged system.

That image of careful calibration generally turns out to be a bit misleading, however. Often shortly after leaving a country, I read comments by movement leaders that indicate that issues I had thought were settled are still subject to internal debate. In several visits to Egypt in 2008, 2009, and 2010, most leaders seemed to suggest that the Brotherhood would run a small number of candidates (one or two dozen) for parliamentary elections scheduled for late 2010, a far smaller number than the 150 candidates it ran in 2005. But then, in the summer of 2010, movement leaders suggested that a boycott and a more substantial participation were both still on the table. And they both were—the Brotherhood wound up filing as many candidates as it had in the 2005 elections but then switched to a boycott between the first and second rounds of voting. In Jordan,

I heard in 2006 that participation in parliamentary elections slated for late 2007 was all but settled. But even after the party indeed decided to run candidates, some members (including the party's secretary-general) continued to question the decision. In subsequent visits I was told that support for the boycott option had dropped among the leadership, but then the party decided not to run in the 2010 parliamentary elections.

The decision to participate in a particular election and the calculations about the extent of participation are deliberated, but calculations are difficult and internal discussions are contentious. A more accurate image than one of a deliberate and strategic movement would therefore be a game of musical chairs, in which the decisions about whether to participate, how many candidates to run, and which ones to run are the subjects of constant motion; decisions are final only when the music stops (or, to abandon the metaphor, when the filing deadline comes). Even a movement that has participated in the past is likely to dither over whether to participate in a particular election, and if so, how many candidates to run. The decision to run any candidates means forgoing the threat of a boycott, which (as described in Chapter 2) is one of the few bargaining chips a movement can deploy to affect the terms of political participation. Debates are less likely to focus on the legitimacy of participation on religious grounds than on the advisability of doing so under a particular set of rules. Even after a decision to participate has been made, the movement will immediately face the question of how many candidates to run (at least in parliamentary elections): running more candidates can be taken as a threat by other political actors (particularly in the regime) that the movement is considering breaking the unwritten rule that it lose. Running fewer candidates can send different signals: under some circumstances, it may communicate to the regime that the movement does not seek to win; under other circumstances, the message may be sent to militant followers that the movement does not accept the rules of the game. A movement that fields candidates for a minority of seats signals that it is willing to live temporarily by the rules of semiauthoritarian politics but also strongly suggests that its main horizons lie outside the formal political process.

We can see this game of musical chairs operating in the most sustained way in Egypt. Under the constantly shifting terms of Egyptian semiauthoritarianism, the Brotherhood cautiously moved into openings while striving hard to avoid being trapped into making permanent organizational commitments to a primarily political strategy.

In its first incarnation, the Egyptian Muslim Brotherhood dabbled in electoral participation but ultimately found that its internal preferences on the issue were irrelevant: the movement was banned by the pre-1952 regime (its political activity had, after all, extended beyond electioneering to paramilitary training and—with or without the authorization of the senior leadership—urban terrorism). The second incarnation of the Egyptian Muslim Brotherhood, as it reemerged in the 1970s and 1980s, resumed where the movement had left off before being suppressed. In the 1970s, it did not regain legal status, but it found some limited opportunities to resume modest participation. While its friendliness toward participation rapidly increased from the time of the movement's reemergence through the 2005 parliamentary elections, the political environment in which the Brotherhood was active showed less consistency. The Egyptian political system in its semiauthoritarian periods offered real and substantial openings to the movement at certain points but at others showed the Brotherhood its most ferocious face. The result was to spark debate within the movement about the relative emphasis on politics and political participation.

There was little advocacy of total withdrawal or its opposite, conversion to a completely political strategy. It is true that some observers, such as Mona El-Ghobashy, noted a shift in the movement's approach from "politics as a sacred mission to politics as the public contest between rival interests."[4] Alongside that acceptance of normal political activity, however, was a continued insistence that the movement would never forget the breadth of its agenda and that "participation in elections is a means and not an end."[5] The debates that occurred were between those who saw politics as more central (and unsurprisingly, those who developed greater skills in the political sphere, which they were eager to deploy) and those who emphasized, practiced, and valued it less. The first pole gained adherents for much of the period of the Brotherhood's reemergence, but their arguments and claimed benefits lost their luster in the final years of Mubarak's presidency.

The Brotherhood's reemergence initially brought about concrete attempts to enter the political process at two levels. First, parliamentary elections were occasions for individual Brotherhood members to run for parliament as independents (or as members of one of the recognized political groups). But while such candidacies clearly took place with the tacit support of the Brotherhood, they required no commitment from the organization as a whole to participate in or support the campaign.

Second, the younger generation of political activists on Egyptian campuses had, in a sense, entered politics even before they entered the Brotherhood. By competing in student association elections, they chose to campaign on general

---

4. Mona El-Ghobashy, "The Metamorphosis of the Egyptian Muslim Brothers," *International Journal of Middle East Studies* 37, no. 3 (2005), 374.
5. Gamal Hishmat, personal interview, Cairo, July 2009.

ideological issues (emphasizing, to be sure, their determination to meet the specific needs of students). And when they graduated and entered professions, they continued this record of political involvement in Egypt's professional associations. The Brotherhood not only coaxed in a large number of those students but also managed to convince those who did join about the necessity of peaceful change and working within the boundaries of the existing system. Youthful energy was thus channeled by wizened patience to produce the move into more sustained political activity in the 1980s.

Indeed, it was during the 1980s that the move into politics gradually shifted from the tactical and opportunistic level of dabbling to a more strategic (if generally still cautious) set of campaigns. About a decade after the Egyptian political system had become semiauthoritarian, the Brotherhood finally stepped up its politicization in a major way. During the 1980s, the movement came to dominate some key professional associations and also was poised to take up the role of leading the political opposition in the country's parliament with a level of parliamentary activity that began to eclipse that of the non-Islamist opposition.[6]

But the Brotherhood's success began to create problems for the organization as it discovered that semiauthoritarian politics does not move in a consistently liberalizing direction. In the professional associations, the rise of the movement allowed its younger leaders to establish a strong base and create a political space where they could articulate a broad critique of regime policies on a wide range of matters not restricted to professional concerns. That not only produced some tensions within the associations but also generated a strong backlash from the regime. Some of the leaders of the professional associations from the Brotherhood concluded that they had pushed too far too quickly.[7] They reacted by consciously pulling back on their rhetoric, activities, and level of domination in the associations. The diminution of their activities was not fully voluntary: the regime introduced and enforced a new law for professional associations that was clearly designed (and generally worked) to wrest control of most of the bodies back out of Islamist grips.[8]

A similar trajectory of forward movement and forced retreat was followed in parliamentary elections: the Brotherhood's gains of the 1980s were met by a series of legal and extralegal steps to curb the group's ability to compete. In the 1990s,

---

6. See Hasanayn Tawfiq Ibrahim and Huda Raghib 'Awad, *Al-dawr al-siyasi li-l-jama'at al-ikhwan al-muslimin fi zill al-ta'adduduiyya al-siyasiyya al-muqayyada fi misr* (Cairo: Al-Mahrusa, 1996); see also El-Ghobashy, "Metamorphosis of the Egyptian Muslim Brothers," p. 378.

7. See Geneive Abdo, *No God but God: Egypt and the Triumph of Islam* (Oxford: Oxford University Press, 2000), chap. 4.

8. The most thorough coverage of the Brotherhood's role in association politics is Carrie Rosefsky Wickham, *Mobilizing Islam: Religion, Activism, and Political Change in Egypt* (New York: Columbia University Press, 2002), chap. 8.

parliamentary elections became less friendly turf for the Brotherhood. Despite the reluctant admission by the regime of independent candidates (forced by a series of Supreme Constitutional Court rulings), a variety of techniques ranging from arrests of leaders to cutting the telephone lines of campaign workers obstructed the Brotherhood's ability to campaign on behalf of its candidates. The movement complained vociferously through any legal channel it could, but it also reacted with a clearly enunciated policy of self-restraint. Leaders constantly reiterated that while they sought to run, gain seats, and use them to present and argue for their vision, they had no immediate plans to govern Egypt. They demonstrated this by running candidates for a minority of seats and often refusing to challenge leading members of the governing National Democratic Party. Indeed, the movement not only disavowed a majority but also repeatedly stated that it would seek no more than one-third of the seats; with more than that it might have the ability to block any constitutional amendment proposed by the majority.

When asked, Brotherhood leaders claimed that their decision to participate in politics was a strategic one that was no longer contested internally. They admitted to ongoing debate within the movement, however, on how much to participate. Part of that debate was over how to read the prevailing political environment: How many seats would they be allowed to win? Was the administration of the election likely to be so unfair as to prevent meaningful opportunities? How much should the movement coordinate its position with other movements?

A large part of the debate also reflected a clash of priorities, though movement leaders discussed this less openly. On the one hand were leaders who came to view political participation as central to the Brotherhood's mission. 'Abd al-Mun'im Abu al-Futuh, for instance, one of the architects of the Brotherhood's plunge into politics, argued that the change the Brotherhood seeks must come from societies and not from leaders, implicitly criticizing those who wanted to focus only on quiet persuasion of leaders or even seizing control of the polity in an effort to Islamize it.[9] It was this view that led him to argue for a strong commitment to involvement in political life and elections (and later, as will be seen, for a partial withdrawal).

On the other hand, some leading Brotherhood figures worried that excessive political involvement would only generate a backlash; they wished to work far more on developing a cadre of firmly committed followers—a vanguard that could lead the Islamization of the society at a later date. Such figures, often referred to as "Qutbists" by their opponents, were influenced less by the radical aspects of Sayyid Qutb's approach (which they worked hard to interpret out of

---

9. See the Collection of his articles in 'Abd al-Mun'im Abu al-Futuh, *Mujaddidun la mubaddidun* (Cairo: Tatwir li-l-nashr wa-tawzi', 2005).

existence) than by his emphasis on the need to develop a committed vanguard to lead an Islamic revival. These figures did not reject participation but sought to shift the emphasis to organizational and other work. When Muhammad Badiʿ was elected general guide in 2010, for instance, he quickly reiterated the movement's commitment to political participation (repeating the "participation, not domination" slogan) despite his reputation as a *tanzimi* (advocate of internal organizational work) and even a Qutbist.

The fullest flowering of the efforts of the first camp came in 2005, when the Brotherhood won one-fifth of the seats in parliamentary elections. But just as some leaders concluded that they had overreached in the professional associations in the 1980s, the strong parliamentary showing generated a vigorous debate within the movement's leadership, especially as the harsh regime backlash showed no sign of abating. Muhammad Habib, the deputy guide of the Brotherhood at the time and neither a *tanzimi* nor a Qutbist, made no secret of his feeling that the Brotherhood would have been better served by contesting fewer seats.[10] Sympathetic intellectuals began to moot the suggestion that the Brotherhood withdraw from politics for a period and focus on organizational, propagandizing, and missionary work until the situation improved.[11] And by 2010, even Abu al-Futuh, the leader most identified with the political approach, began to claim that an extended suspension of electoral activity—for as long as two decades—made sense. He insisted that such a step would not be abandoning politics but only forgoing elections. Electoral activity could be resumed when other political forces arose and the Brotherhood no longer faced the regime in comparative isolation. (That moment actually came much sooner than Abu al-Futuh hoped; it took not twenty years of waiting but only a few months before the semiauthoritarian regime fell in a popular uprising. At that point, his electoral enthusiasm returned so strongly that he broke from the movement to run for president.)

The movement as a whole rejected even a temporary suspension of electoral activity, and in 2010 it rebuffed efforts to coordinate an electoral boycott by all opposition forces. Positions had now switched; it was the politically minded within the movement who argued for a boycott and those who sought to preserve other movement goals who worried that such a step might be seen as too confrontational (and indeed too political) by the regime. The period of repression definitely strengthened the hands of the latter camp, but even they decided to boycott when it became clear that the election would be administered in such a way as to exclude them nearly completely from the parliament.

---

10. Muhammad Habib, personal interview, Cairo, July 2009.
11. Muhammad Salim al-ʿAwa, an influential independent Islamist intellectual, began making this argument in 2007.

Two lessons stand out from this experience: first, the Egyptian Muslim Brotherhood moved to grasp the opportunities semiauthoritarianism presented and to retreat when semiauthoritarian rules shifted to discourage its participation. Second, while it responded, it did so slowly, unevenly, and only after extended (and sometimes divisive) deliberation.

Forming a Party But Keeping Its Leash Short

A second difficult decision is whether to form a political party and, if so, how to structure it (in particular, how to configure its relationship with the broader movement). Indeed, the issue of forming a party is not simply difficult for the movements; it is confusing for researchers. In Jordan, it is not unusual to meet an Islamist leader who wears three hats, with leadership positions in the Muslim Brotherhood, the Islamic Action Front, and a prominent Islamist NGO (such as the Islamic Center). Yet each body insists on its legally distinct nature, internal procedures, and autonomous status. In Kuwait, I have spoken with Islamist leaders about the possibility that the movement and the party may go their separate ways. In Palestine, Hamas members elected to the parliament insisted in my interviews with them that they were elected on as members of the "Change and Reform List" electoral list and its platform—one that emphasized domestic issues—leaving the status of the movement's ambitious agenda on the struggle with Israel less clear. And those placed by Hamas in ministerial positions stressed that their task was to serve the nation, not to pursue movement goals. But what insiders perceive as a potential rift between movement and party, outsiders tend to see as an attempt to hide the movement's creeping tentacles.

A political party may be ideally suited to take advantage of any legal openings and to turn out the vote in elections—but it also has all the liabilities discussed earlier in this chapter (such as fostering new leaders and new followers, imposing a new legal framework, generating new interests, and diverting movement resources). The balance within a movement between what Kenneth Greene has called "office-seekers" and "message-seekers" can be deeply altered by the creation of a new structure dedicated to a focus on politics.[12] Both the benefits and costs increase as the party becomes more autonomous from the main movement. Few movements have contemplated converting the entire movement into a party, since that would mean favoring politics over all other aspects of the movement's

---

12. Kenneth F. Greene, "Creating Competition: Patronage Politics and the PRI's Demise," Kellogg Institute Working Paper 345, December 2007, available at http://citeseerx.ist.psu.edu/viewdoc/download?doi=10.1.1.126.5276&rep=rep1&type=pdf.

mission. But they have fretted and argued over how long a leash to give a party. The more open a political system, the more the leadership will be enticed by the possible rewards accompanying a relatively costly decision to form an autonomous party. In the long run, such a step may be difficult to reverse not only because of the sunk organizational costs but also because it has fostered the rise of a group of leaders whose perspective is based on their position within an electorally oriented party.

The four movements under examination have reacted to the pressures on party formation in different ways. In Egypt, Brotherhood leaders began discussing the option of forming their own party since shortly after the Egyptian political order moved to a formal multiparty system in the late 1970s. By the end of the 1980s, the movement had approved the idea in principle. But that general decision simply deputized the Guidance Bureau, the Brotherhood's top executive arm, to make a final determination on the timing and form that the Brotherhood's foray into partisanship would take. The bureau never found the time appropriate until after the Mubarak regime fell and even then moved cautiously and uncertainly Under semiauthoritarian conditions, the movement simply never found the moment right—in 2010, Sa'd al-Katatni, the head of the Brotherhood's parliamentary bloc and a member of the bureau, opined that even applying for a party license would be "signing the Brotherhood's death certificate."[13]

The situation in the other three countries has been only slightly more welcoming. In Jordan, the movement formed a party as soon as the law allowed but has kept it on a short leash. And the party has been viewed with an increasingly wary eye by the regime. In Palestine, Hamas formed an electoral list, but the political system collapsed before it was clear whether a real electoral party would have evolved. The movement that has made the most significant investment in an autonomous party is Kuwait, but even there the movement-party tensions have continued. And the Kuwaiti regime has placed limits in its own way by refusing to allow parties legal status and declining to bargain with existing blocs as blocs (or, in effect, proto-parties).

Let us turn our attention to Jordan, where the legislative framework has been most welcoming and the experience of managing movement-party relations the most sustained. The IAF was founded in 1992 to take advantage of Jordan's

---

13. The information in this paragraph on the internal deliberations within the Brotherhood over the period is based primarily on interviews with two Brotherhood leaders, 'Abd al-Mun'im Abu al-Futuh and Sa'd al-Katatni. For some of the historical debate on political parties in the Brotherhood, see Tawfiq Yusif al-Wa'i, *Al-fikr al-siyasi al-mu'asir 'and al-ikhwan al-muslimin* (Kuwait: Maktabat al-Masar al-Islamiyya, 2001), chap. 4. For an analysis of the recent debate within the Egyptian Brotherhood, see Khalil al-'Anani, *Al-ikhwan al-muslimun fi misr: shaykhukha tusari' al-zaman* (Cairo: Maktabat al-Shuruq al-Duwaliyya, 2007).

political opening and its new, relatively permissive, political party law. A political party seemed a logical complement to the movement's various organs for realizing its broad mission of reform and Islamization. At the time of the IAF's founding, a minority of leaders wished to register the Brotherhood as a whole as a political party; another group was suspicious of the attempt to move definitively toward a greater political emphasis.

The compromise decision—to form a party distinct from the movement—managed to resolve the issue, and even those who had opposed the decision rushed to gain positions in the new party. But while the general matter of establishing a political party was resolved, the relationship between the party and the movement as a whole remains ambiguous and a source of continuous maneuverings and tensions.

Indeed, the IAF was a far less autonomous body than had been promised. To this day, the IAF and Brotherhood have interlocking leaderships. The IAF leader is informally selected by the Brotherhood (more formally, the Brotherhood generally forwards its suggestions to the IAF, which ratifies them as a matter of course). IAF members from the Brotherhood are expected to follow Brotherhood positions and decisions and can be disciplined if they fail to do so. Thus the failure of IAF leader Bani Arshid to back IAF candidates led to his trial in a Brotherhood court rather than a party one. When the Brotherhood supported the idea of a "constitutional monarchy" in 2009, the IAF was expected to echo the call. On both occasions, however, the matter was too divisive within the movement to make its decisions stick: Bani Arshid's trial was eventually shelved and the constitutional monarchy initiative obtained growing support but some (including Bani Arshid himself) continued to distance themselves from the theme.

Why have movement-party relations been so difficult and contentious? Because the rewards for fuller politicization (in the form of an autonomous, politically minded party leadership) have been murky, shifting, and balanced by some liabilities.

It is clear that there are some rewards. The formation of a political party has probably allowed the Islamist movement to cultivate its political skills and strategize more effectively about how it wishes to manage its political positions and its electoral participation. While pre-1993 elections saw some conscious strategizing by Brotherhood leaders, there was now a specialized structure dedicated to politics; there was also a clear and identifiable party label to communicate to voters the names of favored candidates, provide an umbrella campaign, and attract independents sympathetic to parts of the movement's message. And the party was largely successful in imposing decisions in designating candidates, though the process has at times been difficult. Before 2007, the IAF sought to devolve much of the authority over candidate selection to its branches to ensure that it would run locally viable candidates, but the national organization worked to maintain some balance among internal factions in its slate. In 2003, it brought in almost entirely new faces to communicate that it was a movement rather than a collection of leading personalities; the move also helped ensure that the decision about participation could not be construed as a product of the personal ambition of older leaders. In 2007, the national organization imposed a smaller, more ideologically uniform slate as a result of internal struggles as well as an effort to communicate a less threatening image to the regime (though its leaders claim to have followed the wishes of the base in most instances and vehemently denied any agreement with the government on the list[14]). In most elections—including the 1997 and 2010 balloting, which it boycotted—the IAF has faced a few defections from movement members who decided to run on their own; in general, the party has been firm in disciplining such defections.

The benefits of forming an autonomous party have been qualified in three ways, however. First, they are limited by the nature of the Jordanian political system. It is clear that the IAF has been welcomed into politics only on the condition that it lose; the prize of parliamentary seats it has been offered comes with the clear message that it cannot use those seats to pass any laws or to shape policy.

Second, the benefits are uncertain. In the middle of the first decade of the 2000s, for instance, the movement's clear commitment to politicization did not prevent a set of regime moves against it. In 2006, IAF deputies were arrested; in 2007, the party charged that the most conciliatory slate of candidates it had ever submitted was the victim of rigging (an allegation the regime seemed to confirm at least explicitly in 2010 when it pledged itself to fairer conduct of electoral administration).

Third, and more subtly, the formation of the IAF has made for a more rigid division between movement supporters and opponents. Creating a party was intended to have the opposite effect of attracting independents to the Islamist banner. And indeed, some of the IAF parliamentarians have not been Brotherhood members. But the prominent political role played by the IAF—and the strongly oppositional cast of its rhetoric—has contributed to a polarization. Earlier generations of Jordanians often passed in and out of the movement almost noiselessly: since the Brotherhood focused largely on social activities of a less controversial nature, it attracted figures who were closer to the regime (and indeed, some leading pro-regime politicians were members in their youth). But the political role of the IAF has made such shifting political loyalties less likely.

---

14. See, for instance, the interview with Ruhayl Ghurayba: "Ghurayba: The Differences with the Movement Are Being Settled and the Probability of Its Split Are Denied," *Al-ghad,* 12 October 2007.

The response of the Islamist leadership to the uncertain and limited nature of the benefits is to keep the party on a fairly short leash. The cultivation of a politically skilled cadre is a welcome development, but the movement is not yet ready to allow a completely political logic to dominate one of its wings. Oddly, that short leash is itself a gift to a regime looking for pressure points against Islamists. In the Jordanian case, the toothpaste-tube nature of the Islamist movements offers Islamists the opportunity to squeeze themselves into whatever openings arise—but also allows the regime many places to squeeze the movement. The multiple exposures were illustrated most forcefully in 2006 when mounting political and security concerns about the movement led the regime to seek to hem it in; ultimately, the IAF, the Muslim Brotherhood, and the movement's largest nongovernmental organizations were all caught in the complex tangle. In June 2006, at a time of escalating tensions between the movement and the regime, four members of the IAF (including firebrand Muhammad Abu Faris) were arrested after visiting the funeral tent erected by Abu Mus'ab al-Zarqawi's family. While many IAF activists considered the visit an embarrassment, the arrest led the party to rally around those detained. So the next month the regime moved toward a more subtle path. The cabinet used a report by the public prosecutor alleging irregularities in the management of the Islamic Center, the largest NGO associated with the Islamist movement, to replace the organization's board. The message was clear: the radicals' political activity was endangering the movement as a whole. Throughout the region, Islamist leaders reacted to the Jordanian move with alarm, seeing it as "economic punishment" (as the general guide of the Egyptian Brotherhood termed it four years later) for political overreaching.[15]

The Temptations and Frustrations of Alliances

When discussing the issue of cross-ideological alliances with opposition leaders in the Arab world, I have found that it takes little more than a minute to hear talk of common aims and lofty objectives give way to suspicions, grievances, and complaints about unrequited affections. The potential rewards of a broad opposition alliance seem strong. Why it is that Islamist leaders seem so ambivalent on the subject?

Movements investing in politics will have to make a series of decisions about cultivating allies: Should a broad opposition front be formed to press for deeper change even if it means crafting a program that focuses only on the

---

15. See Muhammad Badi''s weekly message of 15 April 2010, available at http://www. ikhwanonline.com/Article.asp?ArtID=63452&SecID=213.

least common denominator among ideologically incompatible movements? How should a movement react if the regime offers it benefits or even a limited tactical alliance denied other opposition actors? Is a movement better served by cultivating ties with other Islamist parties (such as salafi or Shi'i parties where they exist) or does such an alliance prevent cooperation with non-Islamist groups and expose the more mainstream movement to charges of hidden extremism? Once in parliament, does it make more sense to reach out to ideological rivals and opponents to secure specific legislative gains or to maintain ideological purity in an effort to communicate to followers the movement's sincerity and fidelity to principles?

The stakes behind such decisions are high for both regime and opposition. For the regime, a long-term, strategic alliance among opposition forces is likely to be based on demands for democratizing reforms; such a development would be threatening indeed. Short-term tactical alliances among opposition forces, by contrast, may be merely annoying. Regimes will therefore seek desperately to forestall strategic alliances with divide-and-rule tactics and even raw repression. But they may tolerate tactical alliances.

For Islamist movements, therefore, a strategic alliance with other opposition forces is a risky and confrontational path. And it is a difficult one. Tactical alliances are often easy to make—and to break. Long-term pacts among opposition forces require a much more serious commitment to coordinating actions, programs, and strategies. A purely political movement might be willing to throw in its lot with a cross-ideological alliance. A social movement with broader nonpolitical objectives will likely find such a path less attractive, since it may mean subordinating nonpolitical objectives to a set of political goals. It may also mean firm commitment to a fully oppositional strategy and permanently forgoing some of the benefits that might arise from coming to a separate accommodation with the regime.

We can understand the debates and the implications of various decisions best in Kuwait, in large part because the potential rewards of a broad alliance are greatest there. In Kuwait, the party leadership has more autonomy; the fractured nature of Kuwaiti society means that Islamists will never secure a majority without forging alliances; and the political environment is on the more liberal end of the semiauthoritarian spectrum. But even there, cross-ideological alliances have been short-lived and formed only over short-term tactical goals. The Kuwaiti case demonstrates that even in seemingly favorable circumstances, semiauthoritarian politics and the broad-based nature of Islamist movements makes strategic opposition alliances difficult to form and even harder to sustain.

Growing involvement in politics—and in particular the formation of Hadas— has required the movement to think seriously and strategically about alliances with other political forces. Even in a fully democratic environment, such alliances would be necessary: with a significant Shi'i minority, a good portion of the population voting in accordance with tribal allegiances, liberals and economic elites suspicious of Islamists, and an Islamist scene that includes salafis and other competing groups, it is virtually inconceivable that the Muslim Brotherhood or Hadas would ever attain a majority vote. Should it wish to form a majority, Hadas will need coalition partners.

Kuwaiti Islamists face decisions about alliances on two occasions: general elections and parliamentary voting. In both cases, the movement's growing politicization has led to greater friendliness toward tactical alliances (and even flirtation with strategic alliances), but the results have often been frustrating.

First, with regard to elections, balloting in Kuwait seems to encourage various kinds of alliances; voters are allowed to select four candidates, and the top ten vote-getters in each district earn parliamentary seats (before the 2008 elections, voters were given two votes in smaller districts, and the top two vote-getters went on to parliament). Rather than run a full slate of candidates, Hadas runs one or two and then seeks to form vote-swapping pacts between its supporters and those of reasonably congenial individuals or movements. (These limited tactical alliances are sometimes publicly announced and sometimes communicated privately to strong supporters.) Famed for their party discipline, Hadas leaders have always hoped to be able to work the system to their advantage. In order to maximize their chances for success, they allowed district campaign managers to take the lead in negotiating the arrangements they saw as most promising.

The results have been disappointing. Hadas has worked to seek out like-minded candidates, generally those who were socially conservative and often from the salafi camp. Because such potential allies often operated as individuals or small groups, negotiations were protracted and complicated. Ultimately, Hadas leaders have come to suspect that some potential allies (especially among the salafis) deliberately dragged out negotiations over alliances with Hadas while secretly forming different alliances in order to outmaneuver Hadas. In the end, in both 2008 and 2009, Hadas found itself more the target of other alliances than the beneficiary of its own.

If elections drove Hadas away from potential allies, what about alliance formation in parliament after elections? Again, such alliances seem a very attractive path: the Kuwaiti parliament has some authority, and a cohesive opposition bloc would be able to bring down ministers, sketch a legislative agenda, and perhaps move Kuwait toward a constitutional monarchy. But in parliament, the Islamist movement has had only a little more success than it has with elections. Before the formation of Hadas in 1991, movement members of parliament tended to line up between government and opposition in a floating group of independents, tribal deputies, and socially conservative deputies. The government could generally assemble its own majority (sometimes including Islamists and sometimes not) by attracting loyal and "service" deputies interested in obtaining government benefits for their districts or tribal members. But in the 1980s, Islamists gravitated more toward opposition ranks on issues of parliamentary prerogatives, pushing in effect for a more liberalized political system. Their growing prominence in Kuwaiti society, however, deepened liberal fears, and contests between Islamists and liberals over control of the student association and other bodies made the rivalry too intense for common parliamentary interests to overcome.

The formation of Hadas seemed to be a step in a different direction: it was connected with an unambiguous Islamist commitment to electoral participation and restoration of the constitution, and indeed, ideological rivals across Kuwaiti society (including salafis and some Shi'a) joined in pressing for political reform in the wake of the Iraqi invasion of 1990. Once parliament was restored in 1992, however, opposition unity crumbled. Hadas chose to align itself quite clearly with salafi and independent Islamists, leading to prolonged ideological rivalries for over a decade. Yet as much as Hadas cast its lot with the right side of the Kuwaiti political spectrum, its ability to form a cohesive Islamic bloc was limited: salafi deputies remained contemptuous of Hadas as being more political than religious in inspiration, and independent Islamists lived up to their label by often being impervious to coordination. While Hadas had a reputation for being less confrontational than other opposition groups, the ruling family did not always find Islamist forces much easier to work with than their non-Islamist counterparts. In the 1996 parliament, in which the Islamist bloc held fifteen seats, tensions between parliament and the government grew so strong that the prime minister and crown prince finally asked the amir to dissolve parliament—the first time that Kuwait had moved to early elections.

In the following decade, Hadas leaders moved to construct broader and more strategic alliances across the political spectrum. Their goal was to force through a set of political reforms that would move Kuwait in the direction of a constitutional monarchy; they hoped they could find common cause with various political forces that all favored a more powerful parliament and limits on the influence of the ruling family. Suspicions among potential allies, especially over social questions, ran very deep, however, and Hadas often found that one set of alliances undercut another possible set. (For instance, when Hadas worked with other political groups on a law governing the collection of alms, Shi'a deputies complained that the proposed law was written in conformity with Sunni practice and might undermine their own alms collection; an assurance by a Hadas deputy that Shi'a could avail themselves of the exemption under the draft law for non-Muslims only inflamed matters.)

Among liberals, Hadas was seen as suspect on two grounds. First, despite its recent oppositional history, Hadas was regarded as being insufficiently dedicated to political opposition. Such suspicions were based in part on the traditional priorities of the Islamist movement in Kuwait. The diverse activities associated with the movement led it to value protected social space; an overly confrontational or politicized attitude might endanger aspects of the movement that benefit from official acquiescence. And even in the 1990s, when Hadas emerged as an opposition party, its potential partners continued to see it as too quick to cut separate deals with the government to protect the status of the Islamist movement more generally (especially in the educational and charitable arenas). While there was a rough consensus among the diverse opposition groups on the requirements of political reform (an enhanced role for parliament, greater fiscal transparency, genuine political accountability, electoral reform, and diminished dominance of the ruling family over the government), Hadas's potential partners often charge the movement with insufficient enthusiasm for the cause. In the 1990s, there may have been some justice to this charge, because Hadas was quite willing to concentrate on elements of its agenda that set it against other opposition groups (especially in the cultural realm), but in the past decade its dedication to the cause of political reform seems to have run quite deep.

Second, Hadas found itself suspect on almost the precise opposite grounds—not that it was lukewarm in opposition but that it was masking deeply radical sentiments. Part of this fear came from events and movements elsewhere in the region; while Kuwaiti Islamists have completely eschewed violence, it is not uncommon for critics to charge in private that Hadas differs from more radical groups only in its ability to put forward a gentler image. As long as political violence is common in the region, there is probably little that Hadas can do to dispel such doubts, which are based on nothing that Hadas has said or done but instead on the enthusiasm with which some radical Islamist groups elsewhere have embraced violent means.

Thus it should be no surprise that the parliamentary coalition pressing successfully for electoral reform in 2006 utterly failed to build on its success. As described more fully in Chapter 5, the "bloc of blocs" managed to negotiate a reform program but dissolved in mutual suspicion after only a few months. In subsequent parliamentary debates, Hadas deputies found themselves sometimes able to coordinate with some of the chamber's other Islamists (they managed, for instance, to form a small "Change and Reform" bloc) and could occasionally participate in broader reform coalitions on specific issues. But overall, the ability of the ruling family to divide the opposition proved more powerful than Hadas's efforts to find strategic partners for reform.

By 2007, with Hadas's coalition-building strategy in shambles, the party reacted by gyrating between joining the government and stridently opposing it. The results sparked ridicule by the movement's adversaries and even confused some members as well as neutral observers. (In a 2007 meeting with some party leaders, I asked about their oppositional stance, and my questions were parried with an insistence that under some conditions they would support the government. What I did not know—but they clearly did—was that one of my interlocutors in that meeting would be appointed a minister the next day.) And when Hadas turned to opposition, it no longer sought a broad, cross-ideological coalition but instead went back to the path of the early 1990s by forging links with other conservative and Islamist deputies.

Semiauthoritarianism does not make opposition alliances impossible. But it leaves the government so many tools to divide, rule, co-opt, and repress that it would be a bold Islamist leadership indeed that decided to shift to a wholly political strategy, postponing much of its Islamic agenda for the sake of opposition unity, and face down a determined regime. And even if it cast its lot with such a choice, the well-founded suspicions among all opposition actors engrained from years of succumbing to divide-and-rule tactics would make an alliance difficult to sustain.

Using the Parliamentary Bloc

In March 2006, I was in Ramallah at the time of the first parliamentary session after Hamas's stunning electoral triumph. I had arranged to interview a few of the new parliamentarians as well as the incoming deputy prime minister. Most Hamas deputies were staying in the same Ramallah hotel, so my interviews were spread out over an evening in the hotel lobby. As I sat on a sofa with a series of deputies, I noticed that every hour on the hour, a crowd of bearded men crowded around the television to watch the news on Al-Jazira. They were, of course, newly elected parliamentarians interested in watching themselves: their initial session was the first story on every news broadcast. But while they took tremendous pride in their organization's accomplishment, they were clearly unprepared for it. I began one of my interviews with a parliamentarian who had been designated a press spokesman with what I thought was a soft question: "What are the first pieces of legislation you would like to work on?" The answer was an awkward and quite prolonged silence. Hamas had won the first parliamentary elections it had contested and the eyes of the world were on it, but the movement had no firm idea of what it wanted to do.

The problem of managing the parliamentary bloc was acute for Hamas since it had both a strong majority and an almost total lack of political experience. But even comparatively wizened movements that do not enjoy a majority find that gaining seats in parliament faces them with difficult organizational choices: Who determines the parliamentary agenda and how? What issues should be emphasized and why—should the movement work to secure policy and legislative changes, articulate an alternative vision of a just social order, emphasize its opposition credentials, show its fidelity to religion, or advocate broader political reforms? Should priorities and decisions be made by the parliamentary bloc, the party, or the broader movement? On occasion, a parliamentary vote might force a basic choice on a difficult issue; a movement's penchant for platitudinous statements on divisive issues will be of no use when an up-or-down vote is taken. Such a choice famously faced the German Social Democratic Party in supporting war credits at the outbreak of World War I.

In this section, we will focus on the Egyptian movement and will discover how semiauthoritarianism offers opportunities for developing a broad agenda but almost no chance of implementing it. The result is a diverse agenda but also an ability to avoid the difficult choice that faced the German socialists.

The creation of a Egyptian Brotherhood parliamentary bloc has raised some issues of coordination and priorities, but these have been less acute for the Brotherhood than might be expected, for two reasons. First, unlike some other Islamist movements (such as the Islamic Action Front and Hamas), all MPs associated with the Egyptian Brotherhood are full members of the organization. While the Brotherhood has sometimes offered support to candidates it finds ideologically close, only movement members are affiliated with the parliamentary bloc. They are therefore fully subject to movement discipline. (Formation of a political party, begun after the January 2011 revolution, has already opened the possibility of attracting nonmembers to the party's electoral banner.) Second, not only are MPs drawn from the ranks of the Brotherhood membership, but most top movement leaders (even some of those regarded as *tanzimis*) have served a term in parliament. Service in parliament raises a member's public profile and boosts his prominence within the movement (though nonpolitical routes to prominence are still probably more consequential). Thus movement leaders are themselves familiar with and accustomed to dealing with parliamentary politics.

The 2005 elections—and the formation of a bloc of eighty-eight Brotherhood MPs—created new issues for the movement. In particular, two challenges emerged. First, the movement was not initially well positioned to support the work of so many parliamentarians. Its Cairo headquarters was set up to support the Guidance Bureau, not a large bloc of parliamentary deputies. And the parliamentary apparatus itself, with its professional staff and research services, was still firmly in the command of pro-regime figures. Yet the Brotherhood deputies were determined to demonstrate their ability to produce expert questions, offer proposals, and even draft laws on all matters of importance in Egyptian political life (and indeed, they succeeded). The Brotherhood leadership therefore moved to offer the parliamentary bloc whatever support it needed; at first, just like the Hamas parliamentarians, the Egyptian deputies all stayed in the same hotel while parliament was meeting, holding seminars and training sessions as well as discussing positions and strategy.[16] Later the group moved to a more permanent structure that allowed the MPs to continue their coordination. Brotherhood deputies quickly established themselves as the most active within the body.

Second, the new group of MPs could have emerged as a distinct bloc within the movement, expert in political participation and oriented toward maximizing its parliamentary effectiveness and electoral fortunes. As one leading Brotherhood MP stated to me in 2006, "We have to remember it is not the Muslim Brotherhood that led to our success. It is the people." Candidates were generally selected by local Brotherhood branches for their reputation for public-spiritedness and probity, which ensured a particularly effective set of candidates but also figures with strong local reputations. And the movement as a whole allowed the bloc considerable autonomy in deciding how to act in parliament.

While the movement therefore handled the first challenge—providing support to parliamentarians—fairly successfully, the second challenge remained partly latent. Semiauthoritarianism prevented leaders from facing the full burden of developing a wholly political face for the movement. The parliamentary deputies simply did not have the opportunity to present a coherent political strategy that relied primarily on elections and parliament. Hopes were high in 2005 that they would be able to use parliament to articulate a full and persuasive vision of a reformed Egypt. The deputies actually showed considerable early success in that mission: they were able to sketch out a full agenda that moved far beyond the cultural and religious issues that had drawn the passion of past parliamentarians.[17] To be fair to their predecessors, the contrast with past blocs was relative rather than absolute; Brotherhood deputies in previous parliaments had been able to raise a host of issues related to economics and political reform, and the 2005 deputies hardly dropped cultural and religious issues. But armed with more deputies and greater expertise, discipline, and determination to show the viability and breadth of the Brotherhood's vision, the 2005 bloc was far more extensive

---

16. Shehata and Stacher, "Brotherhood Goes to Parliament."
17. See Amr Hamzawy and Nathan J. Brown, "The Egyptian Muslim Brotherhood: Islamist Participation in a Closing Political Environment," Carnegie Middle East Center Paper 19, Carnegie Endowment for International Peace, March 2010.

in its range of interests and activities than any of its predecessors. Corruption, press freedom, health care, constitutional reform, judicial independence—on all these issues, Brotherhood parliamentarians peppered ministers with questions, pushed the speaker to place debates on the agenda, and pursued draft laws in committee and plenary sessions.

But if the ambition of articulating a vision was partially met, Brotherhood deputies were forced to confront the difficult reality that they could do virtually nothing to implement that vision. Convinced in 2005 that they bore the weight of popular hopes and needs, Brotherhood deputies spoke as if they had a tremendous public duty to meet the society's expectations. And they could not. "We have come down to earth," one prominent parliamentarian told me in the summer of 2009. The possibilities of parliamentary Islamism in semiauthoritarian Egypt had been pushed to the limits and found wanting.

Entering the Cabinet

Finally, a few movements have been faced with a difficult decision when invited to join a cabinet. In a 2005 public forum in Ramallah, I was present when Hasan Yusif, a prominent Hamas leader, was asked whether his movement would impose the *hijab* if it won control of the Palestinian Authority's Ministry of Education. He responded with a politician's waffle: "The Palestinian Authority has no authority, so the question is meaningless." His dodge showed that his movement as a whole had no answer to the question of whether it would enter the government or what it would do if it did—it had gone through enough internal squabbling over whether it should even run. In the semiauthoritarian systems prevailing in the Arab world, the offer of participation in the cabinet generally provides only a sliver of authority: a movement is offered a handful of ministries, giving it the opportunity to have only limited influence over specific policy areas while simultaneously implicating the party or movement in broader government policies that it would prefer to oppose.

While most movements have occasionally faced the question of accepting a cabinet position,[18] we will probe the problems posed in the Jordanian case, in which Islamists have entered the cabinet but in a junior capacity. The Jordanian experience suggests that Hasan Yusif's statement is exaggerated but still generally applicable: under semiauthoritarianism, Islamists can accept a position of

---

18. On the Egyptian case, see Barbara Zollner, *The Muslim Brotherhood: Hasan al-Hudaybi and Ideology* (Abington, U.K.: Routledge, 2008), pp. 27–28.

authority only if they also accept a mild dose of co-optation and a heavier one of impotence.

The Jordanian movement has been able to act fairly coherently in parliament, but it has been more hesitant regarding participation in the executive branch. Perhaps fortunately for the movement, it has only rarely been faced with the question. Its opportunities actually came more frequently when Jordan was more fully authoritarian and the Brotherhood less focused on politics. In 1957, it was invited into the cabinet (and according to some accounts, as mentioned in Chapter 5, even offered an opportunity to head it) but found the prospect too intimidating to contemplate: its leader at the time was said to have answered that the movement was prepared to support rulers but had no wish itself to rule. The movement did not object in principle to having its members serve as ministers, but it was divided in practice. As mentioned earlier, Ishaq al-Farhan's acceptance of a ministerial post in 1970 led to his suspension from the movement (though he later returned to play a prominent role in different capacities).

With the advent of semiauthoritarianism—and the movement's strong showing in the 1989 parliamentary elections—Jordanian Islamists again came face to face with the prospect of joining the cabinet. For a significant if strident wing of hawks, the answer was simple: "The Muslim Brotherhood and any regime that does not apply Islam should not be in the same trench."[19] For the majority of the movement, however, the question was tactical rather than ideological, but that only made the decision more difficult. The movement did not have the experience to develop a clear strategy for the question of participation and the cabinet. Although Brotherhood ministers served for a brief period, the movement concluded that it had not been fully prepared for the experience and that it risked being co-opted or having its opposition to policies (especially matters connected with the Arab-Israeli dispute and the peace negotiations then occurring under the Madrid framework) necessarily muted by the requirements of cabinet discipline.

Ever since the movement lost its cabinet positions, the question of participation in the cabinet has (mercifully, in the eyes of some members) been only theoretical. With the signing of the Jordanian-Israeli peace treaty, it has become increasingly unlikely that the IAF will be invited into the cabinet or that it would accept such an invitation. It should be noted, however, that the movement has not rejected the matter in principle and that some leaders suggest that the existence of the peace treaty would prevent them only from accepting portfolios that would require them to deal with Israeli officials.

---

19. This and similar comments are repeated in Muhammad 'Abd al-Qadir Abu Faris, *Safahat min al-tarikh al-siyasi li-l-ikhwan al-muslimin fi al-urdun* (Amman: Dar al-Qur'an, 2000).

A Farewell to Arms?

A few movements might face still one more difficult choice beyond these five: whether to disarm. Of the movements studied here, only Hamas has a full and influential armed wing at present, but the Egyptian Muslim Brotherhood had a "special apparatus" that included some paramilitary elements in the 1940s and 1950s, and the question has also arisen in less pressing form in Jordan and even Kuwait. In any discussions with Islamist leaders, the issue of violence and an armed wing provokes an aggressive defensiveness: outside the cases of Palestine and Iraq, the leaders vehemently disavow any endorsement of violent means, but they also sharply defend Hamas and the necessity of resisting occupation in Iraq and Palestine. Indeed, their position is so strongly stated that it can lead to a different, more embarrassed kind of defensiveness when the subject is raised of the Iraqi Islamic Party (regarded by Brotherhood movements as a kindred movement but also one that cooperated with the United States–led program of political reconstruction).

Several Muslim Brotherhood groups have actively dabbled in violence in the past. The Egyptian Muslim Brotherhood's "special apparatus" still sparks political controversy in Egypt. Today's Brotherhood leaders alternate between disavowing the group's past activities and insisting that they were unauthorized or exaggerated. The reputational effects have been so severe that the Egyptian organization has been battling them for half a century. The Egyptian Brotherhood and some other Brotherhood organizations (including the Jordanian) also participated in military efforts against Israel, but those live on primarily in Brotherhood lore and have not been repeated for six decades (with the exception of a short-lived and limited attempt in Jordan to align with some Palestinian efforts in the late 1960s). The Syrian Muslim Brotherhood was embroiled in a violent conflict in the 1970s and 1980s with the regime there, but in the Brotherhood's account the primary combatants were some splinter groups and an unusually aggressive government. Finally, the Kuwaiti Muslim Brotherhood formed some groups to combat the Iraqi occupation, but those elements quickly converted to peaceful political activity when Kuwaiti sovereignty was restored.

The issues raised by a willingness to use violence or to form an armed wing are less ideological than they are reputational and organizational. The ideological issue is resolved for most movements: however much they root for Hamas, their strong preference in their own countries is to work peacefully within the system. But that ideological stance is buttressed by the high costs that the existence of an armed wing has posed for both reputation and organizational coherence. This lesson has been learned the hard way.

Reputation

The reputational costs can best be illustrated by the problems experienced by the Egyptian Muslim Brotherhood. Since its reemergence in the 1970s, the movement has repeatedly and emphatically rejected using violence in Egyptian politics to achieve its goals. Youthful Islamist activists of the 1970s and 1980s often split on the issue; those who agreed to reject violence gravitated toward the Brotherhood, and those who were less categorical gravitated toward more radical groups. The Brotherhood has been tested, to be sure: its supporters have been arrested and harassed, and the old regime showed little hesitation in using thuggery as well as more legally sanctioned force against Brotherhood activists. The Brotherhood has steadfastly refused to respond in kind.

So why does the issue of violence continue to pose a problem for the organization? The Brotherhood can control its current behavior but not its past: the legacy of its use of violence in the 1940s and 1950s continues to be raised in public discussions. The reputation for violence has not been forgotten by those opposed to (or even merely suspicious of) the Brotherhood. The existence of the "special apparatus" of the 1940s and 1950s was routinely invoked under Husni Mubarak to justify widespread arrests. In 2006, a martial-arts demonstration by Brotherhood members who were students at al-Azhar was trumpeted as a sign of the revival of a Brotherhood paramilitary group; some of the periodic round-ups of Brotherhood leaders were accompanied by vague but dark charges of the creation of a secret section (or a "Qutbist" wing) of the Brotherhood. Abroad, the history of the special apparatus probably matters less to the movement than the Brotherhood's current support of Hamas in Palestinian politics; Hamas's embrace of violent "resistance" is unambiguous and unembarrassed. While the Egyptian Brotherhood lends material and moral support to Hamas, it insists that the circumstances faced by the movement's Palestinian comrades is so different that there is no contradiction between that support and the Egyptian movement's peacefulness at home.

There was a vicious cycle provoked by the Brotherhood's violent clash with the regime half a century ago. Egypt's semiauthoritarian rulers regularly cited that history to justify their periodic harsh campaigns against the present-day organization. This aggravated an existing Brotherhood tendency toward secrecy in internal operations (for instance, the movement kept its internal regulations confidential until recently; the results of the 2010 internal elections for the movement's consultative council were similarly not released). Brotherhood leaders explained that naming names only exposed those people to arrest; even announcing an internal election has sparked a wave of repression. In short, the more open the organization becomes, the more the Egyptian regime rediscovers its fully authoritarian roots, driving the movement back into secrecy. But the secrecy that resulted sparked continued suspicion by outsiders that the Brotherhood is maintaining something like the older "special apparatus"—thus justifying the repression.

Organization

There is another internal legacy from the Brotherhood's experience with the "special apparatus," one that has been more significant internally. An armed wing is almost necessarily underground, and it therefore forces a broad movement to attempt to unify a far-flung public movement with a small, secretive, tight-knit armed wing.

When the Egyptian movement tried to blend the public and the secret wings, the effect was to undermine organizational coherence (the first half of the 1950s saw contests between members of the "special apparatus" and those who sought to disband it). And it took half a century to overcome the problem. The veterans of that organization within the organization continued to play a strong leadership role in the Brotherhood and sometimes were viewed as constituting a clique within the tight circle dominating the movement. They tended to either avoid or downplay the violence employed by the special apparatus.[20] Such avoidance hardly assuaged skeptics. The salience of the issue is now declining only because of the passage of time: the movement's general guide from 2004 to 2010, Mahdi 'Akif, a member of the special apparatus in his teens, may have been the last group leader to have brought that background to his post.

For Hamas, the organizational issues are particularly acute. The organization, in contrast to the other Brotherhood movements, was born to resist. And while its leaders will sometimes speak of resistance in very general terms—considering its political and social activities at times as a form of resistance—Hamas has left no doubt that armed action against Israel is central to its conception of resistance. The movement can engage in ideological circumlocutions when attempting to justify its targeting of Israeli civilians (arguing, for instance, that civilians are potential soldiers or that Hamas targets civilians only in response to the Israeli targeting of Palestinian civilians), but it shows no such bashfulness about its military activity more generally. Indeed, it is the prolonged periods of inactivity that seem to cause more discomfort as its leaders insist that they are still a resistance organization despite their momentary quiescence.

---

20. See, for instance, Muhammad Mahdi 'Akif's comments on the subject in an interview: "Mahdi 'Akif: I Requested a Dialogue with Mubarak a Thousand Times ... and Let him Try Once," *Al-shuruq,* 13 February 2009.

Hamas's resistance activities have the full support of its counterpart organizations. Islamist movements in other Arab countries explain that while they disavow violence for their own part—as one Muslim Brotherhood leader in Kuwait told me, "changing with the hand is not our way [*kharij min adabiyyatna*]"—they heartily endorse what they regard as resistance to foreign occupation.

Including resistance in its activities and making it central to its identity has profound organizational effects for Hamas. First, the organization early on constructed a compartmentalized cell-based military wing in order to prevent key arrests from disrupting the organization as a whole. That step ensured that military commanders had some autonomy from the rest of the organization, aggravating problems of coordination and enabling some Hamas leaders to commit the organization by using this autonomy in an ambitious manner. The 2007 seizure of power in Gaza, for instance, undertaken by the military wing, appears to have been more brutal and extensive than some within the movement expected. Second, retention of resistance means that a portion of the organization is underground, an anomalous characteristic for a political party in an open political system. The movement is less transparent in its leadership and decision-making structures—and even in its membership—in part because of its partially secretive nature. Finally, its retention of an armed wing ensures that the movement has difficult relations with whatever political authority controls the territory where it operates. This was true of the PA before Hamas won the parliamentary elections, but it was even true of the PA under the Hamas-led government: this situation made it difficult to determine who was speaking for the movement and may have forced the political authorities to follow the policies set by the armed wing rather than the other way around.

Organizational Effects of Participation

How have the opportunities presented for political participation affected the organization of Islamist movements in the Arab world? A broad movement facing the sets of choices explored in this chapter will often seek to postpone decisions that commit the organization fully to a path of partisanship, participation, and politicization. It will seek to grasp opportunities that carry less permanent implications. Organizational costs for participation that move beyond dabbling can be high. With semiauthoritarian regimes constantly rewriting the rules of political participation, a deep and irreversible commitment (in the form of an ideologically critical parliamentary vote or the formation of an autonomous party) is often best avoided. Commitments to participation are therefore likely to be slow and uncertain even when they do come. And regimes might prefer such tentativeness. A movement that is fully committed to participation not only signals that it is focused on gaining political power; it may also be more difficult to pressure.

Thus, judging by the experiences of Egypt, Jordan, Kuwait, and Palestine, we should take note of two consistent themes. First, movements generally respond by reconfiguring their organizations to take advantage of whatever opening they find—but they tend to do so slowly and can show some internal strain. Second, they generally leave a line of retreat, working to protect their nonpolitical activities and ensuring that the movement's goals are not forgotten by the entrance into the political process.

Seizing Opportunities

Islamist movements grasp opportunities—sometimes with alacrity, sometimes with deliberation, and occasionally with diffidence. But grasp they do. This can be shown in each of the areas discussed in this chapter.

First, with regard to participation, all the movements here have responded to semiauthoritarian elections by running more candidates. On occasion a movement will boycott (as the Egyptian Muslim Brotherhood did in 1990 and 2010 and the Jordanian Islamic Action Front did in 1997 and 2010), but even when it does so, leaders insist that it is specific electoral grievances rather than an ideological opposition to elections that lead to such an extreme measure. Only Hamas rejected participation on broader grounds (its 1996 boycott of parliamentary elections was justified by the movement's rejection of the Oslo Accords), but that step provoked opposition within the movement and formation of a splinter party—and was reversed in time for the 2006 parliamentary elections. Movements also generally work to calibrate the scale of their participation to the degree of opportunity, but they argue internally (sometimes vociferously) about what the opportunities are.

Second, movements file for party status wherever they can do so and in accordance with whatever legal framework exists. Jordan allows parties, and the IAF was the first party formed under the more liberalized 1992 party law. Kuwait tolerates parties but accords them no legal personality, and Hadas therefore operates in a formal but unrecognized manner. Palestine permits electoral lists, and Hamas formed "Reform and Change" in order to participate in elections. Semiauthoritarian Egypt permitted parties in theory but restricted them in practice and barred religious parties. The country's Muslim Brotherhood therefore decided in theory that it would form a party but postponed practical implementation until the constitutional, legal, and political environments were more permissive (as they finally became in 2011).

Third, Islamist movements form alliances. They do so slowly and cautiously, but also with growing confidence. Before plunging so heavily into politics, the Islamist movements studied here generally shunned allies. Leaders remained convinced that this would only provoke the authorities; they were also often dismayed at the nonreligious orientation and behavior of non-Islamist groups and fearful of the strength of leftist or nationalist forces. On occasion (such as in Jordan in the 1950s through the 1970s and Kuwait in the 1960s and 1970s), this set of attitudes made Islamists in many countries seem more loyal than opposition. As they grew in size and experience, and as other opposition movements lost a good deal of their vitality and organized constituencies, and—most important— as the opportunities of semiauthoritarian politics beckoned, Islamist movements have become friendlier to cross-ideological alliances, though generally of a tactical nature. Currently, leftists and nationalists (and liberals now as well) are the ones who fear Islamist strength rather than the other way around. And in the process of enlarging their prominence in the opposition, Islamists have clearly solidified their position as firmly planted in the opposition camp.

Fourth, Islamist movements have allowed parliamentary blocs to develop some autonomy and to pursue a broad legislative agenda. Egyptian Brotherhood members proposed laws to make the judiciary more independent; Jordanian IAF MPs have complained about prices of basic commodities; Kuwait's Hadas has pursued issues related to the use of public funds; and Hamas used its brief period of enjoying a clear legislative majority to develop a broad agenda that ventured far from the "resistance" and religious themes that had propelled the movement since its inception.

Fifth, the movements discussed here have accepted the idea of participating in the government. For Egypt's Muslim Brotherhood, this long remained only a theoretical point, but it was one underscored by the movement's willingness to endorse a second presidential term for Husni Mubarak in 1987. Jordan has sent members into the cabinet, though not since the IAF was formed. In Kuwait, Hadas has accepted a cabinet position on occasion. And Hamas formed the government in 2006.

With regard to violence, all the movements studied here have agreed to disavow it in domestic politics. Egypt's Muslim Brotherhood formed its infamous "special apparatus" in its first incarnation but has consistently disavowed any intention of re-creating it. Jordan's Brotherhood flirted with support for Palestinian attacks on Israel in the aftermath of the 1967 war, but its role was negligible and the subject has been dropped. Kuwait's Brotherhood organized armed resistance to the short Iraqi occupation but disarmed immediately after the forced Iraqi withdrawal. And Hamas has insisted that it would turn its arms against Israel, not against fellow Palestinians—a position that was suspended quite emphatically in June 2007, when the movement seized control of Gaza; it also found itself involved in clashes with Fatah and other Palestinian factions earlier. But its attitude toward such internal violence remains both embarrassed and defensive; Hamas leaders insist that they resorted to violence extremely reluctantly and that they did so with restraint and only in self-defense. On some occasions, but not in all, such a claim is fair.

Investments but Not Commitments

If Islamist movements seize opportunities, they always look for an escape route as well. The benefits of political participation in a semiauthoritarian setting are real but retractable. And the movements' leaders insist that their project is the long-term comprehensive reform of the society, not the exercise of political authority tomorrow. As a result, the organizational changes discussed are rarely pursued without qualification or with permanent commitment to a purely political path. We come now to the hedges and qualifications to the decisions made in the various areas considered in this chapter. In each area, Islamist movements have left a route of retreat.

First, with regard to participation, the slogan of "participation, not domination" has become widely accepted among the movements as the wisest course. The only movement that broke the rule was Hamas, by pursuing a majority of parliamentary seats. That decision seems to have been made carelessly by Hamas leaders, was viewed as a mistake even by sympathetic Islamists elsewhere (I have heard leaders in Egypt and Jordan express the view directly that Hamas erred in seeking a victory), and is regarded as something of a disaster by many Islamist leaders in retrospect. To be sure, they hold Israel, Fatah, the United States, and Western powers more generally responsible for that mistake, but it is still one that they have learned from: in the fallout from the Hamas victory, other Islamist movements in the Arab world have insisted they have no wish to win an election anytime soon.

Second, while Islamists have formed parties everywhere they are allowed and in accordance with the extant legal framework, nowhere have they been given much autonomy. Egyptian Islamists moved to form a party only after the semiauthoritarian regime fell; the IAF's leash from the Muslim Brotherhood seems to have grown short indeed; Kuwait's Hadas has more autonomy but its electoral troubles in recent years have led to a resurgence of the role of its Muslim Brotherhood founders; and Hamas's electoral "Change and Reform" list never developed into even a proto-party. When asked, some Islamist leaders mention the Moroccan PJD as a positive model for the greater degree of independence it has established from the mother movement, but even the Moroccan experience is hardly an unalloyed example of electoral success and organizational independence.

In the case of cross-ideological alliances, the greater willingness to build bridges rarely progresses past cautious tactical steps. Where non-Islamist opposition forces are weak, Islamists feel they have less to gain and non-Islamist fears are greater. The experience of the movements studied here suggests that political involvement is closely connected with the rise of leaders who seek to forge connections and make appeals more general, but nowhere have the opportunities created by participation allowed them to dominate decision making within the movement. (The more general issue of ideological evolution and commitments will be considered in Chapter 7.) Nowhere have leaders come forward who have been able to build a sustained and strategic cross-ideological opposition coalition. The most sustained attempt to do so in Kuwait led to meager results.

Political involvement has led all the movements here to accord some autonomy to their bloc of parliamentary deputies, but the movements tend to retain control over major decisions (such as whether to support or withhold confidence from the parliament). Parliamentary deputies and blocs have been accorded the freedom necessary to develop full legislative agendas, sometimes quite extensively, but, as noted, these tend to supplement rather than replace the traditional religious and cultural focus. No bloc has attempted to impose positions on the movement; on rare occasions when there has been disagreement, the movement has retained its dominance. For instance, Hamas as a movement successfully curtailed initiatives by some of its deputies to introduce Islamizing legal reforms, convinced that such a step was politically premature at best.

When offered the opportunity to enter the government as a very junior partner, none of the movements here showed much enthusiasm for doing so. The Egyptian movement has not yet been faced with the option, the Jordanian has accepted the idea in principle but avoided it in practice, Kuwait's Hadas has accepted cabinet positions but sometimes regretted doing so, and Palestine's Hamas shows no sign of having seriously considered the possibility before it found itself sucked in by the logic of its 2006 victory (since the 2006 elections, however, Hamas has shown great tenacity in maintaining its grip on power, even while reiterating, however unpersuasively, that it did not seek rule as an end in itself). Hamas is an important exception, therefore—but its growing appetite for governing authority has, if anything, diminished the appetite of other movements.

Regarding an armed wing, all the movements considered here (again with the obvious and important exception of Hamas) dropped any dalliance with such an idea before plunging into politics. As a result, none really faced the question of whether to disarm before running for office. The experience of these movements suggests that even the bounded opportunities provided by semiauthoritarian politics are enough to persuade the movements to reiterate (sometimes constantly) their rejection of resort to force in domestic politics. But the example of Hamas suggests as well that participation within such boundaries may not be enough to persuade a movement to disarm. In other words, semiauthoritarian participation has not shown any ability to reverse a decision to build an armed wing, but once a movement has disarmed, robust participation may prevent backsliding.

Organizationally, Islamist movements react positively but guardedly to semiauthoritarian opportunities. How does participation in semiauthoritarian politics affect their ideological development? In the next chapter, we will find that ideology follows a pattern similar to that of organizational change.

IDEOLOGICAL CHANGE
Flirtation and Commitment

In 2005, Muhammad Mahdi 'Akif, then general guide of the Muslim Brotherhood in Egypt, was asked by a journalist what Egypt needed most. He responded with one word: "Freedom," and then repeated it for emphasis. "Freedom is a basic part of the Islamic order," 'Akif claimed. "If it is absent then the slogan Islam is the solution has no value; it becomes the problem not the solution."[1]

The choice of the word "freedom" seemed odd, not simply because Brotherhood critics hardly viewed the group as a liberating force, but even more because 'Akif was embracing the slogan at a time when an American president who was profoundly distrusted in the region was himself promoting a "Freedom Agenda" for the Middle East. The Egyptian "mother movement" was not alone in the Islamist camp in launching an effort to position itself as a force for political reform. During the first decade of the twenty-first century, Islamist activists throughout the Arab world were emphasizing such issues as free elections, freedom of the press, judicial independence, separation of powers, constitutional reform, and curbs on official corruption. The Islamic shari'a would sometimes be cited but often vaguely, and movements began to proclaim that they aimed at creating not a religious state but only a "civil state with a religious reference." Statements, platforms, and proposals for political reform came thick and fast from movements in those Arab countries that permitted elections.

---

1. "The General Guide of the Muslim Brotherhood Affirms to Al-Dustur: Now ... Freedom Is the Solution," *al-Dustur*, 15 June 2005, p. 8.

In Jordan, the Islamic Action Front and Muslim Brotherhood developed political reform proposals that culminated in 2009 with a call for a constitutional monarchy. Kuwait's Islamic Constitutional Movement attempted to form a reform coalition, and its leaders spoke quietly of a constitutional monarchy as well. Even Hamas, the "Movement of Islamic Resistance," fielded its candidates in 2006 parliamentary elections under the banner of "Change and Reform" and modified the Muslim Brotherhood electoral slogan from "Islam is the solution" (*al-islam huwa al-hall*) to "Reform is the solution" (*al-islah huwa al-hall*).

The formula was a winning one, to an extent. It garnered the Islamists more votes, at least for a while. The common cause of political reform made possible some limited coalitions with other opposition actors and piqued international interest. But strong electoral performances also prompted considerable fear and harsh countermeasures. And in only one place did it result in victory. In Palestine, Hamas won a large parliamentary majority—one that it realized was within reach only shortly before the balloting. The surprise was not wholly pleasant, either for Hamas or its Islamist sympathizers in neighboring countries, as we saw in previous chapters. Thus, in July 2009, a leader of the Muslim Brotherhood in Egypt explained that under conditions prevailing at that time, the upper limit for the movement was to compete for one-third of the seats (and many leaders wished to run a much smaller number of candidates): if the Brotherhood won more than one-third, it would be able to block some parliamentary action and that meant participating in governing.[2] The Brotherhood had high hopes to reform Egyptian society in many different ways, but governing was not part of its short-term plans.

If Islamists' primary goal was to win elections, the reform fad would be easy to explain. Movement leaders, sensing a series of opportunities throughout the region, might logically seek to rush to the head of the reform parade, assure skeptics that their intentions were limited, safe, and laudable, and in the process garner popular support from societies suffering from the accumulated problems caused by unaccountable regimes. But winning elections was generally not an option; it was certainly not a short-term priority. After Hamas's victory, several regional movements took pains to make clear that they did not expect to win majorities; they even made it impossible to do so by running candidates in a minority of races.

The combination of actions in the first decade of the 2000s—running many candidates but rarely enough to win, developing popular electoral programs but insisting that politics was only a part of the group's mission—was a little puz-

---

2. Muhammad Mursi, personal interview, Cairo, July 2009; Sa'd al-Katatni, personal interview, Cairo, March 2010.

zling. But the history of political activity by Islamist movements has shown many twists and turns, in the words used, the ideas stressed, and the programs pursued. How do we understand the ideological changes and programmatic evolution of the movements? How does running affect their rhetoric and positions?

Ideology, as mentioned in Chapter 3, can be sticky. Shifts have costs: they generate suspicion among rivals and supporters alike as a sign of insincerity or opportunism. Indeed, Islamist leaders insist that they and their movements are consistent and never waver in their fixed principles. When I began to ask Muhammad Mursi, a senior leader of Egypt's Muslim Brotherhood, about changes in the movement's rhetoric over the last generation, he interrupted me to dismiss the question impatiently: "Change? What change? The word 'change' is not in our vocabulary."[3]

Islamist movements with broad agendas have no difficulty entering politics, but they begin to confront vexing questions when they go beyond dabbling. How do they respond? More specifically, how (and how much) does their ideology change under the pressures of political participation? Entering elections and formal politics confronts Islamists with demands from various sources. Most of our frameworks for understanding the electoral agenda, ideology, and programs of political parties in democratic systems are based on the assumption that their goal is some combination of winning seats, holding office, and shaping public policy. But what if winning is neither an option nor an immediate priority? How do movements with broad agendas, ones that neither seek nor expect to govern (at least in the short term) decide to pitch their programs? What if they are broad movements with other goals, some of them far from politics? What rewards do they look for and how do they respond to them?

In the previous chapter, we considered the organizational effects of political participation in semiauthoritarian conditions. We saw movements that were generally willing to make significant investments in politics but balked at any steps that required ongoing commitments to such activity. What are the ideological effects of participation in a semiauthoritarian setting—especially for a broad movement that, as we saw in the last chapter, is loath to jettison its wide-ranging agenda in favor of a primarily political strategy?

In answering these questions, our primary source of information will be the ideological statements of the movements themselves: the writings of leaders, the statements they make in interviews, and, above all, the formal positions and platforms the movements issue. These documents often spark some skepticism since they amount to mere words. Not only is talk often dismissed as cheap, but the

---

3. Muhammad Mursi, personal interview, Cairo, July 2009.

statements of Islamist movements can be vague and confusing. Many platforms read as if they were written by committees, and they usually were. But these are no reasons to dismiss them. For ideological movements, words and ideas matter. Vagueness is in itself an important indicator of a movement's political orientation, as we will see.

Indeed, platforms are probably best viewed as the location where leaders of a movement are forced to address different audiences at the same time. They must communicate core beliefs to followers and reassurances to skeptics; platforms are attempts to placate or threaten rulers while motivating followers. And they are occasions for movement members to speak to each other and resolve the content of their collective position, their immediate priorities, the range of acceptable opinions, and their common talking points in public debates.

In this chapter, we will approach the question of ideological change in three steps. First, we will examine the general ideological approach of Islamist movements, emphasizing those issues on which they are most often pressured to change. Those areas include rights and freedoms, Islam, the nature and extent of opposition, and democracy.

Second, we will examine those pressures—who asks them for what sorts of ideological commitments. Islamist movements are pulled sharply, and sometimes in different directions, by followers, the broader public, other opposition actors, and regimes. We will work to understand the nature of these pressures in general and consider the issue of women's political rights in Kuwait as an illustration of how these pressures operate.

Finally, we will examine how Islamist movements actually respond in a semiauthoritarian setting. What changes are they likely to make and how deeply and specifically are they likely to commit to ideological changes when operating in a semiauthoritarian environment? For each of the four issues mentioned, we will examine how a particular Islamist organization responded, selecting a movement that was subjected to particularly strong or sustained pressure. Strong pressure will reveal the maximum likely effect of semiauthoritarian politics on movement ideology; sustained pressure will allow us to probe the effect over time. We will focus on how the Egyptian Muslim Brotherhood has responded to pressure on rights; how the Jordanian movement has responded to pressure on Islam; how Kuwaiti Islamists have responded to pressure on the nature and extent of their political opposition; and how Hamas has handled pressure on democracy.

Overall we will find a pattern similar to what we found with organizational change: Islamist movements evolve ideologically in order to respond to political pressures, but their ideology is not infinitely plastic. They keep most of their commitments to such positions fairly general, preserving lines of ideological, rhetorical, and even programmatic retreat.

The Range of Islamist Political Vision

As we explored in Chapters 4 and 5, Islamist movements have positioned them-selves in a number of different ways. The general nature of their ideology leads to programmatic plasticity and allows leaders some flexibility, but not an in-finite amount. The overall project of the movements remains fixed: reform of the individual and the society along Islamic lines. But such reform can take many different forms. Some political positions are obvious: a general emphasis on reform and a strong opposition to corruption are easy political positions to take because they generate little opposition, especially if they are not given de-tailed content.

As they increase their political involvement, however, the movements come under pressure to define the nature of their priorities and programs in more specific terms. Before we consider how they respond to that pressure, we will examine four issues that have become particularly prominent. Our goal in this section is simply to understand the range of views within Islamist movements. How far can the ideological vision of the movements stretch?

Freedoms and Rights

Islamist movements have wrestled with their support for—or reservations about—the full panoply of freedoms and rights, a contentious topic in Arab politics. As a general rule, political rights, especially freedom of political speech and expression, have loomed large in Islamist platforms. As a result of their own experiences with official harassment, arrests, and restrictions on liberties, Is-lamist leaders have steadily come to embrace the idea that political rights must be respected and that existing Arab regimes fall far short of their obligations in this regard.

Economic rights have also sometimes figured in Islamist political discourse. While generally suspicious of Arab socialism and respectful of individual prop-erty rights, Islamist movements have still shown a strong inclination toward both populism and nationalism in economic policy; they have also been sympathetic to the idea that states have an affirmative duty to provide for the minimal basic needs of their citizens.[4]

Nevertheless, Islamists' endorsements of freedoms and rights are hardly ab-solute; their leaders may yearn for some liberties, but they are not fully liberal.

---

4. On Islamist economic thought, see Bjorn Olav Utvik, *Islamist Economics in Egypt: The Pious Road to Development* (Boulder, Colo.: Lynne Rienner, 2006).

In particular, there are four significant limitations to their embrace of liberal freedoms. First, while they support a strong measure of political liberty, their tolerance for individual rights drops sharply in the social realm (where they are far more likely to stress the rights of the society and of a divinely sanctioned order than an individual right to act in accordance with personal values and convictions). Second, protection for artistic freedom has been a problematic issue for some Islamists, especially when it extends to material that might seem blasphemous. Third, religious freedom is often circumscribed. While Islamist movements accept that non-Muslim communities have a separate set of rites and practices, the Islamic nature of the entire society places religious freedom within certain bounds (such as restricting senior state positions to Muslims, not recognizing conversions out of Islam, and insisting that individuals may choose a recognized faith but not that each individual is free to devise whatever set of practices he or she may wish). In all these areas, Islamist leaders assert that they are not violating individual freedoms but merely ensuring that those freedoms are exercised in a manner that does not provoke social chaos, promote immoral values, or lead to the denigration of religion. Fourth and finally, Islamist movements insist on seeing calls for women's rights through a shari'a-based prism. Personal status law, for instance, is to be based on a set of reciprocal but not identical obligations between husband and wife; family law is not to be gender-neutral.[5] Similarly, standards of modesty in public appearance and conduct exist for both men and women, but they are not identical. And for many Islamists, older strictures reserving specific positions of authority for men (chiefly head of state and sometimes judge) should still inform current practice.

Yet for all these restrictions, a slow evolutionary change is evident in many Islamist movements: there is clearly a growing comfort in casting their demands in rights-based terms. Movements might have their religiously based reasons for adopting specific positions, but they have been learning to present these in a less exclusivist manner. As a political claim, for instance, women's head coverings can be presented as a religious obligation or as a matter of religious freedom (that those women who wish to cover should not be obstructed or limited by state authority). Islamist movements in the Arab world have shown signs of shifting their emphasis to the latter kind of claim as they come to feel it has broader resonance.

---

5. It must be noted that shari'a provisions are the starting point for all personal status law governing Muslims in the Arab world; Islamist movements are not asking for change here as much as insisting on fidelity to prevailing interpretations. They show some willingness to consider amendments in the personal status law but often balk at changes that they feel are based on flimsy interpretations of the Islamic legal heritage.

Islam

An Islamist movement that no longer favored some role for Islam in public life would no longer be an Islamist movement, and no such evolution has taken place in the Arab world.[6] When it enters the political realm, an Islamist movement will by definition draw on its understanding of Islamic principles in developing its platform; more ambitiously, it is likely to insist that the state support and reflect those principles. Given the rich tradition of Islamic jurisprudence and the centrality of the Islamic shari'a to many conceptions of Islamic politics,[7] Islamist movements have thus gravitated toward presenting their political program as an implementation of—or at least drawn heavily from—the shari'a.

But what does an emphasis on the Islamic shari'a mean in practical political terms? In earlier decades, Islamist leaders tended to concentrate on general symbolic issues (such as favoring constitutional provisions declaring Islam the official religion or requiring the head of state to be a Muslim) and on bringing shari'a-based rules into legal force in a few highly visible areas (such as banning the sale of alcohol in Kuwait). These efforts attracted such attention that they often obscured an underlying accommodationism: the existing political order (sometimes monarchical, sometimes republican, and always with the bulk of law in force derived from non-Muslim sources) was rarely contested. Hasan al-Banna himself accepted the Egyptian constitution as consistent with shari'a, rejecting only specific laws.[8] Even when Islamist movements began to push for somewhat stronger constitutional language (declaring the principles of the Islamic shari'a

---

6. By way of analogy, such a movement might be seen in the path followed by the Christian Democratic parties of western Europe. In 2009, Germany's Christian Democratic Party presented an election platform that contained only the briefest mention of the Christian nature of its vision as well as passing references to the importance of churches (http://www.kas.de/upload/themen/programmatik_der_cdu/programme/2009_regierungsprogramm.pdf). Turkey's AKP might be seen to have followed a similar path, though it would probably be more accurate to describe it as a coalition that includes a significant Islamist element as well as one willing to work within (while recasting) an officially mandated laicism. Egypt's al-Wasat party presents itself in similar terms. Denied legal recognition in the Mubarak regime, the harsh legal environment reinforced the party's tendency to downplay the specifically Islamist character of its approach. By the time the party was accorded legal status in 2011, the tendency to stress the "civil" rather than the "religious" nature of its ideology had become deeply ingrained. (It was the al-Wasat party that pioneered the formula of being a "civil party with an Islamic reference" that the Brotherhood later adopted, though the phrase is capacious in meaning.

7. Scholarship on the role of the Islamic shari'a in contemporary Islamic political thought has grown quite large. I have tried to contribute to this body of work with "Shari'a and State in the Modern Muslim Middle East," *International Journal of Middle East Studies* 29, no. 3 (1997): 359–376; "Islamic Constitutionalism in Theory and in Practice," in *Democracy, the Rule of Law and Islam,* ed. Eugene Cotran and Adel Omar Sherif (The Hague: Kluwer Law International, 1999); and "Debating the Islamic Shari'a in the 21st Century: Consensus and Cacophony," in *Shari'a Politics: Islamic Law and Society in the Muslim World,* ed. Robert Hefner (Bloomington: Indiana University Press, 2011).

8. See *Majmu'at Rasa'il al-Imam al-Shahid Hasan al-Banna* (Beirut: Mu'assasat al-Risala, 1970), pp. 170–174 and 215–218.

to be "a" main source of legislation and later "the" main source), the practical implications of such a move were likely quite limited, especially if the enforcement of the provision was left to existing constitutional structures.[9]

In the 1950s, however, some leaders began to move in a more ambitious direction, provoked by four developments in Egypt. First, the deterioration of relations between the regime and the Muslim Brotherhood led to less accommodationist attitudes. Second, the achievement of full legal independence (marked in 1949 by the abolition of the Mixed Courts) and the development of comprehensive new legal codes opened wider possibilities and prompted widespread discussion of the proper relationship between the Islamic shari'a and the legal framework. Third, the Egyptian regime became increasingly intrusive in religious matters (folding separate personal status courts with shari'a-trained judges into the regular court system, for instance). Finally, the growth of the Muslim Brotherhood led to its inclusion of lawyers and even some prominent judges, who devoted considerable attention to the proper relationship between Islamic law and the Egyptian legal system.

Indeed, it was during the early 1950s that two polar positions began to crystallize, personified by two prominent judges who joined the Brotherhood. The first, 'Abd al-Qadir 'Awda, argued Muslims were obligated not simply to ignore but to combat those laws that contradicted the shari'a: "The Islamic shari'a is the basic constitution for Muslims, and all that agrees with this constitution is true and all that violates it is invalid, whatever the changes of time and the developments of opinion in legislation, because the shari'a came from God by way of his prophet, peace be upon him, to work by it in each place and time."[10] The second, Hasan al-Hudaybi, also insisted that the Egyptian legal order be brought into line with Islamic legal strictures, but he was comfortable with almost all the parliamentary and liberal provisions being considered for Egypt's constitutional order. He subscribed to a fairly expansive and permissive view of the Islamic law, stressing that implementation had to be gradual and interpretations appropriate for current conditions.[11] That broader approach—ultimately more influential in Brother-

---

9. This effort began in Syria but soon spread elsewhere. On Syria, see Radwan Ziyada, *Al-islam al-siyasi fi suriya* (Abu Dhabi: Emirate Center for Strategic Studies and Research, 2008).

10. 'Abd al-Qadir 'Awda, *Al-Islam wa-awda'na al-qanuniyya* (Beirut: Mu'assasat al-risala, 1985), p. 62.

11. Al-Hudaybi noted, for instance, that the early caliph 'Umar is said to have suspended the punishment for theft during a time of famine; similarly, if economic circumstances were hard, then the full panoply of criminal punishments should not be mechanically applied. This example has emerged as a standard way to affirm the criminal provisions of the shari'a while avoiding any implication that they should be immediately applied.

On al-Hudaybi's stand on legal and constitutional issues, see his *Dusturuna* (Cairo: Dar al-Ansar, 1978). I am grateful to Barbara Zollner for bringing this short book to my attention; she believes it was written in connection with debates about writing a new Egyptian constitution after 1952. Such

hood circles when it reemerged in the 1970s—insists that positive legal rules be consistent with the general goals of the Islamic shari'a and that they not violate those shari'a-based rules that are incontrovertibly authentic and clear.[12] This has allowed the eventual endorsement of the idea of a "civil state with an Islamic reference (*marja'iyya*)," a formula that has gained increasing currency among Islamist movements over the past decade.

'Awda and al-Hudaybi represent two poles of an internal debate, but there have been other influences on the ideology of Islamist movements on the question. In Jordan, for instance, the approach of Hizb al-Tahrir (also founded by a judge, this time one in the Palestinian and Jordanian shari'a courts who turned away from the Brotherhood's approach) has been followed by some factions of the Islamic Action Front (Hizb al-Tahrir's political program consists of the insistence that a proper ruler, generally a restored caliph, enforce shari'a, and it counsels only patience if such a ruler does not now exist). In many countries, salafi movements, with their strict textualism, have been influential; such movements tend to focus much more attention on appropriate law and practice and much less on politics and state structures. 'Awda's radicalism within the Egyptian Brotherhood gave way to a distinctive approach led by Sayyid Qutb; similarly unyielding on the requirement to follow Islamic teachings strictly, Qutb focused on the necessity of individual and small group ("vanguard") reform as first steps rather than immediate political change. Qutb's declaration of all existing societies as *jahili* (un-Islamic) has been too radical for most Brotherhood movements, but his emphasis on individuals and groups was very much in keeping with Brotherhood methods, and Qutb remains influential for that reason.[13]

The various positions within Islamist movements generally do not stand in logical contradiction to each other. All agree that an Islamic polity should be based on Islamic norms and operate in accordance with Islamic law. But that vague position—one that would attract widespread popular support in most Arab societies—can be applied in a number of different ways. Differences focus on two issues: what is to be applied and by whom?

---

timing would explain al-Hudaybi's fairly undemanding view of what allowances the constitution should make for Islam. In an interview from the same period, he articulated some principles (such as election of leaders and mandatory education) that should be included in the Egyptian constitution, thus implicitly endorsing the idea of a constitutional text even within an Islamic legal framework (*Ruz al-Yusuf*, 27 December 1952, p. 7).

12. This position is hardly restricted to the Muslim Brotherhood and indeed has become close to a consensus position. See my "Debating the Islamic Shari'a."

13. Brotherhood members seeking to reconcile their respect for Qutb with rejection of *takfir* (declaration that purported Muslims are apostates) insist that Qutb aimed his criticisms at the society as a whole and did not denounce particular individuals.

First, what is the content of Islamic law? Some activists, perhaps following partly in al-Hudaybi's footsteps, focus more on general principles (speaking often of *maqasid al-shari'a,* or the shari'a's goals, and the necessity of interpreting legal rules by relying in part on discerning *maslaha,* or the public interest) and on not violating very clear Islamic legal precepts. They often insist that the shari'a is to be applied in a way that is not burdensome on individuals and the community and cite the principle of centrism (*wasatiyya*) in support of their general approach. Others are far more demanding and far more textual in their approaches. Why, for instance, seek a centrist path between good and evil (as I once heard a salafi put it)? Why let political considerations or social convenience influence the determination of God's will and instructions?

Second, whose voice is authoritative? What is the relative role of the general population of Muslims, legal scholars, the official religious establishment, and constitutional structures and procedures (such as parliaments and courts)?

That such questions have grown more acute and difficult for the movements is in large part a result of their escalating political involvement. A general social movement does not necessarily need to spell out all its positions, but a would-be political party with legislative and governing ambitions is often expected (and motivated) to spell out what laws it wishes to enact.

How Much Loyalty, How Much Opposition?

Movements in Egypt, Jordan, and Kuwait have, at times, been regarded by other opposition forces as too close to the regime; at other times, the same movements have posed as the most strident critics of the regime. Some have even crossed the line from serving as loyal opposition to constructing armed wings. The issue of loyalty and opposition is not merely one of tactical positioning. It carries serious ideological dimensions: how much does an Islamist movement present itself as a supporter of the existing order and how much does it claim to offer a comprehensive alternative vision?

Islamist movements emerging from the Muslim Brotherhood show a fairly similar pattern in Arab states. The original movement and its offshoots in the countries under consideration here began as largely social, educational, and charitable movements that sought to cultivate friendly relations with rulers. After a period of such activity, the growth of these organizations led to some initial political involvement. But that political involvement was limited and aimed primarily at fostering a greater role for Islam in public life and political debates. While the movements certainly struck an Islamic pose in such participation and could be very critical of specific policies or practices, they were generally not sharply oppositional in nature.

In some countries where Islamist organizations retained some freedom (such as Kuwait and Jordan), a rivalry developed with other political forces that were less religious in nature and often on the left. In such cases, this exposed the movement to the charge (sometimes accurate) that Islamists had a favored relationship with the government. (Even in the Palestinian case, an analogous criticism was that Islamists were long granted favorable treatment by Israel, which sought to undermine the Palestinian national movement.) But the relationship, guarded and even testy rather than cozy, decayed everywhere it existed, and the Islamist movements shifted more clearly into opposition.

In those Arab states less permissive of autonomous social organizations, there was generally no room for Islamist movements, and they were often harshly repressed (as happened in Egypt in the 1950s and 1960s and in Iraq and Syria under Ba'th rule beginning in the 1960s). In the Syrian and Egyptian cases, the clash between authoritarian government and Islamist opposition led some within the movement to engage in political violence. Often the most determined participants in armed confrontation, however, were not members but instead those who left or disavowed the umbrella of the larger movement, convinced that it was excessively cautious and conservative in its approach. The shift from authoritarianism to semiauthoritarianism in some Arab states has led to a greater official toleration for Islamist movements, though only within vaguely specified and constantly shifting "red lines." In such societies, Islamists generally strike a sharply oppositional pose, but they also attempt to calibrate their participation to prevailing political realities and emphasize their peaceful nature and willingness to work within existing legal channels.

Democracy

The range of debate among Islamist leaders on democracy is actually far less than many observers might expect.[14] The Islamist movements considered here have rarely rejected democracy on ideological grounds and have often strongly endorsed it. In their earliest incarnations, the political programs of Brotherhood-inspired movements focused on opposition to imperialism and support for the Palestinian cause; they devoted less attention to matters of internal governance but were willing to participate in parliamentary elections. At present, most movements have become extremely strong advocates for political reform; in the past

---

14. One interesting general work on the subject is 'Amr al-Shubaki, ed., *Islamiyyun wa-dimuqratiyyun* (Cairo: Al-Ahram Center for Political and Strategic Studies, 2004).

two decades, calls for democratization have become a standard part and sometimes even a centerpiece of their programs.

But Islamist movements have not merely varied in degree in their support of democracy. Three qualitative differences in their positions have emerged over time. First, some have displayed ambivalence about the word "democracy," not so much opposing its usage but preferring terms with greater Islamic connotations, most notably "consultation" (*shura*). Hesitation about using the word "democracy" has abated markedly among most movements in recent years, however. Second, Islamist movements have varied considerably in their attitude toward nondemocratic regimes; indeed, they have taken almost every conceivable position from accommodation to strident denunciation.

Third, while the term "democracy" has created ambivalence and hesitation at times, the idea of partisanship has presented a far greater obstacle. Indeed, Islamist movements have had a much easier time with democratic mechanisms than with political pluralism. Hasan al-Banna, the Muslim Brotherhood's founder, evinced distrust of partisanship out of a fear that it would divide the Islamic community, though he did not treat existing parties as illegitimate. Those Islamist movements that choose to form distinct political organs seem at times to avoid the term "party" (though they are hardly alone in this reluctance), preferring terms such as "front" or "movement." The distrust of partisanship is of course not an Islamist monopoly; it is just as deeply rooted in some strains of liberal and especially republican thought. But in the case of Islamists, hesitancy concerning political parties has a religious coloration stemming from a concern that the community of believers (and, by extension perhaps, the citizens of a nation-state) should not be divided and encouraged to place individual and group interests above that of the whole. Resistance to partisanship has abated among most Islamist groups in recent years, but it has not disappeared.

The Pressures of Openness: Navigating among Opportunities and Threats

The semiauthoritarian environment that emerged in the Arab world in the late twentieth century—with its uneven tolerance for organizing and debate and its firm antipathy to allowing fully competitive elections—placed a variety of ideological pressures on Islamist movements that want to pursue broad goals but also to seize any opportunity for political activity that is offered. In a fully authoritarian political environment, not all actors are relevant nor is much detail demanded of movements far removed from everyday struggles over politics and policy. But when such systems open, the range of actors interested in specific commitments from Islamists grows.

Seekers of Commitments

Four actors are most relevant in semiauthoritarian conditions. First, core followers, attracted to the movement for its espousal of clear religious and moral principles, will want to know that political involvement has not led the leaders to sell their souls. Islamist leaders can evince considerable flexibility in their interpretation of Islamic teachings and even Islamic law, but followers will demand that their positions on such issues do not shift quickly according to political expedience. They will want their leaders to articulate and defend a fairly conservative social vision and will look for firm guidance on issues of religious virtues in public life. An Islamist movement that forgets to mention God, the Qur'an, and the Islamic shari'a, or that appears to empty its understanding of Islam from any legal content, sounds entirely vacuous when it invokes religious themes. A movement that wishes to motivate its core followers or that feels no need or opportunity to reach out to new constituencies will likely feel compelled to pay close attention to this base.

Second, the broader public—those not hostile to appeals to Islamic values but also not involved with the movement—may not object to religious rhetoric and will often be attracted to a movement for its ability to convey a spirit of probity and piety. But such potential supporters will look for practical commitments to serving constituent needs, pursuit of public policies in such areas as health care and employment, and incorruptibility. Popular causes (and perhaps especially national ones) might also resonate with those who are potentially sympathetic but uninvolved. Such themes can often take on a religious coloration but they cannot be exclusively so lest the Islamist movement appear impractical. A movement seeking to perform impressively in the electoral arena, even if it did not aim to win, would logically feel drawn to casting its programmatic commitments in broader and more practical terms.

Third, other opposition movements (at least those that are not religious in nature), religious minorities, feminists, many intellectuals, and sometimes foreign government and nongovernmental actors will press for specific commitments on liberal rights and freedoms. They are likely to be satisfied by bromides for only a limited period before demanding answers to questions on issues ranging from the face veil to censorship. Few Islamist movements will siphon many votes from those in this camp. But reassuring such audiences still has a payoff: it is often the ticket to international respectability and the level of protection that this can bring. It also creates a better environment for building opposition coalitions. In recent years, Islamist movements have shown more interest and sophistication in approaching human rights organizations, foreign researchers, and even liberals within their own societies.

Finally, existing regimes will demand fewer ideological commitments and more practical ones: will the movement respect the vague and shifting red lines that it sets? And more critically, will it forswear victory? Steps toward ideological evolution that broaden Islamist electoral appeal can be far more threatening than narrowness and rigidity; many Islamist leaders feel that it is not coincidental that periodic crackdowns (particularly in Egypt) often target individuals who package Islamist messages in more liberal terms because such presentations have broader appeal.

For all these actors, but especially for regimes, democratic commitments are less at issue than is often assumed. The complaint that Islamists favor "one man, one vote, one time" is pithy but not generally reflective of most critics' concern. Such a formulation implies a fear that Islamists will bar a second competitive election, but most of these actors are much more focused on what Islamists might do with a victory in a first one. Rulers and some opposition actors worry that Islamists are actually too democratic (in the narrow sense of favoring majority rule). An Islamist commitment not to win is far more reassuring to those who currently hold power.

The areas of commitment listed here are not only varied; they are sometimes in tension. Core supporters might react positively to the sorts of red meat appeals that would alienate broader audiences and dismay liberals and foreign observers. Reassuring Islamist appeals to liberals might cause concern in ruling circles that the opposition may be trying to overcome the limitations that semi-authoritarianism imposes. Development of economic populism might provoke non-Islamist opposition leaders to fear that Islamists wish to rob them of their own constituency rather than form cross-ideological alliances. Not only are such pressures likely to push in different directions, but bowing too quickly to any of them will risk accusations of insincerity from skeptical observers and of obsequiousness from core supporters.

Over time, Islamist movements have learned how to develop general rhetorical commitments that communicate a religiously inspired vision to core supporters and a soothing message of tolerance and flexibility to those who are less persuaded by their central message. But increasing political involvement will lead to pressure for more specificity—and for Islamist movements and their opponents, the devil is (figuratively, but almost literally) in the details. These are treacherous waters for a movement to navigate, to be sure.

Hadas and Political Rights for Kuwaiti Women

The issue of women's political rights in Kuwait provides a striking illustration of the complexity of these calculations. Until 2006, women were barred from voting and running in parliamentary elections. In taking positions on removing either of these restrictions, Kuwaiti Islamist leaders found many eyes looking over their shoulders. In this section, we will probe how the movement attempted to avoid committing itself because of conflicting pressures but also how it crafted a cautious position when it finally had to make a decision.

In formulating its stance on women's political rights, Hadas sought to appeal to Islamists (concerned over a perceived threat to conservative social and religious values), a broader public (generally, if not overwhelmingly, in favor of female suffrage), and a potentially large electorate (Kuwaiti women, who, after they were actually granted the vote in 2006, made up a majority of voters). It also had to worry about rivals in the Islamist camp (who often outflanked Hadas in fealty to conservative interpretations of Islam) and liberal critics (for whom women's rights were a litmus test of the movement's willingness to accommodate itself to liberal values). And Hadas had to manage relations with a ruling family that had pledged its support for full political rights for women. Were the movement completely unprincipled, it still would have had enormous trouble developing a position. And on this issue, its principles were not actually the biggest problem. Many Hadas leaders saw nothing objectionable in (and some favored) political rights for women. (Hadas rank-and-file followers, by contrast, did not want their leaders to seem soft in defense of virtue.)

Hadas attempted to meet these pressures as though it were threading a needle. In 1999, the amir, likely reacting in part to international pressure, issued a decree allowing women to vote shortly before an election; in doing so, he cited a constitutional provision allowing him to issue decrees with the force of laws if parliament was not meeting, provided he submitted them to the parliament at its next session. Hadas was able to stand against the step by citing not the issue itself but instead the amir's abuse of a constitutional tool designed only for national emergencies. With Hadas support, the newly elected parliament overturned the decree.

That let the movement off the hook for only a few months as women's rights activists, sometimes acting with government support, continued to press parliament on the issue. Hadas held intensive internal discussions, allowing various points of view to be aired and consulting with various religious authorities. The movement finally argued that its opposition was more cultural than religious and that it could accept women's right to vote but was far more reluctant to endorse the right of women to run for parliament or serve as ministers or judges. This exposed the movement to ridicule for seeming to split hairs, hedge, and compromise on matters of principle. Such maneuvers could not be used indefinitely when actual draft laws were presented for parliamentary voting (though on one motion, Hadas deputies managed to abstain). In the end, when presented with a vote on full political rights for women, Hadas deputies felt compelled to oppose the measure, fearful perhaps of losing their core followers.

Party leaders were probably relieved, however, when they finally lost and women obtained political rights. The defeat removed a source of division and eased pressure on the movement (and allowed it to reap some credit when the speaker of a European parliament, apparently unaware of Hadas's stand, led the chamber in applause for a visiting delegation that included Hadas parliamentarians in recognition of the Kuwaiti parliament's action). And the outcome also allowed Hadas to pivot quickly to frame the issue of women's rights in its own terms. The movement soon developed its own women's rights legislation, which was based on a more paternalistic than liberal conception of those rights: it protected women from working in dangerous occupations or late at night and offered support for those who chose to forgo working outside the home for child rearing. This set of positions angered some liberals as a perversion of the very idea of women's rights, but it proved politically popular, attracted support inside and outside the party, and allowed Hadas to set its own agenda rather than appear simply to be an obstacle.[15]

In addition, the party quickly reacted to the new electoral environment by forming its own women's branches to ensure that it could campaign effectively among all members of the newly enlarged electorate. Indeed, it came up with an internal quota for women in leadership bodies that was almost Scandinavian in spirit. The party held off on nominating its own female candidates (though some leaders have privately expressed a wish to break that barrier), but it paid no political price among women voters for its opposition to the law granting them political rights.

The issue of political rights for women, therefore, illustrates how an Islamist movement like Hadas responds to contradictory pressures: the preferred path is to frame and define the issue in its own terms; failing that, it might follow strategies to parry and finesse. When confronted with the necessity to make a decision—for instance, because of an impending vote or because its more supple responses begin to become costly in terms of the movement's reputation—it will take a definitive stand, but only as a last resort. And in this particular case, having taken a stand, it then moved quickly to change the subject.

---

15. For more details on Hadas's proposals, see the pamphlet "Woman: Vision and Work Program" issued by the party in May 2008.

The question of women's rights in Kuwait is an especially helpful example of the complexity of pressures, but it was unusual in one respect: the issue was resolved. The areas of ideological change we are most concerned with are those that lend themselves more to management than to definitive resolution. Rights, Islam, opposition, and democracy are all areas that evolve over time.

In the remainder of this chapter, we will attempt to understand how Islamist movements change ideologically on these four issues under the pressures of semiauthoritarian politics. On the subject of rights and freedoms, we will probe the evolution of Egypt's Muslim Brotherhood; such issues have been central to debates within and over the Brotherhood over the past two decades. For changes in the ideological role for Islam, we will examine Jordan because the Brotherhood's relationship with the various actors (supporters, broader public, other opposition, and regime) has been framed partly in terms of the movement's positions on religious issues. Kuwait will prove the most fertile ground for understanding how semiauthoritarianism affects the balance between loyalty and opposition, mainly because the opportunities presented to the movement seem so large. Hamas will provide a fruitful example of the evolution of attitudes toward democracy because it is the only movement to have won an electoral majority.

Egypt: Rights and Routes of Retreat

From its birth, Egypt's Muslim Brotherhood has confronted the challenge of crafting its message in a way that appeals to (and draws on) a religious framework but simultaneously attracts, appeases, or soothes the various external audiences. Does greater political participation strengthen the impulse to push ideological commitments in a more flexible and general direction? Does interaction with non-Islamist political factors act (perhaps in a Rawlsian fashion) to encourage broad appeals to public reason rather than specific appeals to the religious beliefs of movement members? Does it encourage movements to go even further than general platitudes to specific ideological commitments to various rights and freedoms or to constitutional political processes? The Egyptian experience suggests that semiauthoritarian participation had such effects, but only halfway. It encouraged a move to less rigid generalities but discouraged specific commitments. This is a lesson that the Brotherhood learned the hard way—by trial and error. When it moved toward soothing and general but vague language, it managed to balance the various pressures. When it contemplated more specific and detailed commitments, it paid a price and beaten a quick retreat into platitudes.

The Quest to Pin Down the Brotherhood

The Brotherhood's position on rights and freedoms can be pushed in more liberal or less liberal directions. On the one hand, the religious discourse of the Egyptian Brotherhood can lead the movement into an exclusionary set of positions. And the Brotherhood in Egypt generally pursues a conception of state authority that bases it far more on the public interest than on the rights of individuals and groups within the society. Issues of morality—involving consumption of alcohol or sexuality, for instance—are not merely private concerns for Brotherhood members but legitimate areas for public policy to impose restrictions on individuals. Further, the historical legacy of Islamic jurisprudence on which the Brotherhood seeks to draw generally assumes (and often requires) rulers to be Muslim males; women have rights under the shari'a (and real legal protections in marriage and inheritance) but generally based on an assumption that they are a weaker party. Non-Muslims are also accorded protections, but their rights certainly fall short of full civic equality.

On the other hand, the Brotherhood can also retreat from such positions by suggesting general support for freedoms, citing general shari'a-based principles rather than specific rules, and insisting that the movement respects all liberal rights and freedoms not at direct variance with Islamic teachings. It can insist that even on those matters for which those teachings guide behavior in specific ways, this should be done by persuasion rather than coercion—an approach that respects the freedom of individuals to choose. And Brotherhood leaders have usually insisted as well that they accept Egypt's constitutional text, even if they sometimes propose modifications in it to increase its Islamic coloration.

Opponents of the Brotherhood in Egypt are thus more likely to scour Brotherhood statements for their positions on the difficult questions of women's rights, citizenship for non-Muslims, and cultural restrictions. They are less likely to be mollified by general statements on comparatively easier issues of political process and specifically political freedoms. And skeptics will look for specifics. In 1997, Mustafa Mashhur, then the movement's general guide, made a reference to Egyptian Christians as *ahl al-dhimma* required to pay the *jizya* (that is, they exchanged protection from the Muslim polity in return for payment of a special tax, thus enjoying something short of full citizenship), a statement quoted again and again by Brotherhood critics ever since.

Given such external pressure, it should not be surprising to find that the Brotherhood attempts to respond. In a thorough examination of the evolving position of the Egyptian Muslim Brotherhood toward democracy, Chris Harnisch and Quinn Mecham describe Brotherhood leaders as "turning to the Qur'an to support political preferences derived through recent political experience, rather than devising their political preferences textually."[16]

But if the semiauthoritarian context of the Sadat and Mubarak years provided some opportunities for a movement willing to shape its political preferences to prevailing conditions, the benefits were limited—and the ideological commitment they provoked were therefore likely to be more suggestive than definitive. Leaders were motivated in this regard not only by carrots but also by sticks. Mona El-Ghobashy writes of the evolution of the Muslim Brotherhood:

> Electoral authoritarian regimes such as Egypt's show that party adaptation is still possible and even considerable, but not due solely to damaging losses at the ballot box. Instead, parties in electoral authoritarian regimes adapt to fend off state repression and maintain their organizational existence. It is not Downsian vote seeking but, rather, Michels's self-preservation that is the objective of a party in an authoritarian regime, self-preservation defined broadly to include jockeying for influence and relevance with the public and influential international actors. If the Ikhwan have responded with such flexibility to the threats and opportunities of their authoritarian environment, one can speculate how much more they would acclimate themselves to the rigors of free and open electoral politics undistorted by repression.[17]

The speculation El-Ghobashy mentions is just that: gray-zone regimes tend to produce gray-zone movements willing to hint at ideological softening but only in a general way that stops short of a costly commitment. And when they move into more specific territory, they are often quickly beaten back into retreat.

In its increasingly bold forays into politics in the 1980s, 1990s, and first decade of the 2000s, the Egyptian Brotherhood produced a series of platforms and documents designed to spell out its vision. The movement took these documents extremely seriously: they provided an occasion for the movement to iron out its own positions and priorities; leaders also regarded them as something close to contractual documents with voters, not merely explaining Brotherhood positions but obligating those elected to follow them as pledges. Hardly at a loss for words, the Brotherhood had no trouble articulating its vision for a politically reformed Egypt in some detail—and in a form that increasingly mirrored that of other opposition groups. The salience of political reform increased in the

---

16. Chris Harnisch and Quinn Mecham, "Democratic Ideology in Islamist Opposition? The Muslim Brotherhood's 'Civil State,'" *Middle Eastern Studies* 45, no. 2 (2009), 195–196.

17. Mona El-Ghobashy, "The Metamorphosis of the Egyptian Muslim Brothers," *International Journal of Middle East Studies* 37, no. 3 (2005), 391.

Brotherhood's rhetoric, particularly in the early 2000s. But on issues of cultural expression, citizenship, and gender, the Brotherhood's positions moved more slowly (or, more accurately, retreated into ambiguities). On cultural freedoms, for instance, Brotherhood MPs would take up cudgels against books that were perceived as an offense to religion and public morals. But at the same time, they would deny pressing for state censorship, arguing that they wished not to ban a work but only to remove state support for such material. (In a country in which much cultural production is state-supported in some form, the distinction between censorship and removal of state support can become less sharp, however.)

And what of citizenship rights? Were all Egyptians to be accorded full equality? Or if they were to operate in a manner consistent with the shari'a, what were the shari'a-based requirements and limitations?[18]

In approaching these questions, Brotherhood leaders were forced to respond to the dictates of their own conscience and their interpretations of the Islamic heritage, but they were also caught by the need to respond to various internal and external constituencies. Their ideological development was facilitated by the role of prominent intellectuals sympathetic to the Brotherhood's project who developed a set of interpretations of the Islamic legal heritage friendlier to liberal values. Based on the belief that Islamic law is by its very nature flexible and designed to be adaptable to a wide variety of social and political circumstances, such intellectuals not only pressured the movement from the outside and provided a supportive climate for the movement's ideological development along more liberal lines; they also provided a ready set of arguments to be deployed in internal debates.[19]

Thus some within the Brotherhood—not coincidentally, those most committed to political activity—began to echo some of the arguments developed outside the Brotherhood. The movement began to copy the splinter Hizb al-Wasat (see

---

18. On some of the ambiguities in the Brotherhood's positions, see Khalil al-'Anani, *Al-ikhwan al-muslimun fi misr: shaykhukha tusari' al-zaman* (Cairo: Maktabat al-Shuruq al-Duwaliyya, 2007), chap. 5.

19. One good English-language treatment of the thought of such intellectuals is Raymond William Baker, *Islam without Fear: Egypt and the New Islamists* (Cambridge, Mass.: Harvard University Press, 2003). See also Bruce Rutherford, "What Do Egypt's Islamists Want? Moderate Islam and the Rise of Islamic Constitutionalism," *Middle East Journal* 60, no. 4(2006), 707–731. Carrie Rosefsky Wickham's forthcoming book on Egypt's Muslim Brotherhood will also be very helpful. Those interested in reading the works of the thinkers themselves should consult Yusuf al-Qaradwi, *Dirasa fi fiqh maqasid al-shari'a* (Cairo: Dar al-Shuruq, 2006); Tariq al-Bishri, *Al-wad' al-qanuni bayna al-shari'a al-islamiyya wa-l-qanun al-wad'i* (Cairo: Dar al-Shuruq, 1996); and Muhammad Salim al-'Awa, *Al-islam wa-l-'asr, hiwar: muhammad barakat* (Cairo: Maktabat al-Shuruq al-Duwaliyya, 2007). In this last book, for instance, al-'Awa makes an argument for citizenship and also for the modern state as an institution as being something that premodern Islamic fiqh (jurisprudence) did not encounter. In so doing, he justifies departing from long-received traditions in Islamic jurisprudence, viewing them as historically bound and not appropriate to current circumstances.

Chapter 5) and call for a "civil state with a religious reference." 'Abd al-Mun'im Abu al-Futuh, the leader most identified with the political tendency, began to argue that atheists should be accorded full freedoms (and merely denied state support); he also claimed that he had no objection to a Christian head of state.[20] Not all within the movement were willing to go this far, however.

The Platform: Paying the Price for Specificity

Peppered for years with demands for specific answers and driven by criticism that it spoke with too many voices, the Brotherhood finally began to attempt to answer questions regarding its positions and resolve internal debates by drafting a party platform. The contest in the Egyptian Muslim Brotherhood over a party platform is worth examining in some detail since it illustrates the struggle between generalities and specific commitments in a semiauthoritarian setting in a particularly accessible way. And it is in a sense an exception that proves the rule: the Brotherhood paid a price for its foray into specificity and therefore immediately retreated.[21]

The occasion for the platform was a response to a hypothetical question that the Brotherhood need not have answered: what positions would a Brotherhood-sponsored political party take? The benefits of issuing a detailed platform were not tangible, but they seemed clear enough at the time: a comprehensive document would demonstrate to the Egyptian public that the Brotherhood had a full program; assure critics in the political elite (and perhaps abroad) that the movement was comfortable in the world of democratic politics; and begin to resolve debates within the movement over pressing political questions. But pursuit of each of these benefits carried a risk: specific commitments might alienate some followers, feed ammunition to unfriendly critics, and split the movement—all for the sake of a political party that could not be formed under existing law. As drafts were developed and circulated, the risks materialized but none of the benefits did, prompting the leadership to shelve the project as inappropriate for Egypt's political environment.

---

20. See 'Abd al-Mun'im Abu al-Futuh, *Mujaddidun la mubaddidun* (Cairo: Tatwir li-l-nashr wa-tawzi', 2005).

21. I have analyzed the draft platform in more detail with Amr Hamzawy in "The Draft Party Platform of the Egyptian Muslim Brotherhood: Foray into Political Integration or Retreat into Old Positions?" Carnegie Paper 89, Carnegie Endowment for International Peace, January 2008. As I note there, the draft platform excited tremendous discussion in the Egyptian press. See also Marc Lynch, "The Brotherhood's Dilemma," Middle East Brief 25, Crown Center for Middle East Studies, Brandeis University, January 2008. Also see Kristen Stilt, "How Is Islam the Solution? Constitutional Visions of Contemporary Islamists," *Texas Journal of International Law* 46 (2010), 73–108.

In 2006 and early 2007, Brotherhood leaders solicited suggestions and questions from any available source.[22] A committee then went to work drafting a program. In the summer of 2007, a draft was circulated to a small number of intellectuals outside the Brotherhood for reaction and comment—but it was quickly leaked, provoking widespread debate within the movement, within the broader society, and even internationally. The draft was enormously detailed on a wide range of subjects, from judicial independence to tourism to telecommunications. It took strong positions supporting political rights and freedoms. But two details designed to bring the document into line with many leaders' understanding of Islamic requirements proved to be the focal point for debate and convinced critics that the movement's commitment to rights was superficial. First, the draft proposed the establishment of a council of religious scholars to determine when laws clearly violated unambiguous shari'a provisions; and second, the document opposed selecting women and non-Muslims for some senior state positions.

The Brotherhood suddenly found itself on the defensive in public debates for a document it had not yet endorsed; it was also deeply (and openly) divided internally about how much to relax ideological strictures in these areas when turning the draft into a final document. The more politically inclined, for instance, argued that restricting the position of head of state to Muslim males was both religiously outmoded (the shari'a-based ideas of such issues having been developed for a very different institutional context, before the construction of the modern state) and politically unnecessary (no Christian was ever likely to win the presidency in a democratic election). But incorporating more liberal provisions on such matters into a subsequent draft of the platform would alienate not only some members of the leadership (who charged their colleagues with having forgotten Islamic law) but also much of the grassroots membership. As one Muslim Brotherhood leader said, "We presented the first draft to all and we accepted criticisms and we made changes. But we cannot satisfy everyone."[23]

And they did not. In the end, the Brotherhood took three steps in response to the public debate over the platform. First, it disavowed the council of religious scholars and placed its faith in the country's Supreme Constitutional Court to implement Article 2 of the country's constitution (stating that the principles of

22. A piece I wrote with two coauthors for the Carnegie Endowment was in part a reaction to the Brotherhood's solicitation for questions. See Amr Hamzawy, Marina Ottaway, and Nathan J. Brown, "What Islamists Need to Be Clear About: The Case of the Egyptian Muslim Brotherhood," Policy Outlook, Carnegie Endowment for International Peace, February 2007.

23. Tariq Salah and Munir Adib, "The Brotherhood Delays Announcing the 'Amended' Platform Fearing Fissures," *Al-misri al-yawm*, June 27, 2009.

the Islamic shari'a are the chief source of legislation). Second, the Brotherhood implied that it was primarily the position of head of state that was a matter of concern (and not all senior state positions) for the movement, and that its opposition to a non-Muslim or a female filling that post was firm. But it hinted as well that the opposition was simply a Brotherhood position rather than a proposed constitutional requirement and that the Brotherhood would not question the constitutional legitimacy of a Christian or non-Muslim who was democratically elected. Or as some Brotherhood leaders sought to spin the decision: if a Christian or a woman wished to be president, he or she should not join the Brotherhood but would need to find another group to support his or her candidacy.

The third and perhaps most significant step was simply to drop the platform. The document was a draft for a party that was not about to come into existence. The Brotherhood was finding that it was paying a price for responding to questions that it did not have to answer. General answers that paper over differences rather than specific answers that commit the movement (but also alienate key actors inside or outside the movement) make far more sense in such a situation.

In short, the Muslim Brotherhood was experiencing precisely the sorts of tensions to be expected when an ideological movement is tantalized by the prospect of electoral gains. How quickly—or even whether—it responds by giving the specific ideological and programmatic and policy commitments demanded by skeptics (on issues involving Islamic law and women's rights most particularly) depends in significant measure not simply on ideological debates within the movement but also on the expected response from a host of external actors. And in the prevailing restrictive environment, in which Egypt's semiauthoritarianism was showing its harshest face, leaders concluded that in 2007 they paid the price of clarifying commitments without reaping the benefits. They learned their lesson. In developing a platform for the 2010 parliamentary elections, for instance, the Brotherhood steered clear of the issues that had given it such headaches in 2007. Only after the 2011 revolution did they dust off the project, and then they took months to tinker with it before releasing it to the public.

Jordan: Evolution of Islamic Themes

The Jordanian Muslim Brotherhood's approach to Islam is testimony to the complexity of the various ideological eddies and currents that affect the development of a movement as it increases its political involvement. Indeed, the Jordanian movement's navigation of issues related to Islam has become much more difficult as it has seized semiauthoritarian opportunities.

What had been a manageable effort to satisfy core followers without alienating the government (from the movement's beginning until the 1980s) became a much more complicated struggle with the emergence of semiauthoritarianism and the resultant increase in political activity. Now it was necessary for the movement to respond not simply to core supporters and official suspicions but also to broader sympathizers and non-Islamist political forces.

The Jordanian Islamist movement has been influenced by its greater political involvement to recast its message in broader terms. But while the investment in politics has paid off with some success, it has also increased ideological demands on the movement and strains within its own ranks. And those difficulties have been accentuated by the refusal of the movement to allow more autonomy to its various specialized wings in politics, social activism, education, and propagandizing. The closely interlocked nature of the movement (described in Chapter 6) has maintained organizational flexibility, allowing the movement to be active simultaneously in many different spheres. But the tight links among these various movement bodies have also ensured that ideological struggles in one area are transferred to other wings of the movement.

A Comfortable Pious Pocket

In its first few decades, the political stance of Jordan's Muslim Brotherhood might best be described as pious hectoring. Appealing primarily to a devout middle-class group of followers, the movement used a fairly strict Islamic yardstick to measure public policies and government actions. It was not afraid to criticize official actions that contravened the religious principles (and social conservatism) of the group's loyal followers; it tended to couch all its arguments in religious and shari'a-based language. But it did not allow its stand on specific issues of interest to develop into a broader critique of the political system.

In the 1950s and the 1960s, the Muslim Brotherhood—at that time a smaller movement focusing mostly on nonpolitical work but with a foot in the political process—was thus able to take a fairly strident set of positions on issues related to Islam and Islamic law without paying the high political price of sustained repression. It showed a predilection for cultural issues and perceived offenses to religious values in Jordanian public life. Movement deputies used their parliamentary seats to call for implementation of Islamic law and to condemn cultural practices deemed non-Islamic (such as the visit of an ice-skating troupe whose members wore costumes deemed excessively revealing). The movement's positions on many issues, ranging from Palestine to the Islamic shari'a, were strong and uncompromising, and the language of some of its deputies was sometimes shrill. While most of its concerns were specifically religious, it could advance

outside that realm into foreign policy, especially regarding Jordan's foreign alignments and the Palestinian cause. The Brotherhood denounced a U.S. aid offer in
1957 with the slogan "No reconciliation [with Israel], no dollar, no atheism, and
no imperialism." But because it did not link its opposition to the foreign policy of
the regime with support for Arab nationalism (then often closely associated with
an Egyptian regime that treated its own Brotherhood with remarkable harshness), the movement's positions were more annoying than threatening to the
regime. And in general, the Brotherhood stayed squarely within the boundaries
of peaceful opposition. It often supported calls for political openness but did not
prioritize the issue.

These positions—and the rhetoric deployed in support of them—frequently
alienated other political actors and contributed to the movement's status as
slightly out of the center of Jordanian political struggles. But political isolation in
a politically closed system was not a high price to pay, especially for a movement
that was allowed to pursue its nonpolitical agenda unimpeded. The movement
avoided opposition coalitions and membership in the cabinet, explaining its political opposition in terms of the government's failure to implement Islamic law.[24]
But if the movement was strong in some of its language and politically isolated,
it was not deemed extremist or threatening by the regime: for all the movement's
occasional thunder, some of its specific demands could be met and the movement pursued no political strategy other than complaining if they were not.

This stance, fairly uncompromising in rhetoric but focused on religious (and
select other) issues, was one that married the movement to its core supporters. It
also made internal differences and relations with the regime largely manageable.
There were some who wished to take a more cooperative line with the regime
and others who prided themselves on principled opposition. The result was an
uneasy compromise—or perhaps more accurately, an unsteady compromise, because there was a constant contest over how much the movement's stress on
fidelity to Islamic law should place it in an oppositional stance. And there were
periodic tensions with the regime and occasional repressive measures. Still, the
pocket the movement created for itself was small but comfortable.

Navigating Outside the Pious Pocket

The Brotherhood began to move outside that pocket as Jordanian politics opened
up in the late 1980s. The emergence of Jordanian semiauthoritarianism occasioned the movement's growing political involvement, its formation of a politi-

---

24. Indeed, see Abu Faris, *Safahat min tarikh,* for a history of the movement that stresses its oppositional nature specifically on shari'a-based grounds.

cal party, and its increasing investment in electoral and parliamentary activities. These have led Jordanian Islamists to emphasize a set of Islamic themes that cut a broader swath but seem to run far less deep. The effect has been to increase the movement's programmatic reach, attract the attention of a broader set of potential constituents, and create opportunities for tactical partnerships with other political forces. But there have been costs. The turn toward politics and the ideological adjustments this required have led the movement to pose a greater challenge for a regime that has set out its own agenda of religious platitudes. Additionally, it has made the Islamist current less coherent and its divisions more apparent. Finally, and most paradoxically, the escape from a narrow ghetto of rigidly religious supporters may be leading the movement into a larger but still confining Palestinian ghetto.

The entry of the movement into mainstream politics gradually led most of its leaders to cultivate a broader view of the Islamic shari'a. Movement intellectuals have taken part in the general shift in Arab Islamist discourse toward emphasizing the overall goals and the diverse richness of the Islamic legal tradition and de-emphasizing specific shari'a-based legal provisions. For instance, the IAF's 2003 platform echoed past themes when it called for application of the Islamic shari'a, identifying it as a religious obligation and the basic goal of the party. But it gave remarkably few details, and where it cited examples, it used very gentle terminology, such as suggesting that certain parts of commercial law be modified in a way that was consistent with the Islamic shari'a. The platform pointed as well to the supreme goals of the shari'a, a common way for Islamist movements to portray pursuit of the shari'a as consistent with public welfare and not an imposition or set of burdensome restrictions. The approach became one of firm dedication to Islam and Islamic legal principles but also an inclination toward gradualism and persuasion rather than radical and imposed change.

This shift made it possible for the movement to construct a broader agenda. Political reform and economic grievances could now be portrayed as integral parts of an Islamic agenda, based on the argument that the Islamic path offers solutions to social and political problems. For instance, the movement participated in general calls for political reform and spoke up for what it perceived as the economic needs of citizens, arguing that these positions flowed from a religiously based dedication to the public welfare and general Islamic principles such as consultation and justice. Movement leaders now claimed that their pursuit of the shari'a led them to champion political freedoms and oppose fuel price increases.

Previous generations of movement leaders sometimes resisted talk of "democracy," instead favoring "shura" or claiming that "democracy" could be implemented only within Islamic strictures (and therefore sometimes favoring the term "shuracracy"). Current leaders have lost all their timidity about the imported term. And they have adopted the self-description of their party as "a civil party with a religious reference" used by other Islamist movements in the region.

In October 2005, the IAF issued its most detailed reform program, a document so full of liberal and democratic ideas and language that a leader of a secular opposition party was forced to confess that it differed little from the programs of other parties. And indeed, the new broader understanding made it possible to engage with a wider array of political actors. Other opposition forces have found that they could make common cause with an Islamist movement that in an earlier generation had stood aloof from their concerns. International interlocutors seeking congenial Islamists found leaders conversant with the discourse of human rights and political reform. In my 2007 visit to IAF headquarters described in the previous chapter, one participant mentioned that Amnesty International had just issued a report criticizing Jordan's human rights record. Party leaders of various persuasions immediately gathered around a computer screen to read the report, clearly interested and gratified that their complaints about political developments in Jordan, increasingly lodged in the terms of political reform and human rights rather than a religious vocabulary, had found some international resonance.

But this shift has not always been an easy one for the movement, and there have been some signs of retreat in recent years. The ideological effects of the foray into increased political activity became apparent gradually. In 1989, the movement still stressed implementation of the Islamic shari'a as one of its conditions for supporting the government; in 1993, its platform called for banning satellite television in Jordan (presumably because of its unmanageable content).[25] Even as late as 2007, the movement found itself in a complicated position when it argued in support of dropping criminal penalties for press offenses (because some in the movement insisted that offenses against religion should be maintained as criminal). And some within the movement have been troubled by what they see as the dilution of the movement's religious orientation. Of course, the broader discourse that has been increasingly adopted can still be portrayed as true to the movement's Islamic principles as long as those principles are understood in the most general terms. In two different conversations with a leading dove (in 2005 and 2007), I asked whether the movement was deemphasizing the shari'a in favor of political reform and economic issues. His response both times was, "But this *is* the shari'a!" Still, such talk makes others nervous that the party is compromising on its core in favor of a more pragmatic approach. One

---

25. Bassam al-'Amush, *Mahattat fi tarikh: jama'at al-ikhwan al-muslimin fi al-urdun* (Amman: Dar Zahran, 2008), pp. 274–275.

leading hawk, for example, proclaimed that "pragmatism means conceding principles and fixed positions, and this is something we cannot do," and admonished that "parliamentary elections are a means," not an end. While they make noise, such figures have not boycotted political activities or the IAF's parliamentary role. Indeed, one of their firebrands (Muhammad Abu Faris) even accepted the chairmanship of the parliament's legal committee, putting him in the position of participating in composing man-made legislation, an unusual task for a militant shari'a advocate.

Thus political activity has made for a more difficult balancing act. Within the movement, latent ideological tensions have become more apparent. The necessity of taking votes in parliament or developing positions on a wider range of issues has made the earlier process of papering over differences more problematic. Outside the movement, there have been new opportunities to build alliances, but every political success has also caused an increase in official suspicions. The various tensions have not been easily contained within the party but have spread to other bodies. They have led to bitter divisions within the Muslim Brotherhood; entangled the movement's main social arm, the Islamic Center; and led to disputes about the movement's newspaper.

As if these internal struggles are not enough, the movement's calculations are greatly complicated by the regime's own adoption of some of the reformed Islamist vocabulary and use of the arguments of "centrism" for its own purposes. In 2005, the Jordanian regime sponsored an international conference in order to oppose radical interpretations of Islam, denounce violence and charges of apostasy (*takfir*), and support Muslim unity. It committed itself very publicly to the resulting "Amman Declaration," insisting that it offered a truer picture of Islamic teachings than those advanced by radical forces within the Muslim world. And it used the Amman Declaration as a litmus test for Brotherhood: important regime figures questioned whether the Brotherhood was hinting at far more radical ideas than those endorsed in the officially sponsored Amman Declaration. When regime-movement tensions escalated over the next year, more conciliatory Islamist leaders attempted to fend off charges of extremism by inducing the movement to issue a 2006 statement finding parts of the Amman Declaration it could support and distancing itself from some radical ideas. But while it rejected *takfir* of Jordanian society, the statement was more equivocal concerning *takfir* of individuals; it also could not deny that those with more radical views on the matter remained within the movement. Five days after the first statement, the movement's leaders added a statement that explicitly affirmed their acceptance of the Amman Declaration. But many leaders resented the defensive tone the movement had struck; their resentment only deepened when the expected payoff for the statement failed to materialize and the regime proceeded with harsh measures against the movement (including placing three parliamentarians on trial and maintaining the seizure of the Islamic Center, as mentioned in Chapter 5). Thus the attempt to placate the regime only succeeded in widening splits within the movement; eighteen of the forty members of the Muslim Brotherhood's consultative council—the organization's key policymaking body—submitted their resignations to protest the movement's statements.

Confronted with the limits of semiauthoritarian politics, the advocates of a broader way to cast Islamic issues began losing ground within Jordan's Islamist movement. In 2010, for instance, they failed to bring the movement to fully endorse a proposal to pursue an ambitious program of political reform as an Islamic project. But at the same time, the movement did denounce any attempt to side with the United States in Afghanistan (as the Jordanian regime was then quietly doing) as unbelief (*kufr*). A partial reversion to a more strident but more specifically religious discourse seemed under way. And when a protest movement erupted in Jordan in 2011 (one that sought to emulate the Egyptian and Tunisian movements while stopping far short of calling for regime change), the Islamists showed strong ambivalence. Those more politically inclined leaders sought to join the effort and use it to press for a constitutional monarchy while the traditionally more strident voices held back, less anxious to choose political reform as the issue on which to confront the regime.

Kuwait: Navigating between Government and Opposition

In Kuwait, the Islamist movement operates under a milder brand of semiauthoritarianism. The movement has escaped the harsh repression or the sustained harassment that movements elsewhere have experienced. And the opportunities have sometimes been far greater—to form alliances, to bring down ministers, to enter the government, and even to pass an occasional law. But these opportunities have tantalized the movement and made it hesitate between two strategies. On the one hand, Hadas could enter the cabinet and pursue a limited agenda, perhaps related to a religious or moral issue in a specific field. On the other hand, the movement might instead choose to eschew short-term and modest gains and instead pursue its vision of a constitutional monarchy with a full party system in which it alternates between government and opposition. Earlier in this chapter, we saw how Hadas was caught on the issue of political rights for women. Its dance on aligning itself with the government or the opposition is similar but far more sustained; it has moved back and forth between the two. As a result of living in this semiauthoritarian netherworld, Hadas experiments with both strategies; it reaches for both roles but fully grasps neither.

Paradoxically, we have seen that increasing participation in semiauthoritarian politics often induces Islamist movements to find a stronger oppositional voice. And Hadas was indeed created in part to play such a role: to operate as the politicized arm of the Islamist movement and to pursue some of the benefits of a broadly oppositional program. In the previous chapter, we saw how the movement has sometimes worked to forge alliances with ideological rivals in pursuing a broad program of political reform. Loose and shifting coalitions, some of them spearheaded by Hadas, have been able to bring down individual ministers and even force the unprecedented parliamentary questioning of the prime minister on two occasions. But any more ambitious or constructive agenda has been completely unrealized.

The opportunities dangled in front of the movement as well as the costs of being shut out of power suggest that the party would be unwise to close all doors to a more cooperative position, and Hadas has never rejected the idea of participation in the cabinet in principle. In fact, in recent years, the party has attempted to leave all doors open, finessing the various pressures and opportunities, by adopting the campaign slogan "Responsibility." The word was carefully chosen: it is designed to communicate to the general public that the party places the national interest above party or individual interest; it also allows the party to present itself as standing above the rivalry between parliament and cabinet that has paralyzed Kuwaiti politics in recent years. The slogan communicates to the government that Hadas does not oppose for opposition's sake and to potential allies that Hadas will be businesslike in its relations with other forces.

If "Responsibility" allows Hadas to pursue loyalty and opposition at the same time, the slogan is still too vague to tell party leaders what to do if they should be offered seats in the cabinet. An actual position of responsibility makes ambiguity impossible, and when it has been offered a seat at the cabinet table, the party has reacted in a consistently inconsistent manner. Hadas has felt its greatest tensions—and perhaps made its most significant miscalculations—on precisely this question. Over the past twenty years, Hadas has seen the amir reach out to some of its members or its close allies—but the offer is usually of a single post rather than a general role in policymaking. It is difficult to decline such a position; having an ally in the Ministry of Religious Affairs in the 1990s, for instance, allowed the establishment of the Public Foundation (see Chapter 5); having a senior member serve as minister of oil not only gave Hadas a voice in a vital area but also seems to have allowed the party to hire a number of its younger members in a critical state office. Holding the Justice or Communications ministries allows the party to show its integrity and competence; it can live up to its slogan of

"Responsibility." And what is difficult for Hadas as a whole to turn down is even harder for an individual leader to decline: on two occasions, leading members of the party have been enticed into the cabinet despite the movement's opposition, leading to bitter public squabbles. Acting responsibly in such contexts has some costs, especially because it forces the movement to hold its rhetorical fire when it would prefer to criticize policy. As a result, on several occasions when Hadas entered the cabinet, it came to rue its decision.

The gyrations between government and opposition were on full display late in the first decade of the 2000s. In 2007 and again in 2008, a leading Hadas member accepted the Oil Ministry with the party's full endorsement. That led Hadas to support some cabinet decisions that predated its participation; when the government abruptly (and without explanation) caved in to parliamentary opposition on those decisions, Hadas leaders felt they had been tricked into loyally fighting a battle that was not their own. They decided to withdraw their minister from the cabinet and quickly dropped any inhibitions in their willingness to criticize the government; in order to reestablish their opposition credentials, they moved to haul the prime minister into parliament for formal questioning (a step that led the amir to dissolve the parliament and call for new elections rather than have the prime minister submit himself to such an indignity). As a result, Hadas leaders found themselves compelled to explain to a confused electorate why a cabinet whose policies they had supported one day became a target of such contempt the next. In 2009 balloting, they were saddled simultaneously with having been part of the cabinet and having incurred the ire of leading members of the ruling family.

In sum, the environment of Kuwaiti semiauthoritarianism is a bit milder than that of many states in the region and the room for maneuver is greater. But that has only sharpened the dilemma of whether to work as an ally of the existing order or its reformer. It has also made calculation of appropriate tactics difficult; the movement has sometimes found that if it attempts to strike out in every direction at once, it falls down.

Palestine: Hamas and Democracy

The ideological effects of participation—and the limits of those effects—are most dramatically on display in the case of Hamas. The trajectory of Hamas's attitude toward democracy is clear—diffidence evolving into interest evolving in turn into a central ideological and rhetorical element in the movement's program—and closely mirrors that of its sister movements. The primary differences are that Hamas's path was more rapid and more extreme than that of the other movements and that it was partially reversed: Hamas's attitude toward democracy was put to the test after it won the 2006 parliamentary elections. The interpretation of the test results is a matter of deep controversy domestically and internationally. There is less room for debate that the political system itself, already weak, failed in a potential democratic transition. During all this evolution, Hamas showed one further characteristic common to its counterpart movements: true to its self-image as a practical movement, its evolution came very much in response to a shifting environment; for all its emphasis on holding fast to fixed principles, Hamas's ideology clearly is defined in part by what the movement does. In other words, Hamas's commitment to democratic principles followed its involvement in democratic politics rather than the other way around.[26]

Moving to Embrace Democracy

The pre-Hamas Muslim Brotherhood showed little interest in democratic institutions and practices, and indeed, there were few to be found in Palestinian politics. The structures governing Palestinians in the West Bank and Gaza were generally authoritarian. With the exception of Jordanian parliamentary elections (which included West Bank Palestinians until 1967), the limited opportunities for democratic politics that did exist (very limited elections in Gaza before 1967, municipal elections under Israeli rule in 1976, and occasional student or professional association elections) drew little Muslim Brotherhood interest. When a more activist generation of leaders began to emerge in the Muslim Brotherhood in the 1970s and 1980s—the group that eventually formed Hamas—their level of social and political engagement led them to participate more in student and association elections, but their behavior was regarded by other factions as blending thuggery with politicking.

When Hamas was founded in the late 1980s, therefore, it had only a scanty foundation in democratic practice and virtually none in democratic ideology. Its initial orientation reflected this experience, but its political engagement suggested other possibilities. At first, its ideological pronouncements were very long on resistance, relatively long on religion, and quite short on democracy. But there were three elements present at the founding that suggested the possibility for evolving in a different direction.

First, Hamas was unambiguously committed to social and political involvement. This is what marked its departure from the Palestinian Muslim Broth-

---

26. This is a major argument of Jeroen Gunning, *Hamas in Politics: Democracy, Religion, Violence* (New York: Columbia University Press, 2008).

erhood legacy; it also distinguished Hamas from other Islamist parties and movements (such as Hizb al-Tahrir, which mimicked the Palestinian Brotherhood's previous aloofness, and Islamic Jihad, which focused only on resistance).

Second, the movement prided itself not merely on its engagement but also on its popularity. Hamas leaders were strongly oriented toward Palestinian public opinion, often allowing it to guide tactical decision making, especially on questions related to means of resistance and methods of political participation.

Third, Hamas inched toward accepting pluralism. Its track record of collegiality was very much adulterated by a strong competitive streak; Hamas's major decisions were often motivated by a desire to outflank its rival groups. But the movement ventured beyond the Brotherhood's rejection of the leftist and nationalist partners and began to speak a more accepting language about coordination and the need to forge a common Palestinian agenda.[27]

Democracy itself was not much of an issue for any Palestinian group in the late 1980s when Hamas was founded, but the creation of the Palestinian Authority in the mid-1990s opened some new electoral structures, and Hamas found itself forced to define its role. Here it felt contrary pressures: it rejected the Oslo Accords that made the elections possible and sharply constrained the authority of the Palestinian entity being created. But Hamas also felt the pull of its commitment to social and political involvement and its sensitivity to public opinion (much of the population of the West Bank and Gaza was enthusiastic about electing a president and a council). What is remarkable about Hamas's decision making was that the debates (which were intense) were primarily carried out over the practical implications of participating rather than the abstract ideological principles at stake.[28]

The construction of the PA confronted Hamas with a broader set of questions about its attitude toward a purportedly Palestinian political authority. Once again, political practice led to an ideological evolution: while Hamas continued to reject the legitimacy of the Oslo Accords, it disavowed (in theory and, with some exceptions, in practice) any involvement in intra-Palestinian violence. This placed the movement in a difficult position at times when the PA arrested and even tortured Hamas members (and at one point attempted to shut down a broad swath of organizations informally linked with Hamas). The response of

27. There are many works that focus on Hamas's early ideology, including Andrea Nusse, *Muslim Palestine: The Ideology of Hamas* (Amsterdam: Harwood, 1998); Beverley Milton-Edwards, *Islamic Politics in Palestine* (London: I. B. Tauris, 1996); Ziad Abu-Amr, *Islamic Fundamentalism in the West Bank and Gaza: Muslim Brotherhood and Islamic Jihad* (Bloomington: Indiana University Press, 1994); and Jawad al-Hamad and Iyad al-Barghuti, *Dirasa al-fikr al-siyasi li-harakat al-muqawama al-islamiya, 1987–1996* (Amman: Middle East Publishing Center, 1997).

28. See Shaul Mishal and Avraham Sela, "Participation without Presence: Hamas, the Palestinian Authority and the Politics of Negotiated Coexistence," *Middle Eastern Studies* 38, no. 3 (July 2002), 1–26.

the organization in rhetorical terms was telling: while it blasted the PA actions as craven, it also began to develop a critique of PA practice grounded in the terms of human rights and domestic legality. Hamas leaders began to insist that the PA in general and Fatah specifically were operating in an extralegal manner.

By the time the question of elections arose again, therefore, Hamas had evolved some strains of political argumentation that stressed not simply resistance and Islam but also rights, the rule of law, and constitutional legitimacy. In this it was aided by the development of a reform agenda by its counterpart movements. The decision to enter the 2006 parliamentary elections therefore appeared more of an evolutionary step than a radical break. In agreeing to enter, Hamas negotiated with the Palestinian regime over the electoral law, focusing primarily on the fairness of electoral administration (other factions, by contrast, were more interested in the precise formulas for determining representation and in particular the mixture between proportional representation and district-based voting). And when it produced its 2006 electoral platform, the new vision of political reform, clean and transparent government, democracy, and the rule of law was no longer general and vague but suitable for detailed and lengthy presentation.

Coping with Democratic Success

The surging popularity of Hamas made it easy at first for its leaders to be democrats. And they increasingly placed democracy at the center of their claims to legitimacy, referring to the provisions of the Palestinian Basic Law (a constitutional document for the PA that Hamas had little role or interest in designing), showing themselves more faithful to the text than many of those who had written it. Hamas leaders dismissed criticisms from radical Islamist circles that their embrace of democracy elevated the popular over the divine will; they showed little patience for what seemed to them pointless theological discussions. And they proclaimed their willingness to work with secular politicians and Christians who shared their agenda. In a few years, Hamas had traversed the ideological distance that its sister movements could barely cross in a generation. It was semiauthoritarian opportunities—the knowledge that they could participate, if not win—that pulled the movement along so quickly.

Of course, Palestinian semiauthoritarianism did not work as intended: the opposition won. Victory led the democratic commitments of Hamas to deepen.[29] Embracing constitutionalism and showing an obsessive fidelity to democratic and legal procedure, Hamas leaders found that the legal and constitutional

---

29. On this point generally, see 'Adnan Abu 'Amr, "Al-khitab al-siyasi li-hukumat 'hamas' wa-l-mujtama' al-duwali: al-ta'thirat wa-l-masalih al-mutabadila," *Al-tasamuh* 12, no. 7 (2006).

framework built over the past ten years left them in a powerful position. They turned to a prominent constitutional law professor to serve as justice minister and gave their deputies training in parliamentary procedure (one employee of the parliament told me that the newly elected members spent their time memorizing the parliament's bylaws). The emphasis on legality became particularly marked during this period, merging with and sometimes even eclipsing the democratic populism that the movement had adopted. The new government not only exposed some of the corruption of its predecessor; it also showed an ability to turn its austere ethos into a guide for governing: Hamas parliamentarians traveled by public transportation to work and flew coach on rare international trips.

All the while, Hamas leaders continued to insist that they had not budged in their fundamental principles. Since they had never rejected democracy in principle, there was some truth to this claim, but there was certainly a marked change in the details and tone of their political pronouncements.

There were, however, two flaws in the Islamists' new democratic and constitutionalist fabric, the combination of which proved fatal to Palestinian democracy. First, for all the movement's rigid legalism when it came to internal procedures, there was a continued insistence on the legitimacy of resistance. That meant that the PA could not regulate or bar armed action by Palestinian factions; even the quiescence of Hamas's own armed wing was a matter of its calculation of the strategic environment rather than a deference to authoritative national institutions. Constitutional and democratic procedures could determine who could be taxed and what could be taught, but they were not to guide who could fight and kill the Palestinians' adversaries.

Second, other Palestinian political actors were less punctilious in their approach to constitutional and democratic procedures. The defeated Fatah party began with the sort of shenanigans to be expected from a long-time ruling party startled to find itself out of power (such as encouraging civil servants it had hired to drag their feet in implementing the wishes of the new Hamas ministers and using a lame-duck parliamentary session to rush through legislation). But quite quickly, matters progressed beyond dirty tricks: the president (Mahmud 'Abbas, from the defeated Fatah party) began to threaten to upend the constitutional order by dismissing the government, dissolving the parliament, or calling a referendum. A battle for control of the security services was resolved not through constitutional channels but by the buildup of rival forces by the president and the interior minister.[30]

---

30. On the intra-Palestinian wrangling during this period, see Maryam 'Itani and Muhsin Muhammad Salih, *Sira' al-salahiyyat bayna fatah wa-hamas fi idarat al-sulta al filastiniyya, 2006–2007,* as well as their *Sira' al-iradat: al-suluk al-amni li-fatah wa-hamas wa-l-atraf al-ma'niya, 2006–2007* (Beirut: Markaz al-Zaytuna li-l-Dirasat wa-l-Istisaharat, 2008).

The combination ultimately undermined Hamas's democratic commitments and destroyed the nascent Palestinian democracy. In June 2007, as other countries stepped up efforts to arm and train forces under the president's command, expecting the Fatah-Hamas conflict to be resolved militarily, Hamas's armed wing joined with the security forces under the command of the minister of interior to seize control in Gaza. While the action against presidential security forces was clearly a consensus decision by the movement, the violence and the extreme measures seemed to startle and embarrass some Hamas leaders (especially those in the West Bank, but also even some in Gaza).

Yet even after the brief Palestinian civil war, Hamas showed a continued insistence on its fidelity to constitutional procedure; the rhetoric of its foray into electoral politics had left a strong residue. The movement's leaders strove to show that they were operating in accordance with the terms of the constitutional order wherever possible and that the Hamas-controlled government in Gaza was ruling through regular legal channels and procedures. But just as the movement had adapted to the realities of democratic opportunities, it also showed profound changes under the influence of the collapse of Palestinian democracy and the realities of governing in Gaza. Immediately after Hamas took control of Gaza, President 'Abbas issued a decree amending the electoral law to prohibit Hamas from running.[31] Unsurprisingly, Hamas had no interest in participating in elections from which it had been banned, and when the term of the parliament expired in January 2010, the two halves of the PA could not come to an agreement on how to return Palestinians to the polls. The Palestinian semiauthoritarianism which had emerged between 1994 and 2006—and which was poised briefly to evolve in a democratic direction after the cardinal rule of semiauthoritarian politics was broken by Hamas's electoral victory—had instead collapsed, leaving two fully authoritarian political systems in its wake, one in Gaza and one in the West Bank.

The transformation in Hamas was deep: the movement began to abandon the distinction between movement and government in Gaza, using the military wing to augment the security forces, policing other movements, allowing movement leaders without official position to make decisions that effectively bound the government, and stacking nongovernmental organizations with government supporters. Hamas's construction of a party-state after June 2007 directly contradicted the stance of the movement after the January 2006 elections and ironically bore a resemblance to the path followed earlier by Fatah when it had created the PA in the 1990s. Even the close attention to public opinion began to fade along

---

31. The decree required fidelity to the PLO and to its agreements, conditions that Hamas would be unable to meet.

with the prospect of elections: as Hamas's popularity declined in public opinion polls, the movement simply continued with unpopular policies (especially balking at reconciliation with Fatah). Hamas did not repudiate democracy, but there were unmistakable signs of a democratic retreat.

Openness, Opportunities, and Their Limits

To my knowledge, no Islamist leader has ever proclaimed that "social (or political) being determines consciousness." But that is how they evolve. The movements, dedicated as they are to operating fully within the society, find that the political environment deeply shapes their development.

Openness and opportunities have led to ideological change. More openness leads to more assurances and more willingness to bend ideological principles to assure regimes and critics. The shift from authoritarianism to semiauthoritarianism has led Islamist movements to stress their embrace of peaceful change more forcefully. It has also led them to push their ideological agenda in more general terms—to adduce nonreligious justifications for their existing positions and to deemphasize some of their more specific interpretations of the Islamic religious heritage in favor of more general themes.

But semiauthoritarian regimes generate semiresponsive movements. The semiauthoritarian context, because it denies the possibility of victory to the opposition, places limitations on the ideological commitments of the Islamists. Just as we saw in Chapter 6 with organizational changes, there are important lacunae in the ideological developments of Islamist movements in a semiauthoritarian setting; they work to leave a route of retreat open.

Ideologically (just as we saw organizationally in Chapter 6), there are clear reasons to continue living in the gray zones: avoiding definite ideological commitments allows movements to carefully craft their message to diverse groups. In an authoritarian setting, by contrast, Islamists are generally restricted to appealing to core supporters and (at times) appeasing the regime. But in a semiauthoritarian setting, they have reason to appeal to a broader sympathetic but less committed public as well as to opposition intellectuals and movements that are often more skeptical. For ideological movements that take their statements and platforms seriously—and that use them not only to persuade others about the nature of the cause but also to talk to themselves about what they want—the words they use to describe their positions carry deep meaning for the members. They are weighed carefully.

In the four areas receiving particular focus in this chapter, there were clear—but generally hedged—ideological developments. With regard to rights and freedoms, no Islamist movement has had a problem pressing for political liberalization in general. The emphasis has been consistent; it has even grown grudgingly specific and has also been cast in terms that are less religious in content. But social and cultural freedoms and the full panoply of citizenship rights have been more difficult. It is here that Islamist movements are more likely to feel the pull of various political forces and seek to avoid choosing among them by reference to general formulas or to positions that seem, at least to outsiders, like splitting hairs (such as opposing censorship but favoring withdrawal of state support for books or films deemed culturally or religiously inappropriate). And with general, ambiguous, or overly nuanced positions, it should be no surprise to hear some Islamist leaders thunder about the godlessness of a television broadcast while a colleague sends soothing signals that he is loath to impose his standards on others. If Islamists can claim that their commitment to rights and freedoms has grown (within limits) and gained specificity, they cannot deny that they also retreat from specificity when it costs them too much. The limited rewards of semiauthoritarianism do not encourage anything more.

With regard to Islam, the movements have also shown an interest both in broader interpretations and in casting their arguments in less religious terms. When they move in this direction, however, they encounter not only a degree of internal resistance within their own ranks but also pressure from some competing Islamic forces. Particularly in places where salafi movements are strong (even if those movements do not participate in electoral politics), such evolution on the religious front makes the salafi charge resonate that mainstream and Brotherhood-type movements are really more about politics than religion. We saw in Jordan how growing involvement in semiauthoritarian politics has led to a more general set of understandings of Islamic teachings for politics and society—but also how the real rewards for this evolution may have been exhausted in recent years.

Semiauthoritarian politics has more solid effects in carving out a preferred political space for Islamist movements: that of loyal opposition. Neither dimension of this term should be pushed too far: the movements are loyal in that they generally accept existing constitutional structures, though they clearly want to reform them in some fundamental ways; they are opposition movements, but they do not reject entering the government on principle. In some countries, full authoritarianism pushed the movements into different camps: an exit from politics (the Palestinian Muslim Brotherhood between 1967 and the rise of Hamas), a move fully into opposition (the Egyptian Muslim Brotherhood in the 1950s and 1960s), or a move toward guarded and wary support of the regime (the Kuwaiti and Jordanian Muslim Brotherhoods in the 1950s and 1960s). Semiauthoritarianism has brought the movements closer together: they are now largely above ground and generally willing to work within accepted and legal channels. In the terminology introduced in Chapter 3, they have become relational rather than ideological anti-system parties. We saw in Kuwait how such an evolution has frustrated the movement, tantalizing it with the rewards both of loyalty and of opposition but fully delivering neither.

Finally, semiauthoritarianism has enhanced the role of democracy in the ideology of the movements. The frustrations and limitations of semiauthoritarian purgatory slowly lead Islamist movements to stress the need to relax the unwritten rule of semiauthoritarian politics that the opposition may not win. They do so gingerly at times and emphasize the "participation, not domination" slogan in order to make the call less threatening. But there is no mistaking the gradual increase in Islamist emphasis on political reform that the plunge into politics has brought. The increase is probably greatest in countries where the Islamist movement sees itself as a natural majority. As the experience of Hamas shows, the unlikely event of an Islamist victory solidifies the democratic commitment still further—but it also shows that when that democratic victory was (in Hamas's version of events) effectively denied, the movement begins to revert to a more qualified endorsement of democracy.

All the processes described here work slowly. When there is an unexpected rapid change (such as Hamas's unexpected victory), an Islamist movement generally adapts more slowly and the political system shows itself to be a bit more brittle. It is such less-anticipated changes that provide the starting point for the next chapter.

ARAB POLITICS AND SOCIETIES AS THEY MIGHT BE

In semiauthoritarian politics, movements do not participate in order to win an election and govern. But can their participation affect the workings of the political system or of the society, either over the short or long term? This is a question we have avoided answering, instead focusing on the opposite question: how do semiauthoritarian systems affect the movements? In answering our preferred question, we have arrived at a better understanding of regimes and movements, one that equips us for turning it back around. That is what we will do in this chapter, asking whether Islamist movements can make politics and society different. In doing so, we will find an odd reflection of our insistence thus far on focusing on change within semiauthoritarianism: Islamist movements are too weak and have learned to play along with semiauthoritarian politics too well to be a major force for democratization of the state, but semiauthoritarianism enhances their ability to make social practices more democratic even without regime change.

Thus, after having fended off the teleological temptation to understand all political change in terms of democracy and democratization, we will now briefly succumb to it to a limited extent. Having understood how Islamist movements operate in and are affected by semiauthoritarianism, we are ready to take up the issue of democracy in this chapter. We will do so in both an orthodox and an unorthodox way.

In approaching the question first in an orthodox way, we will focus on procedural definitions of democracy and ask what our findings on Islamist movements suggest about the prospects for fundamental change in the political system.

We will find some unlikely but possible paths to political democracy; we will also find that Islamists are likely at best to play a supporting role in such unlikely transformations if they do occur and that most of the cards do not lie in Islamist hands.

In posing the question in the second part of the chapter in an unorthodox manner, we will shift our understanding of democracy from a purely procedural conception focusing on state structure to one that is more deeply informed by normative concerns and stresses social practice. Islamist movements are often viewed with suspicion by democrats not simply because of their effects on the political system but also because of the social values they propagate. We will therefore ask if Islamist movements are likely to make the society more or less democratic. Here we will find Islamists able to play a more constructive role in some specific ways but overall a highly ambivalent one.

Rewriting the Rules: Islamist Movements and Prospects for Democratization of the State

Movement from semiauthoritarianism to full democracy in most countries of the Arab world is not likely, but its prospect has recently excited mass action in many places. It is possible through either the sudden collapse or slow evolution of semiauthoritarianism. Islamists can play some role in either scenario, but only a limited one.

Semiauthoritarian Collapse

In the case of the unanticipated collapse of a semiauthoritarian regime, what role are Islamists likely to play? Will they help bring down a semiauthoritarian system if it looks weak and help build a democratic one if it promises to emerge? Yes, but only after considerable caution and hesitation.

In early 2011, what appeared to be a stable and reliably semiauthoritarian re-gime in Egypt collapsed after less than three weeks of demonstrations. A military junta stepped in, suspended the constitution, and promised a gradual transi-tion to democratic rule. What Egyptians had come to call a "revolution" augured fundamental political changes, even if the full promise of democratization could hardly be realized overnight.

The downfall of the Mubarak regime came as a surprise even to the activists who sought it. Egypt's Muslim Brotherhood, a movement that had angrily ac-commodated itself to semiauthoritarian politics, was just as astonished as the other political actors. In meetings with the Brotherhood's leaders in the years before 2011, I found them increasingly resentful and bitter about prevailing political conditions in the country but also steadily insistent that they would persevere and maintain a focus on their long-term goals. A complete explanation of the Egyptian revolution is far beyond the bounds of this book, but we can note two salient features. First, the Brotherhood did not aim at revolutionary change until after the upheaval had begun. Second, the regime collapsed not through constitutional means (electoral defeat or constitutional amendment) but through popular demonstrations and military action that upended established procedures. The fundamental rule of semiauthoritarian politics—that the opposition can run but not win—was not broken; it was merely ignored as the rules of the political game were suspended and rewritten. After accommodating itself to semiauthoritarian politics for a generation, and after some initial hesitation, the Brotherhood leapt into the revolutionary fray and picked up the banner of democratic transition.

In the case of the sudden collapse of a semiauthoritarian system, is an Islamist movement likely to play a democratizing role? Will it push political change in a democratic direction or adjust itself to democratic political rules if such rules emerge? Our understanding of Islamist movements in semiauthoritarian systems leads us to hazard a positive answer to these questions but also to acknowledge that we are likely to see considerable hesitation and delay. A movement schooled in semiauthoritarianism, one that invests in politics but does not commit in either an organizational or ideological sense, may be too accustomed to caution and ambiguity to grasp any opportunity with alacrity. And it might also find the transition to operating in a democratic system a substantial challenge, particularly as it comes under pressure to make the kinds of ideological and organizational commitments it has long avoided.

Indeed, the behavior of the Egyptian Brotherhood in 2011 bears out such expectations. Observers scrutinized the statements and behavior of movement leaders, attempting to understand their true inclinations and beliefs, but often missing how much leaders were themselves divided, confused, and uncertain about how to respond to sudden change. The posture and habits developed under semiauthoritarianism left leaders wary of any sudden move. When the demonstrations began on January 25, the movement leadership reacted as it had learned to do over decades, by straddling the fence. It decreed that individual members could participate in the demonstrations but the movement as a whole would not take a stand. When a group of younger leaders took this decree as license to leap into the struggle, and when the demonstrations snowballed, the leadership finally committed itself and called on its members to join in the protests. Even then, the Brotherhood leadership assembled dutifully when summoned by Egypt's momentary vice president for a meeting that most opposition movements boycotted. At critical points, the Brotherhood's involvement helped turn the tide (for example, when it allowed its youth leaders to participate, when it called out its full membership, and when it decided to downplay its own agenda for the sake of a broad revolutionary coalition), but the movement's senior leaders seemed more comfortable playing a supporting rather than a leading role. Those who seek a democratic revolutionary vanguard should not look to an Islamist movement schooled in semiauthoritarianism.

And those accustomed to breaking down Islamist movements into easy categories of moderates and radicals might also be surprised at the tensions that emerged in Islamist movements in the revolutionary climate of 2011. In Egypt it was often the outward looking, more politicized members—especially youth leaders and members of parliament—who, although often described as moderates, pulled the movement into a more confrontational position. Similarly, in Jordan, it was those described as "doves" who hoisted the banner of political reform in conscious emulation of the Egyptian revolution. The "hawks" wanted to step back, uncertain that the political process was worth such an investment or gamble. Zaki Bani Arshid, a hawkish and fiery leader unburdened by party discipline (in 2009, when I asked a Jordanian Islamist about a position taken by his colleague that seemed to depart from the movement's public line, he simply sighed, "Zaki is a problem"), stated directly to me in February 2011 that he would not back calls for a constitutional monarchy because he feared that pressing political change too hard would turn Jordan into another Lebanon. The politicization wrought by semiauthoritarianism led to the emergence of some leaders—generally those more accustomed to forging political alliances and closer to the liberal end of the Islamist spectrum—who were willing to cast their lot more fully with the political process and jump on the bandwagon of fundamental change, but they dragged their movements along with great difficulty.

When the revolution triumphed in Egypt, the reasons for the leadership's hesitation became clear: the movement found the new situation welcome but also challenging. Choices that had been deferred for decades suddenly had to be made. When Egypt's generals decreed a new law allowing the Brotherhood to form a party, the movement made clear that it would finally enter partisan politics. But its leaders then debated and bickered for over two months before announcing that the new party would be fully independent—and that the Brotherhood would send it three members of its Guidance Bureau, approve its platform, and decide the extent of its electoral participation. Even internal movement operations came under tremendous pressure because the senior leadership found that it could no longer explain that repression and arrests would prevent the operation of democratic procedures within the movement. Political openness and prospects for democracy presented the Brotherhood with a far cheerier set of problems than Nasserist authoritarianism, but they were no easier to answer. And the movement was characteristically slow about responding because its leaders were worried about maintaining core principles, holding a disparate movement together, and serving both political and nonpolitical agendas without sacrificing one for the other.

In a revolutionary situation, an Islamist movement structured for semiauthoritarian politics is best seen as a dawdling democrat. But there are other ways for a semiauthoritarian regime to give way to a democratic one. We have considered what happens if such a regime is pushed out by a popular upheaval. But what if democracy comes not because the regime is pushed but because it falls, tripped up by its own mistakes? There are two such paths from semiauthoritarianism to democracy: a sudden one based on miscalculation and a gradual one based on evolutionary change. Are Islamist movements likely to be ambiguous and cautious democrats under these scenarios as well?

Miscalculation and Democratic Breakthrough

Before probing either the sudden or gradual path, let us return to what we have come to understand about semiauthoritarian politics. When we see a semiauthoritarian regime that allows the opposition some freedom but denies it a realistic possibility of electoral victory, and an Islamist movement that bounces between meekness and pushing semiauthoritarianism to its limits, we should not be surprised by the periodic openings, closures, relaxations, and clampdowns. Regimes run to stay in place; Islamist movements push and prod at the limits that are imposed but often spend just as much energy assuring the regime that they will live within those limits. The result combines stability with the appearance of dynamism.

The overall stability should not lead us to view every minor adjustment or maneuver as automatically either serving the regime or hastening its demise. We have seen how political rules under such regimes develop more by a series of tactical adjustments and small decisions than by grand, far-sighted design. Change is by accretion, and its architects are more concerned with fixing yesterday's problem or improvising a structure for tomorrow than in building a bridge to the next century.

This helps us understand what kind of change might augur real democratization and where semiauthoritarian politics is most likely to resist reform. At its most open, semiauthoritarian regimes may permit new formal parties, hold elections according to their legally mandated schedule, negotiate and renegotiate rules of political life, and allow noisy debates to ramble on with only an occasional arrest or scurrilous officially sponsored media campaign to rein them in.

But there are two likely flashpoints where regimes will become particularly resistant and even ferocious. First, when existing parties become able to mobilize real constituencies—or when existing movements with constituencies link themselves to political parties—electoral systems become more difficult to manage. From this perspective, the problem with existing Islamist opposition movements comes not from a weakness in their commitment to democracy; it comes when they become overly committed to democratic change and mobilize their constituencies in the cause. A sense of self-preservation and a focus on the long-term viability of their movements generally prevent Islamist leaders from following that path too enthusiastically.

Second, certain kinds of constitutional reforms, those that would make it possible for existing regimes to lose, will be rejected. Truly independent electoral commissions; constitutional courts that have full autonomy from the executive; entrenched and fair electoral rules—these are the sorts of reforms that regimes are likely to see as existential threats. Opposition movements can ask for them only at the cost of being seen as revolutionary or seditious by the semiauthoritarian rulers.

Because tactics dominate decision making, however, strategic errors are possible. Can either dramatic miscalculation or slow evolution lead to democratization? Can the ferociously enforced borders of semiauthoritarian politics be crossed either because of an unexpected misstep or a series of less-noticed changes? Yes, but both the sudden and gradual paths are fraught with difficulties, and other kinds of systemic change may be the outcome. And most of the keys to change simply do not lie in Islamist hands. Let us examine each path in turn.

What if a short-term maneuver dramatically and unexpectedly backfires? Semiauthoritarian regimes generally have many of the institutions and accoutrements of constitutional democracies: regular elections, parliaments with oversight and legislative authority, written constitutions containing guarantees of political rights, and specialized (and at least nominally independent) judiciaries. The regimes mold such institutions in such a way as to limit their ability to operate in a fully constitutional or democratic fashion.[1] But short-term tinkering can lead to surprising results. Egypt's Supreme Constitutional Court is a body that traces its origin to an emergency presidential decree in 1969 that was clearly (and, over the short term, successfully) designed to bring the judiciary under its control. However, in the 1980s it transformed itself into an autonomous and bold

---

1. I have examined this topic in more detail in *Constitutions in a Nonconstitutional World: Arab Basic Laws and the Prospects for Accountable Government* (Albany: State University of New York Press, 2001).

judicial actor. The Kuwaiti ruling family's extension of the franchise to outlying districts successfully led to the election of a host of loyal deputies in the 1960s but a generation later brought far more feisty, demanding, and outspoken parliamentarians representing the same population.

Elections are particularly plausible sites for miscalculations. In particular, two factors can enhance their unpredictability. First, when senior leaders are divided, they often pursue contradictory—or rapidly shifting—strategies. It is no accident that the most unpleasant electoral surprise for the Kuwaiti ruling family (the triumph of a reform coalition in 2006) came at a time when it was badly divided, distracted by internal family maneuverings, and therefore less capable of a coherent approach. In the Egyptian elections of 2005 or the Jordanian elections of 2007, regime inconsistency and division was provoked by the Islamist movements themselves: regime leaders were uncertain (or disagreed) about whether the Islamist movement should be regarded as a political challenge or a security threat and therefore vacillated between accommodation and co-optation on the one hand and harsher repression on the other.

A second source of unpredictability is the electoral mechanism itself. Sometimes, under international or domestic pressure (or often a combination), regimes will relax their grip slightly by allowing some international monitoring or limited steps toward more neutral electoral administration. In such cases, regimes find more limited tools for controlling outcomes. Those tools are often far blunter—arrests of opposition activists, blatant ballot stuffing, or intervention by the security services.

It can be more difficult to contain the effects of using such blunt and often untested tools. In 2005, the Palestinian leadership attempted to draft an election law that coaxed both the smaller political factions (which wished to see some proportional representation) and Hamas (which wanted to enter without disarming or endorsing the Oslo Accords) into running. But it was working simultaneously to balance among factions in the ruling Fatah party (with some prominent individuals wishing to run as individuals and others preferring a party list system). In short, the leadership was trying to write a law that would be suitable to a semi-authoritarian system: the opposition would run but lose. Doing so while trying to manage internal Fatah tensions led to a fatal series of mistakes, however. A compromise law was finally passed, but it did not prevent some Fatah members from fighting each other over slots (not just metaphorically; gunfire broke out) and others from running as independents (hopelessly fracturing the Fatah vote in some districts). The result was to turn a narrow and largely unexpected Hamas plurality into a landslide parliamentary majority. A similar set of missteps helped lead to the strong showing of the Brotherhood in Egypt's 2005 parliamentary elections (with an electoral system constructed partly by court decisions that insisted on allowing independents to run as well as mandating judicial supervision of balloting). Egypt's rulers were saved from defeat only by the Brotherhood's self-restraint and their own shamelessness—both of them in generous supply—as they called out security forces to beat back potential voters.

Can such accidents and miscalculations lead to a victory by an Islamist opposition and thus a sudden democratic transformation in an Arab political system? Usually not. Three conditions would have to be met for such an electoral result. First, an Islamist movement would have to seek a majority (or at least a blocking minority sufficient to demand a significant share of governing power) or join a broad coalition that sought a majority. But Islamist movements generally run to lose, at least over the short term, by running candidates for only a minority of seats.

Second, the regime would have to accept the outcome. In 2005 in Egypt, the regime intervened heavily in later stages of voting in order to minimize Brotherhood success. In 2006, Fatah loosened its grip on power momentarily but soon reversed itself, seeking to overturn the electoral outcome. Islamists' capacity for learning has encouraged them to expect such a reaction and to seek to forestall it by forswearing victory in advance. The Algerian coup of 1992 that prevented a certain Islamist victory and the aftermath of the Palestinian elections of 2006 are often cited by Islamist leaders in the region as evidence that they should not expect to be allowed to enjoy victory anytime soon.

Third, in some countries, international acquiescence would be necessary to cement a democratic breakthrough. In unusual cases, international support is absolutely critical in instituting or undermining democracy. The restoration of the Kuwaiti parliament in 1992 came after an American insistence was communicated to the ruling family. In the Palestinian case, with the Palestinian Authority's diplomatic and fiscal dependency on non-Palestinian actors, the international attitude (chiefly in the American and Israeli governments but also in key European governments) was critical in bringing the system to civil war rather than democratic breakthrough. In other cases, the international attitude is less critical but still notable. The Algerian coup of 1992 received tacit international endorsement. And the 2005 Egyptian elections were more open in part because of an unprecedented level of international attention.

Only after such conditions are met does it make sense to ask about the intentions of an Islamist party if it won. In the previous chapter, we examined the conditions encouraging Islamist evolution and the possibility for ideological evolution in favor of democracy. An Islamist movement that has been schooled in political patience, coalition building, and iterated elections through a period of semiauthoritarianism will likely make the adjustment to accepting democratic outcomes more easily than one that experiences democratic victory with little experience in democratic politics; certainly we have seen that the frustrations and limitations of semiauthoritarian politics can make democracy loom larger in the rhetoric and political priorities of Islamist groups that are convinced that they represent a potential majority.

A democratic outcome in such a setting depends not simply on Islamist intentions but also on the existence of robust institutions that can function throughout a period of transition. A neutral election commission, a strong and autonomous court system, professionalized and nonpartisan security forces, and a well-established set of parliamentary practices are likely to emerge as critical in ensuring that democratic elections are repeated, and such features are poorly developed or robbed of meaning in a semiauthoritarian context.

The lesson we learned about Egypt's 2011 revolution holds more broadly. The choices made and the patterns that emerge under semiauthoritarianism may be just as important as the ideology of an Islamist movement for determining the viability of democracy. Islamists might be able to facilitate admittedly unlikely routes to democracy by well-timed and clear organizational and ideological commitments. But they are unlikely to drive that process—they are more inclined to hedge their bets because these paths are unlikely.

Democratic Evolution

There is a second path to democratization of semiauthoritarian regimes, one that depends less on a disastrous miscalculation by short-sighted rulers and more on an accumulation of evolutionary changes that ultimately allows the cardinal rule of semiauthoritarian politics (the opposition loses) to be broken. Indeed, such evolutionary paths have attracted more sustained attention from scholars, and their past work can guide our inquiry. They point to two possible routes to gradual democratic transition in which Islamists could play a leading role.

First, disunity within a regime combined with a moderate opposition can lead to democratization by steps culminating in a pact between authoritarian rulers and democratic opposition. At least that is the conclusion of the first generation of scholars studying the breakdown of authoritarian regimes in southern Europe and South America in the 1970s and 1980s.[2] While most of these regimes were fully authoritarian, some (such as Brazil's) were actually semiauthoritarian in

---

2. A large scholarly literature developed on this subject; the most influential work was also one of the first: Guillermo O'Donnell, Philippe C. Schmitter, and Laurence Whitehead, *Transitions from Authoritarian Rule: Tentative Conclusions about Uncertain Democracies* (Baltimore: Johns Hopkins University Press, 1986).

that they allowed some pluralism in the political system. But whether fully authoritarian or semiauthoritarian, these regimes contained different tendencies within their highest levels, with some elements friendlier to limited liberalization (softliners) and others insisting that any opening would weaken the system (hardliners). There was nothing inevitable about the breakdown of such an authoritarian regime, nor would such a breakdown, if it occurred, inevitably lead to a democratic outcome. But if far less than inevitable, one possible path would be a rapprochement between softliners in a regime and those within the opposition (moderates) willing to give some sort of guarantees to the softliners (perhaps to protect certain persons and institutions or to drop radical demands for property redistribution).

The problem for Islamist movements in the Arab world is that they can find few softliners in the regime. Nor can the Islamist opposition easily play its part by sending cooperative signals: the sorts of assurances that oppositions offered to prove "moderation" in other regions are ones that threaten the semiauthoritarian regimes of the Arab world. Any sign that the Islamist opposition leaders are willing to commit fully to politics, to drop or postpone radical demands, or to move toward softer if vague ideological positions suggest a wish to participate in governing. Such steps worry rather than reassure Arab rulers. Chapters 6 and 7 showed that Islamists generally (if gradually and unwillingly) go as far in offering such assurances as semiauthoritarian politics encourages them to do. And they are discouraged from going too far. The real assurance that Islamists can give regimes—and that they generally do give far too easily for would-be democratizers—is to lose elections. That hardly seems like a promising start for a democratic transition.

Softliners may not be completely absent from Arab politics. Arab semiauthoritarian regimes tend to be more opaque in their internal deliberations than Islamist movements, but there often is evidence of a quiet tussle between those who favor more political strategies—enticing Islamist movements into the system, co-opting some leaders, using more cooperative ones to tame and discipline radicals—and those who regard Islamist movements as a security threat. The first group might be seen as a functional equivalent of softliners. In Palestine, such an approach prevailed at times under both Yasser Arafat and Mahmoud 'Abbas; in Kuwait and (especially before the mid-1990s) in Jordan, the regime has sometimes worked to bring Islamists into the fold. But even in these cases, an essential contribution Islamists can make is to show clear willingness to accept subordinate status for the indefinite future (whether they harbor dreams of eventual rule matters far less than whether they are willing to accept a smattering of seats and maybe an occasional social-service ministry). Reaching such understandings becomes more difficult the more powerful the Islamists become. Thus, while such incorporation could conceivably be the beginning of an evolutionary path toward democratic contestation, it has not led that way yet in any Arab country.

There is a second evolutionary path to democratic transition probed by scholars of electoral authoritarianism (a variety of authoritarianism that features regular elections, limited contestation, and domination by a single party—and thus bears a resemblance to semiauthoritarianism).[3] This path depends on a slow change in the position and role of the ruling party. By a series of incremental steps, the dominant party might construct an electoral process over which it loses control. The paradigmatic case for such a process is Mexico, governed by the Institutional Revolutionary Party (PRI) for over seventy years. Two influential studies of the PRI's operation of electoral authoritarianism and its eventual defeat at the polls (one by Beatriz Magaloni and the other by Kenneth F. Greene[4]) differ in some details but tell generally complementary stories that may be suggestive for the Arab world. Taken together, they show how the PRI piled up large electoral majorities not simply to govern (for a long time, the party garnered far more votes than it needed to win) but to project its invincibility and fracture the opposition, dividing it into a group of motivated and highly ideological niche parties that were ill-prepared to present programs attractive to large shares of the electorate. Building a successful patronage machine allowed the PRI not merely to manage governance on a daily basis but also to control overall constitutional structures; it also allowed the PRI to maintain internal coherence and thus succession; finally, it drove the opposition into electoral ghettos. Electoral fraud was hardly necessary to maintain the system in normal circumstances, but it enhanced overwhelming vote totals or perhaps served as a tool of last resort. Over time, however, economic liberalization (stressed by Greene) robbed the PRI of some of the resources necessary to maintain the patronage machine; Magaloni explores not only economic problems but also some side effects of prosperity (voters more receptive to ideological appeals) and institutional change (the creation of a neutral election administration, which ultimately oversaw the PRI's undoing by depriving it of the ability to use fraud as a last resort). Opposition leaders not only found incentives for coordination as the PRI's hold on the system wavered. They also responded effectively to the new opportunities, expanding out of their narrow ideological niches and recasting themselves as broad, catchall parties.

---

3. Indeed, Beatriz Magaloni defines her subject as "hegemonic party autocracy," which is a "system in which one political party remains in office uninterruptedly under semi-authoritarian conditions while holding regular multiparty elections." *Voting for Autocracy: Hegemonic Party Survival and Its Demise in Mexico* (Cambridge: Cambridge University Press, 2006), p. 32.

4. Magaloni, *Voting for Autocracy*, and Kenneth F. Greene, *Why Dominant Parties Lose: Mexico's Democratization in Comparative Perspective* (New York: Cambridge University Press, 2007).

Could ruling parties preside over a similar process in the semiauthoritarian systems of the Arab world? Might the self-sustaining regimes find that the mechanisms they craft are slowly slipping from their control; that either social changes stemming from economic growth or deep grievances stemming from poor economic performance are leading to more demanding electorates; that economic liberalization deprives them of patronage tools; that a few constitutional concessions (an independent election commission, for instance) make electoral defeat a real possibility? Might opposition groups learn to coordinate and discover opportunities to reinvent themselves as broad, catchall parties?

Perhaps, but again, probably not. To be sure, the portrait of dominant or hegemonic party autocracies looks quite similar to some Arab political systems (chiefly the republics): regimes that have long lost their ideological or revolutionary élan but have not decayed in their ability to present themselves as inevitable; the piling up of huge majorities based on patronage networks; quarrelsome opposition parties squirreled away in electoral ghettos armed with pure ideologies but bereft for now of means to appeal to most of the electorate; would-be opposition leaders co-opted for the present by regimes that seem unassailable; and dominant parties that manage to skirt internal fractures. The pressures of economic liberalization as well as the state's declining ability to offer ruling parties seemingly limitless patronage resources could threaten the smooth operation of such a system.

Nevertheless, slow transformation of the electoral machinery dominated by a ruling party seems an unlikely path for the Arab world. Ruling parties and electoral machinery exist, but they seem far less critical to the maintenance of the systems. No Arab regime has produced a political entity like Mexico's PRI in its centrality to the political system.[5] Nor has any shown much willingness to consider the sort of constitutional concessions the PRI eventually made.

Some are monarchies and have not even tried. They are structured quite differently and have simply found no need to create a dominant party—in this book, Kuwait and Jordan fit squarely in this category.[6] The Jordanian king and the Kuwaiti ruling family do not participate in elections, so they have hardly

---

5. For another account of how Arab political institutions have been structured to ensure stability and contain or co-opt the opposition, see Ellen Lust-Okar, *Structuring Conflict in the Arab World: Incumbents, Opponents, and Institutions* (Cambridge: Cambridge University Press, 2005).

6. The monarchies of the Arabian peninsula are dominated by ruling families, which Michael Herb has argued is a particularly stable monarchical form since it is unlikely to generate major internal divisions. See his *All in the Family: Absolutism, Revolution, and Democracy in the Middle Eastern Monarchies* (Albany: State University of New York Press, 1999). In this sense, a ruling family might offer all the benefits of the hegemonic party (when the hegemonic party works well) without the danger that the democratic institutions operating on paper will actually come to life.

built a system that would allow for their eventual electoral defeat. Monarchical regimes have kept the opposition atomized and partially co-opted; critical state institutions operate outside constitutional channels. Thus the sort of institutional evolution that facilitated the gradual transformation of Mexican paper democracy into a viable democratic system seems far less likely.

By contrast, most Arab republics have built dominant political parties that resemble the PRI on paper but not in practice. Dominant parties in the Arab world remain highly personalized and do not have the PRI's ability to change leaders regularly. Presidents often produce parties rather than the other way around. This makes moments of succession far more critical affairs—and indeed, in one of the cases studied here (Palestine), the governing party floundered badly and began to decay after its founder's death. But those regimes that weather such moments generally do not find the party a crucial structure in shaping the regime or in managing the transition; they are more likely to wait to ascertain the new ruler's bidding. As with the monarchies (though often less blatantly), critical state and constitutional structures are placed beyond contestation; parties are dominated by the head of state.

Most semiauthoritarian regimes in the Arab world have proven stable thus far in the sense that they have managed to run in place and, despite the constant potential for miscalculation, have corrected for short-term errors. They are not immune from fiscal pressures, the slow effects of uneven economic liberalization, international conflicts, and sometimes domestic disturbance and even insurgency. But these problems are not likely to produce a gradual loosening of their authoritarian nature or a slow emergence of a broad and viable opposition, nor are they likely to breathe life into moribund constitutional procedures. Instead, they have been more likely to lead regimes that either collapse or retreat into fuller authoritarianism, less impeded by established procedures or institutional obstacles.

Where do Islamist movements fit in this speculation about gradual democratization? Overall, Islamists seem willing to consider playing the part either path would demand of them—but because neither path is likely, they still seek to hedge their bets.

The first path, of negotiating a pact with regime softliners, would demand that Islamists actually give guarantees that they generally hint at giving. The second path, of transition through dominant party decay and activation of dormant constitutional mechanisms, demands that they be willing to recast themselves as catchall parties, which they have explored. But while they have shown some interest in playing the necessary parts, they are unlikely to commit fully to one under semiauthoritarian conditions. Motivated by a general reform and a specifically Islamic vision rather than any strategy that prioritizes or hinges on democratization, the movements generally prefer to protect their organizations rather than make risky bets on systemic change.

Should existing rulers face problems, we should not expect sudden or gradual transformation; instead, the most likely outcome is for feckless regimes to soldier on, fragmented oppositions to bicker, and Islamist movements to dither. And if feckless regimes falter in their semiauthoritarian ways, we are more likely to see them lapse back into full authoritarianism or collapse suddenly than gradually transform themselves.

If Arab political systems are to become more democratic, Islamist movements may do their part, but they are hardly likely to be the engine of transformation.

Islamist Movements and Prospects for Democratization of the Society

All our focus thus far has been on democracy in the institutional sense of the term: that is, democracy understood as a political system in which senior positions of authority and major policy directions are determined as a result of competitive elections with widespread suffrage. There is a strong reason that many scholars have followed such a conception of democracy: it is analytically clear and makes it fairly easy to determine whether a system is democratic or how democratic it is. Political analysis is aided by clear categories.

Yet there are other connotations to democracy that an analytically precise political definition does not capture—connotations that are deeply associated with the history of the concept and that resonate (especially normatively) with the way the term is used, both in the Arab world and outside it. We must introduce such connotations with care. We will indeed find that exploring them will yield real insight. But there is reason for social scientists to hesitate before introducing the normative connotations of democracy into political analysis. The oft-repeated cliché about the relationship between elections and democracy—that "democracy is more than elections"—creates deep problems for such analysis. While it captures the reality of nondemocratic elections, the cliché threatens to discard the shred of conceptual clarity still contained in the word "democracy." The claim that democracy is more than elections is too often followed by associating it with a shopping list of all sorts of fashionable procedures and laudatory values from speech guarantees to property rights to tolerance. If democracy is quite literally to be defined by everything in politics that is deemed good, it is clear why we like it so much. But how is any analytical content left in the term?

We will attempt to be more precise here in using two different senses of the term, but neither one will have the analytical clarity of definitions of democracy that center on fair, meaningful, and participatory elections. First, democracy can be—and in fact is—often seen as a mode of governing that is responsive to public discussion. Second, it can refer to a manner of interaction in the broader society that minimizes domination. In using each of these two concepts in turn, we are exploring terrain that is much swampier than the clear procedural conceptions of democracy, but we are also moving to understand democratic practice in a way that often means more to the people trying to engage in it.

When we move, as these more normatively informed definitions suggest we do, from a focus on state structure to an interest in social practice, what do we find out about the role of Islamists? Islamist movements are unlikely to be either the chief obstacle or the major engine of democratization in the institutional sense. But what will be their effect on the democratic nature of society? In other words, even if Islamists are unlikely to make the state operate in a democratic manner, might they make the society more democratic in spirit by fostering public discussion and undermining domination? Will they encourage democratic discussion? Will they inhibit relations of inequality and domination?

Yes, in some ways, but not in others. Shifting our conception of democracy in this way will yield some surprisingly positive though still quite mixed findings.

Democracy as Discussion

Stephen Holmes has defined democracy as "government by public discussion, not simply enforcement of the will of the majority."[7] This conception of democracy certainly draws on some classical elements. The emphasis on governance by public deliberation and debate was part of democracy from the time the term was invented, and in ancient and medieval city-states, democrats were often suspicious of delegating authority to elected leaders, preferring to reserve authority to the entire popular assembly and designating leaders when necessary by drawing lots.

Nor does democracy as discussion simply draw on historical curiosities; it has resonance in the Arab world. In a region in which the institutional mechanisms of majority rule have been carefully structured primarily to reproduce the sound of the ruler's voice, there is real advantage in focusing on free discussion rather than formal institutions. Lisa Wedeen has written of the Yemeni practice of small social gatherings known as "*qat* chews" as "a key place where people are able to exchange conceptions of fair and free elections, while also deliberating about how to respond to the rigging. That exchange and deliberation are the very substance

---

7. Stephen Holmes, "Precommitment and the Paradox of Democracy," in *Constitutionalism and Democracy*, ed. Jon Elster and Rune Slagstad (Cambridge: Cambridge University Press, 1993), p. 233.

of both the development and practice of democracy." She observes that "everyday practices of political participation operate in a context in which, since the civil war, the electoral process has come to be seen by many ordinary citizens, at least until quite recently, as a way of containing popular populist politics, rather than enabling its expression."[8]

Democracy as government by public discussion fits surprisingly well with part of the project of Islamist groups on the Brotherhood model. Engaged in society, such groups see one of their main tasks as promoting discussion about public issues consistent with Islamic teachings; this is at the core of their conception of an "Islamic frame of reference." Stacey Philbrick Yadav has even defined Islamists "as actors who seek to transform the terms of public debate."[9] If Islamist movements are comfortable operating within this conception of democracy, do they promote it?

When we see democracy as government by public discussion, we find that Islamist movements operating in a semiauthoritarian context push the society (and even the polity) in a more democratic direction in three areas: where public discussion takes place, who takes part, and how it is conducted.

First, as for location, Islamist movements push societies in a democratic direction even under semiauthoritarian conditions by opening spaces for discussion on public issues—and perhaps more importantly by forging linkages among various public spheres. This is most obviously the case in the realm of media: while many state-dominated print and broadcast media are closed to views not sanctioned by the regime, Islamist movements have been influential in satellite media, internet, and social networking technologies. But Islamist publicity is hardly restricted to virtual realms. By participating in and encouraging the emergence of a broad array of social organizations in the religious, educational, charitable, and service realms, Islamists have moved into areas that were dominated by states in a previous era. As states have jettisoned their social service commitments under fiscal pressure, Islamist movements have been part of efforts to organize society in a way to ensure that basic health, educational, and other needs are met. While these efforts are often only loosely linked, and sometimes are better seen as grassroots and middle-class self-help projects than as charitable projects, many are still associated with the general Islamist vision.[10] By connecting them, however

8. Lisa Wedeen, *Peripheral Visions: Publics, Power, and Performance in Yemen* (Chicago: University of Chicago Press, 2008), p. 140.

9. Stacey Philbrick Yadav, "Understanding 'What Islamists Want': Public Debate and Contestation in Lebanon and Yemen," *Middle East Journal* 64, no. 2 (2010), 200.

10. See Janine A. Clark, *Islam, Charity, and Activism: Middle-Class Networks and Social Welfare in Egypt, Jordan, and Yemen* (Bloomington: Indiana University Press, 2004).

loosely, to a broad social movement, Islamists have helped such groups form the kernel of a civil society. As Asef Bayat has written, "The very operation of a social movement is itself a change, since it involves creating new social formations, groups, networks, and relationships."[11]

Second, on the identity of the participants in discussions, Islamist movements have often brought members of the middle class, young professionals, students, and societal leaders directly into public deliberations for the first time. They have promoted forms of political and social discourse that focus on public-spiritedness and virtue in societies where cynicism has deep roots; in doing so, they have worked to create an environment in which arguments made in terms of the public interest will find greater purchase.

Finally, as far as the mode of public discussion is concerned, Islamist movements pride themselves on a disciplined and calm speaking style with all interlocutors. While quite capable of giving fiery speeches to their own ranks, Islamist movement leaders direct their followers to speak gently and rationally with opponents. However much their members might sometimes slip from the ideal, Islamist movements present themselves as the face of rectitude and reason, persuasion and self-possession, composure and calmness—not hectoring and threats. One young member of the Egyptian Muslim Brotherhood even referred to those who argue in an angry or irritable (*mitnarviz*) manner as un-Islamic or ignorant (*jahili*) in their conduct. In one training session for Hadas poll workers I attended shortly before the 2008 parliamentary elections in Kuwait, the main speaker gave the party stalwarts a series of suggestions on how to help their party on election day; some had to do with patience and perseverance, and others had to do with self-discipline and presenting a good image: "Mention the name of God" if you find your energy flagging; "Bring a Snickers bar" for when you get hungry; and "Smile!" to make a good impression.

Semiauthoritarian politics has not only allowed Islamists to pursue democratization in public; it has also nudged their internal practices in a democratic direction in three ways. First, it often allows them to operate openly and therefore practice the same kind of internal deliberations that they call for externally. Movements that are fully or even partially underground are necessarily opaque; the relative freedom of semiauthoritarianism has made the movements more democratic internally.

Second, semiauthoritarian politics encourages Islamist movements to reach out to new groups—most notably women. The women's organizations associated

---

11. Asef Bayat, *Making Islam Democratic: Social Movements and the Post-Islamist Turn* (Stanford, Calif.: Stanford University Press, 2007), p. 195.

with Islamist movements have not been particularly influential within the overall body, but their prominence grows along with political participation (and the need to mobilize female supporters to vote). This was most dramatically the case in Kuwait, where the necessity of forming a women's electoral arm brought new female activists into the organization and changed the public face of the movement. Hadas did not introduce women to Kuwaiti public life (and in some ways obstructed their entrance), but once a decision to extend political rights to women was made, the party embraced the development.

Finally, semiauthoritarian politics encourages Islamists to reach out and form alliances with non-Islamist groups. The effects of such engagement are uneven, but under some conditions it entails not merely tactical cooperation but also a greater tolerance for other ideological orientations.[12]

This rosy picture needs two very strong qualifications, however. While Islamist movements might promote (and profit by) public discussion, the effects are not wholly positive. First, their move into politics—and into politics that takes an oppositional form—can promote a backlash from semiauthoritarian regimes worried that the new spaces the movements open up and the links they build are ultimately threatening. The organizational flexibility of Islamist movements and the consequent difficulty of distinguishing where the movements begin and end have led semiauthoritarian regimes to launch crackdowns precisely on those democratic spaces that Islamists have pried open—professional associations in Egypt, a leading Islamic NGO in Jordan, a budding dissident teachers union in Palestine.

It may seem unfair to burden Islamists with the blame for the measures taken against them, but it is possible that a less oppositional approach might prove more democratizing in the long term. Berna Turam's study of the Turkish Gulen movement makes this argument. She suggests that the Gulen movement may aid democracy less by the beliefs it promotes than by strengthening the society in a way that engages rather than confronts or isolates the state:

> I have argued that Islam's major contribution to democratization has not been Islamic horizontal networking. I have highlighted the illiberal and authoritarian tendencies of the projects in which Islamist actors actively participate. I have also argued that although Islamic parties' participation in procedural democracy has played a role in their moderation, the major contribution of moderate Islamic actors has been

---

12. On this issue more generally, see Jillian Schwedler, *Faith in Moderation: Islamist Parties in Jordan and Yemen* (Cambridge: Cambridge University Press, 2006).

prepared by their unintended engagements with the state in everyday sites. The moderate Islamic actors have formed alternative vertical channels between society and the state.... The key to the flourishing of these alternative vertical patterns is clearly the non-confrontational social actors, who have the potential to make sporadic changes in authoritarianism without threatening the system. Although largely neglected so far, non-confrontation is the major characteristic of engagement and potential transition from authoritarian rule in the Middle East.[13]

While the Turkish AKP is often cited as a model for a politically engaged conservative party with Islamist roots, Turam's suggestion is that the democratization of Turkish society has been accomplished by less explicitly political actors. Seen this way, Islamist movements in the Arab world might have to choose whether to emphasize political democratization now or social democratization over the long term.

A second serious qualification to Islamist promotion of democratization as discussion has to do with a possible blind spot in emphasizing deliberation and public debate. Democracy seen as government by public discussion often has two sharp limitations: such discussion is rarely egalitarian in practice, and it privileges certain kinds of arguments over others. Enthusiasm for public deliberation and discussion often leads its advocates to overlook the vast disparities in access to various public spheres and in the ability to cultivate the necessary skills for plunging into public debates. Advocates of deliberative democracy do not always avoid snobbery. And an emphasis on deliberation and discussion often assumes that there is a common interest, or an overriding public interest, that all participants share. It becomes more difficult to practice when there is a plurality of interests or if one assumes the absence rather than the presence of overriding truths. If we share little, then there may be much to haggle over but there is much less to deliberate about.

Both of these blind spots can be turned against the Islamist virtues in the realm of democratization by discussion. In terms of exclusionary tendency, Islamist movements certainly have given greater voices to devout male Muslims and can lean toward a more paternalistic than egalitarian view of participation. In Islamist politics, it may seem that not all voices have equal value. In terms of the assumption of a common interest, Islamists often find themselves confronted with the criticism not simply that they assume a single interest but that they identify it with God's will, leaving them with poor tools to distinguish among

---

13. Berna Turam, *Between Islam and the State: The Politics of Engagement* (Stanford, Calif.: Stanford University Press, 2007), p. 156.

genuine differences in material interests, arguments over interpretation, and impiety. And while they generally steer quite clear of accusations of apostasy, it sometimes seems that the reluctance to do so is more the product of polite manners than pluralist commitments. Islamist politics, in this view, silences voices that cannot cast their views in religious terms. In matters Islamist, when all arguments are turned up, religious ones are trump.

In short, Islamist movements are suspect on a different kind of democratic ground: as good as they may be on balance for deliberation, do they also allow for a large measure of domination?

Democracy and Domination

Democracy has always been associated with equality, and some connection with equality remains central to its appeal. While not demanding a total equality of all members in all respects, a society is more democratic to the extent that it is able to ensure that all voices be considered equally, that all have equal claims on public decision making, and that inequalities and hierarchies, when they arise, as they inevitably will, not simply serve the interest of the dominant. Democratic societies are inclined to be wary of situations in which members cannot speak in their own voice but must have others serve as trustees. Democracy, seen this way, is not simply about equality but also about suspicion of domination. Ian Shapiro, a political theorist who has argued forcefully for the view of democracy as nondomination, writes:

> Rather than think of democracy as a mechanism for institutionalizing the general will, we should recognize its claim to our allegiance as the best available system for managing power relations among people who disagree about the nature of the common good, among many other things, but who nonetheless are bound to live together. To be sure, this view rests on a conception of the common good. But it is a comparatively thin one, best captured by the formulation that it embodies what those with an interest in avoiding domination share.
>
> Indeed, the possibility of diminishing—if not eradicating—domination is often what draws people to democracy. Confronted with the injustices of apartheid or totalitarian communism, they turn to democracy as the instrument of their emancipation because of its constitutive commitment to nondomination.[14]

---

14. Ian Shapiro, *The State of Democratic Theory* (Princeton, N.J.: Princeton University Press, 2003), pp. 146–147.

Shapiro's description of democracy is one that might make Islamist movements uncomfortable despite their "participation, not domination" refrain. They fall short on democracy as nondomination in four respects. But if their own orientation is not fully democratic, the experience of surviving in an authoritarian environment and moving into a semiauthoritarian one has made Islamist movements more democratic.

The first problem from the perspective of domination is that Islamist movements can be exclusionary: they have problems treating non-Muslims as full civic equals. Non-Muslims might receive strong legal protections and be accorded a significant measure of autonomy in the preferred Islamist order, but that falls short of civic equality. But here it must also be noted that the various Islamist movements operating under semiauthoritarianism in the Arab world have greatly increased their (admittedly sometimes vague) embrace of the concept of citizenship, which can provide avenues for more democratic conceptions of the place of non-Muslims.

Second, Islamist movements can often take on a fairly paternalistic attitude; Shapiro's democrats are much more suspicious of the ability of some members of a society to speak for others. The issue is most acute with gender: Islamist movements often embrace a view of family relations that places some of the burden for public representation on adult males. They do not regard women and minors as bereft of individuality or rights, but they sometimes incline to a view that places adult men in a position that might resemble trusteeship. Jasim al-Mihalhal, one of the founders of Kuwait's Hadas, has written of the political benefits of democracy but also its inappropriateness when applied to raising youth; his image of family life is far more paternalistic and hierarchical than his vision of the proper political order.[15]

Again, however, we see some signs of evolution. Islamist movements have not led societies toward incorporating a strong public role for women, but they have sometimes accommodated themselves to it. Outside of family relations, Islamist movements have actually evolved away from paternalism: those who wield authority are held responsible to meet the needs of those subordinate to them. But in the past, such responsibility was often to be met through fostering moral rectitude among leaders rather than seeking the direct consent of the governed. Islamist rhetoric that criticizes existing Arab regimes has often been based on the view that rulers and high officials use authority for their own interest rather than regard it as a social trust. In recent years, however, Islamist movements have increasingly turned to a more specifically democratic critique of regimes. Cor-

---

15. See his lengthy commentary in *al-Watan*, 18 April 2010.

ruption and abuse of authority still figure prominently, but the theme that rulers ignore not merely the needs but also the voices of citizens has become more significant in Islamist political rhetoric.

Third, Islamists embrace state authority a bit too enthusiastically from the perspective of nondomination. Those who regard democracy as a refuge from domination do not eschew state authority, of course, and many would see it properly used as a tremendous weapon to disrupt or correct relationships of domination. But Islamists would sometimes use state authority to enforce moral teachings and limit cultural production offensive to religious values. In a sense, the problem here from a democratic perspective is that the movements' reform agenda is overly broad. Again, it cannot be stressed too much that the Islamist movements studied here have a very ambitious conception of reform. They have deep criticisms of existing regimes but would prefer to redirect rather than remake the state. And in their eyes, the state should be directed toward more sustained promotion of Islamic values.

Finally, Islamist movements tend to have a more robust and ambitious conception of the public good than the minimal one that Shapiro describes. The traditional distrust of partisanship has been discarded, but the underlying attitude—that the community has an overriding interest that should not be lost in the clash of individual and group interests—remains very strong.

Yet in all these areas, subjugation by authoritarian regimes followed by political participation in semiauthoritarian systems seems to have nudged Islamist movements in a democratic direction. Authoritarianism brought home to Islamist leaders how brutal nondemocratic domination can be; semiauthoritarianism can frustrate them with limitations on the democratic process. Egypt is probably the clearest case here; it is unusual to have an extended discussion with a leader of the Muslim Brotherhood without a reference to the group's long experience with official repression and domination. Skepticism of domination has begun to loom larger in Islamist thought and practice, even in the social and personal spheres.

As with many of the changes in Islamist movements described earlier in this book, movement here is slow, general, and reversible. But as semiauthoritarianism has provided limited openings for them, they have generally become more welcoming of inclusive ideas of citizenship, more willing to allow women to play a role in public life, and more supportive of democratic voices and debate, and sometimes even less insistent on state policing of cultural production.

What of coming to terms with pluralism in the full sense of the term? In this regard, it may be best to turn to the choices outlined by Robert Hefner in democratizing Indonesia:

Traditions laying claim to ultimate meanings face a common dilemma: how to maintain a steadied worldview and social engagement while acknowledging the pluralism of the age.

One response to this predicament, a repressively organic one, is to strap on the body armor, ready one's weapons, and launch a holy war for society as a whole. In today's world of bureaucratic leviathans, this option typically involves the seizure of the state and, from there, the forced imposition of organic unity on an inorganic social body. . . .

A second strategy for religion's reformation renounces organic totalism for separatist sectarianism. Like the Essenes of ancient Israel under Roman rule, proponents of this option take refuge in the uncompromised purity of small circles of believers. . . .

There is a third option for a refigured religion, a civil one. Rather than state conquest or separatist isolation, this approach accepts the diversity of public voices, acknowledging that this is, in some sense, the nature of modern things. What follows after this varies widely, but the underlying pluralist premise remains. The civil option may promote *public* religion, but distanced from the coercive machinery of the state. It strides proudly into the public arena but insists that its message is clearest when its bearers guard their independence.[16]

The Islamist movements studied here rejected the first two paths—seizure of the state or retreat from the society—a generation ago, leaving them for radicals and salafis. But they have only begun grappling with the possibilities raised by the third path of civil religion.

---

16. Robert W. Hefner, *Civil Islam: Muslims and Democratization in Indonesia* (Princeton, N.J.: Princeton University Press, 2000), pp. 219–220.

ISLAMIST PARTIES AND ARAB POLITICAL SYSTEMS AS THEY ARE

Shortly after Hamas won the Palestinian parliamentary elections of January 2006, the leader of the Islamic Action Front's parliamentary bloc startled his fellow Jordanians by suggesting that the results could be repeated in Jordan. Not only did he state that under a fair law "Islamists in Jordan would obtain a majority"; he also asserted that they were "prepared to assume control over the executive branch to realize the hopes of the people."[1] A proclamation by an opposition politician that his party was prepared to win and govern would hardly elicit mention in a democratic system. In Jordan, full fidelity to the constitution and the principles of parliamentary democracy amounted to a threat. The regime's interpretation of the remark—that hoping for electoral victory was tantamount to sedition—made IAF leaders backpedal quickly. A few months later, when I asked whether the IAF would run a full slate of candidates in the next parliamentary elections, one prominent leader of the Muslim Brotherhood responded, "We will not repeat the disaster of Hamas."[2] No longer did the party claim to be "prepared" for victory or notify others that they should prepare themselves for an Islamist electoral majority.

---

1. "Islamists of Jordan: Prepared to Assume Authority," *Islam On Line,* 29 January 2006.
2. Na'il al-Musalha, personal interview, Amman, 5 July 2006.

The Effects of Playing by (and Testing) the Rules

Let us begin by reviewing what we have found. Over time, increased opportunities for political participation afforded by semiauthoritarianism will lead a movement to devote more resources to politics. Moving from full to semiauthoritarianism has real effects on Islamist movements. Within each case, we saw clear effects as the system became clearly semiauthoritarian.

And we saw that variation within semiauthoritarianism has effects as well: the response of Islamist movements to semiauthoritarian opportunities is stronger as the systems become more open and when that openness becomes more reliable and sustained. Greater freedom to speak, write, organize, and mobilize lead to more organizational and ideological adaptation by Islamist movements; enshrining those freedoms in clear laws, explicit agreements, and constitutions, or allowing them to continue over time, have a similar result. Constrictions on speaking, writing, organization, and mobilization—or unpredictable or frequent changes—lead to far more guarded responses.

The changes come slowly and unevenly, but they do come. Perhaps more significantly, we have discovered that there are limits to the organizational and ideological effects of semiauthoritarian participation.

Organizationally, a movement enticed and coaxed into running in elections will devote resources to politics, strive to fulfill legal requirements, develop political skills, and allow political leaders in the movement the support and autonomy they need to take full advantage of the political opening, but within limits. Islamist movements will create a party, accord the campaign managers considerable autonomy over writing a platform and selecting candidates, and allow MPs wide leeway in forming a parliamentary agenda and selecting issues for emphasis. But that is as far as they will go: they will not allow the parties full organizational autonomy (except in a formal sense, if required by law); the movements will generally keep a finger (or much more) in selecting the leadership of the party; movement leaders will not allow campaign managers or party leaders the authority to decide the scale of participation; the movements will insist they have a role in determining critical matters (such as whether to enter the cabinet); and while they may allow party strategists and parliamentary leaders freedom to mold platforms and parliamentary agendas, they will do so within bounds established by the movement. Politicization has deep organizational effects; it fosters the development of new leaders with new skills and shorter time horizons. Knowing that, movements will allow politicization to work some of its effects but not to run its full course. The gain for doing so would be too modest.

Ideologically, semiauthoritarian participation will similarly entice and coax movements into real changes, but most of those changes will be general in nature. Movements will feel free to explore and hint at all sorts of ideological development, but they will be far stingier with clear and specific ideological commitments. They will seek to assure those concerned with civil and political rights and freedoms (having a far easier time with political than other rights) but balk at clear and specific statements disassociating the movement from widespread socially conservative practices or unambiguously repudiating elements of classical Islamic jurisprudence; they will pursue interpretations of Islam and Islamic law that emphasize its general goals and more inclusive themes without specifically disavowing more exclusionary or less liberal interpretations; they will settle most comfortably into the role of loyal opposition while they often fret and argue about possibilities for entering the cabinet in a subordinate way; and they will embrace majoritarian aspects of democracy, especially when they are convinced that they represent the majority.

Semiauthoritarian politics leads to parties that have a short leash and to sustained, but also fairly general, flirtation with liberalization of ideology. Islamists will generally run—and acknowledge, if bitterly, that for now they have to run to lose—and turn to good account what they can gain without making unalterable sacrifices for those limited gains.

We have also seen how time and regime credibility work their effects: movements respond slowly and make organizational and ideological adjustments gradually, basing their expectations on regime responses. Each step is internally debated and often contested, enhancing the jerky and sometimes ambiguous nature of Islamist evolution. Evolution is limited not only by the restrictions on semiauthoritarian politics but also by the unreliability of the openings it provides. Regimes that choose not to make credible commitments to liberalization are unlikely to find Islamist oppositions that will make the full commitment to liberalization. And some regimes feel quite content with that result: a fully politicized movement might be a more formidable opponent. The Islamist fear of commitment is based on solid reasoning—cutting off routes of retreat has a real cost, and therefore Islamist movements will not abandon them for ephemeral gains.

There is a less obvious pattern in Islamist responses that we have explored only implicitly: Islamist movements show a great capacity to learn. They do so not simply in the abstract sense of molding organization and ideology in response to their environment but also in the strict and literal sense of studying and deliberating over the lessons of their experience. Islamist movements tend to be enormously reflective: they review their performance, document their efforts and their effectiveness, and continuously study themselves. Each election is followed by a series of studies and debates; each parliamentary session is followed by an accounting and a report; each strategic decision is reviewed for lessons learned. Advice is solicited from the broad membership, from sympathetic outsiders, and even from critics and rivals. (International specialists who develop training programs often report that if their programs are open to all, Islamists are the star students.) Thus the movements are always adjusting their strategies and tactics, fine-tuning their initiatives, and recalibrating their organizations and platforms.

This capacity for learning suggests that we should add some qualifications to our general findings, specifically those having to do with the effects of time. It is true that as the political system opens, Islamist movements respond. But as we saw in Chapter 2, the trajectory of semiauthoritarian regimes is marked not by steadily increasing openness but by constant tinkering with rules, periodic renegotiations (sometimes involving rather brutal means of bargaining), imposition of shifting red lines, occasional explicit warnings, and more-than-occasional implicit warnings. Islamist movements that learn to take advantage of the openings that semiauthoritarian regimes offer will also learn that those openings are not always reliable and that there are sharp limits to what a political strategy can accomplish. Individuals within the movement learn political lessons from experience, of course, but the organizations as a whole show they do as well when they shift priorities and transfer prominence from political to nonpolitical leaders. Some movements (such as in Egypt and Kuwait) betray an odd tension as a result: as those within the movement with political interests learn political skills, the movement as a whole often learns the limits of what politics can accomplish. The result is a struggle over the extent of politicization.

No movement has yet learned that the political game is pointless. But several have learned, sometimes the hard way, the frustrations of semiauthoritarian politics. In Egypt, after four years of dealing with the harsh consequences of winning one-fifth of the seats in the 2005 parliamentary elections, the Muslim Brotherhood selected a new general guide who—even as he pledged to continue the strategy of "participation, not domination"—showed less interest and skill in politics as well as a reversion to an earlier style of addressing the head of state respectfully. The partial turn away from politics helps explain the movement's flat-footed reaction to the revolutionary upheaval that began on January 25, 2011. In Kuwait, the Islamist movement began to reconsider how much it would ever gain in a political process that offered it at best a handful of seats in a deeply divided parliament that lacked tools for positive action. Even Hamas, the movement that managed to break the defining rule of semiauthoritarian politics by winning an election, has shown signs of being uncertain of what its plunge into politics can produce.[3]

---

3. As a partially underground movement, Hamas makes fewer of its internal deliberations known than do its sister movements. But in early 2010, a flurry of speculation was set off in Arab media

Learning is not the only way for movements to shy away from politics. Islamists may pull back not only because they realize the system's limits but also because of their own limitations as their ranks are driven apart by the rapidly shifting rules. The vicissitudes of semiauthoritarianism often set off debates within the movements about how to respond. As noted in Chapter 6, Islamist movements almost never fracture over what to believe, but they argue a lot over what to do. And a semiauthoritarian environment seems to promote such arguing. This is not only because movement leaders differ in how much they value the gains and rue the costs of participation; it is also because those gains and costs do not hold still. When yesterday's safe slogan crosses today's red line, movements must constantly recalibrate their positions and actions. In Egypt and Palestine, debates occasioned by shifting opportunities have broken out in public; in Kuwait, they seem to have been contained in private but still occur. In Jordan, they have gone the farthest, becoming nasty battles that are sufficiently severe to inhibit the ability of the Islamist movement to organize and act coherently. (Since the movements value unity of ranks so highly, this has led some to look to politics with more suspicion.) When disunity reaches the point at which various factions maneuver with their eye more on each other than on the external environment—as may have happened in recent years in the Jordanian movement—the ability of Islamists to learn from and adapt to that external environment is inhibited. A similar process has been under way in recent years in Yemen, where the Islamist-dominated opposition alliance is particularly diverse.[4]

When these patterns are taken together—the insistence of semiauthoritarian regimes that they must win, the reluctance of Islamist movements to embrace politics wholeheartedly, the ability of Islamist groups to learn how to play politics better but also how to avoid playing so much, and the risks that political participation entails for movement unity—the picture is clear: semiauthoritarian politics leads to a cat-and-mouse game that can change in its details considerably without fundamentally changing in its outcomes.

Indeed, the transition to semiauthoritarianism fosters the cat-and-mouse game in an unexpected way. We have found that Islamist movements may actually take on a more consistently oppositional stance the more they are politicized within semiauthoritarian settings. The more they emphasize manifestos, electioneering, comprehensive programs, and parties and the less they emphasize

about a purported letter sent by a Hamas military commander, Ahmad al-Ja'bari, to Khalid Mish'al, the director of Hamas's political bureau in Damascus, criticizing the effects of subordinating the movement in Gaza to the control of the Hamas-led government. The text of the purported letter can be viewed at http://www.palpress.ps/arabic/index.php?maa=ReadStory&ChannelID=70672&h=%C 7%E1%CC%DA%C8%D1%ED.

4. See April Longley, "The High Water Mark of Islamist Politics? The Case of Yemen," *Middle East Journal* 61, no. 2 (2007), 240–260.

promoting piety and righteousness through example, preaching, and charity, the more they are likely to be oppositional. For similar reasons, the less ideologically anti-system they become (that is, the more they proclaim their acceptance of the political system), the more they become relationally anti-system (that is, with political positions farther away from other, less oppositional, actors in the system). In other words, enticing a movement into politics may render it a bigger political challenge. Some regimes have reacted by encouraging movements to reverse some of their politicization.

We have found as well that it is the rules of the game—rules largely set by the semiauthoritarian regimes themselves, as discussed in Chapter 2—that influence how the movements react. When Islamist movements are compared, there is often a tendency to probe the differences among them as if they stem from organizational or ideological distinctions. But our analysis suggests that such an inquiry would distract from the more important source of difference: given a broad movement that seeks a diverse set of goals, it is the rules of semiauthoritarian politics that explain much of the variation and changes in organization and ideology. Chapter 3 opened with Sa'd al-Din al-'Uthmani, of Morocco's Islamist Party of Justice and Development, attempting to compare his party to the Christian Democrats of Europe. The reason the analogy is misleading is not because of an inherent difference between Islamist and Christian movements but because Morocco has a political system very different from those in Europe. (And when European political systems were more semiauthoritarian in their operation—as most were a century ago—the similarities between Arab Islamist movements and European Christian Democratic movements seem much more striking.)

As long as the fundamental rules of semiauthoritarian politics are in place, Islamist movements will likely continue to suggest and even experiment with many things but fully commit to little in terms of an embrace of politics and democracy. There is every reason to believe that semiauthoritarian regimes prefer that situation; an Islamist movement that stressed democratic participation above everything and that threw all its organizational and ideological weight behind such a strategy would be acting in a revolutionary way. And there is little incentive for them to do so.

Other Places, Other Movements

These patterns can be seen quite clearly if we briefly examine different Islamist movements and different settings in the Arab world.

Based on what we found in these four cases, we should expect that an Islamist movement with a broad reform agenda should react to semiauthoritarian openings with organizational investments and ideological adjustments that are significant but also general and reversible. Organizationally, we would expect them to take advantage of whatever legal avenues exist but also to retain some control over political parties (if they are formed) and to reject any attempt to make them drop nonpolitical parts of their agenda. Ideologically, we would expect more general and, from both a liberal and a democratic perspective, more forthcoming statements but a reticence about specific commitments. Islamist movements without such a broad agenda will not react the same way to semiauthoritarianism.

Islamist movements that are acting in either a fully authoritarian or a democratic context should not behave this way. We would expect that movements in authoritarian settings would be less willing to mingle a significant level of political activity with other aspects of their agenda. Those in democratic settings may be far more willing to commit organizationally and ideologically to participation, but they might be a bit sluggish as residual semiauthoritarian habits recede slowly.

Coping with Semiauthoritarianism and Its Equivalents Elsewhere

An admittedly quick consideration of other cases in the Arab world suggests that Islamist movements with broad agendas act as expected in semiauthoritarian systems. In Morocco, Algeria, and Yemen, Islamist movements have been able to participate in the political system. The political systems allow political parties to form, and such party formation has taken place. But Islamist leaders have not allowed those parties full autonomy from the mother movement. (Morocco's PJD probably has the most autonomy, but even there the party has some overlap in leadership with the movement.)

Ideologically, the parties in those countries have hinted strongly but generally at ideological softening. Again, Morocco's PJD has gone the furthest in specificity, ultimately supporting a royal project to amend the country's personal status law in a manner that was controversial from the perspective of traditional Islamic jurisprudence.

The Moroccan experience is noteworthy because it shows that semiauthoritarianism explains not only the nature of the organizational and ideological adjustments but also their extent. Greater and more sustained opportunities lead to more serious and detailed adjustments. And in the first decade of the 2000s, the Moroccan regime was as welcoming as any semiauthoritarian regime is likely to be: the PJD had legal recognition, freedom to articulate its views, and relatively fair electoral administration (albeit with a complex system still stacked against the party). For a brief moment, the PJD was a rare example of a party that was poised to win an election. PJD leaders did not expect to govern Morocco in an unfettered manner, but they did hope to emerge as the largest party in the 2007 parliamentary balloting and perhaps be asked to form the cabinet. They fell short and learned precisely the lesson we would expect—that the party leaders had gone too far in ideological terms; they had sacrificed some of the enthusiasm of their core supporters in an effort to placate the regime and other political actors. In the aftermath of the election setback, and amid some internal turmoil, the party showed some signs of reconsideration and even backpedaling in its strategy. The rewards of organizational and ideological change were less than anticipated, and leaders reacted by using the routes of retreat, albeit in a limited way.

In Yemen, the Islamist movement also faced the difficult question of whether to support a coalition government in which it occupies a subordinate position—and it reacted first by joining the coalition and later by leaving it and seeking to form an opposition alliance. In Algeria, where an already fractured Islamist movement confronted a similar question, a leading Islamist party became a regular part of the governing coalition but very much in a subordinate position (and showed a great deal of internal disharmony in the process). Such a move offers a measure of protection but also risks a taming of rhetoric as well as a degree of tainting, because it forces the party to be associated with public policies it has little influence over.

Full Authoritarianism and the Responses It Provokes

What happens when broadly focused Islamist movements operate in settings that are not semiauthoritarian? We have already explored what happens to them in fully authoritarian contexts; in each of the countries covered in this book, the semiauthoritarian regime followed a fully authoritarian one. Depending on the precise circumstances, the movements may be pushed underground (as in Egypt in the 1960s and, to a lesser extent, the West Bank and Gaza under Israeli rule) or into quiescence (as in Palestinian areas in the 1950s through the 1970s, Jordan in the 1950s and 1960s, and Kuwait in the same period). In such circumstances, the movements will generally focus on self-preservation, disavowing politics temporarily if need be or restricting themselves to dabbling if that possibility seems open. The best current example of a broadly focused movement living under such circumstances is Syria's Muslim Brotherhood; it has been driven underground within Syria, and some key leaders have moved overseas. The movement has also bounced between attempting to form an alliance among expatriate opposition forces and prying its way back into open operation in the country by reaching an accommodation with the regime.[5]

On some scattered but significant occasions, the movements may opt for violent opposition. In Kuwait, the movement moved briefly into violent opposition during the equally brief Iraqi occupation; in Jordan, the movement considered enlisting in involvement in the Palestinian armed struggle but ultimately pulled back, in part because of the unfavorable domestic context and in part because of ideological conflicts with non-Islamist Palestinian movements. For Hamas, an armed wing is an essential part of the movement's organization, and resistance is central to its identity. But even in Hamas's case, the movement claims (with some but not total accuracy) to aim its guns at Israeli targets rather than Palestinian rivals. That is, in the movement's view, it is violent against an authoritarian occupier but not against a semiauthoritarian compatriot.

Coping with Democracy

If authoritarian systems suppress or contain the movements, what about democratic settings? The argument in this book would suggest that the opportunity to compete openly with the possibility of winning also opens the possibility of clear organizational and ideological commitments to democratic politics. But it suggests as well that such an opportunity would present a movement with a fundamental and very difficult choice: is it a tightly disciplined social organization or the kernel of a broad political party? The model that seems so well designed for semiauthoritarianism may not make the transition to democracy easily: it is held together by close personal bonds and a strong sense of mission and thus not well positioned to open its membership doors to the sort of mass following that full democratic politics requires.

In short, we should expect that a fully democratic system would encourage precisely the kinds of ideological and organizational commitments that semiauthoritarianism discourages, but that the road to making them might be bumpy and difficult.

Two Arab political systems, Egypt and Tunisia, may be attempting to test such predictions. Earlier, the Palestinian Authority did as well, but the rapid collapse

---

5. On the Syrian Muslim Brotherhood, see Radwan Ziyada, *Al-islam al-siyasi fi suriya* (Abu Dhabi: Emirate Center for Strategic Studies and Research, 2008); Joshua Teitelbaum, "The Muslim Brotherhood and the 'Struggle for Syria,' 1947–1958 Between Accommodation and Ideology," *Middle Eastern Studies* 40, no. 3 (2004), 134–158; and *Al-ikhwan al-muslimun fi suriya* (Dubai: Markaz al-Misbar, 2009).

of the political system allowed Hamas to escape the slow but powerful pressures of democratic politics. (And indeed, that is precisely the analysis of many Islamists—that the circumstances were simply not right for a democratic breakthrough in Palestine; neither the system nor Hamas was ready for it.)

But if the Arab world contains only embryonic test cases, some other political systems have been able to hold a series of elections in which broadly based Islamist movements have participated. Have such systems been able to entice the movements into making the specific organizational and ideological commitments that their Arab sister movements have been so reticent about under semi-authoritarian circumstances?

Yes, to an extent. The most extended experiment has come in Turkey. Organizationally, the AKP has clearly established itself as an autonomous political party; ideologically, its positions have reached the point that it is sometimes referred to as a "formerly Islamist" party or as an "Islamist-conservative coalition." The party has explicitly accepted constitutionally mandated secularism (while giving it a new meaning in the Turkish context). But those developments came over a considerable time and under the constant threat (hardly an idle one) that a variety of constitutional and extraconstitutional means would be used against a movement that did not make such clear commitments. And ironically, the AKP may have learned its lessons too well, proving so successful at participating in democratic politics that it has found itself in a position to rewrite the rules of political life in Turkey with as yet undetermined results.

Elsewhere few Islamist parties have been afflicted by too much success for their system's good.[6] In fact, in most other countries, Islamists have moved to make the organizational and ideological commitments that democratic systems encourage them to do. But they often earn lackluster rewards, making the path more difficult. One survey of Islamist parties globally found that "Islamic parties have (relative to their starting point) liberalized their stances significantly over the past several decades" but also that "the electoral performance of Islamic parties has been generally unimpressive."[7] When this happens, the party rarely folds; instead, the two roles of social movement and political party simply diverge further, each one toiling away in its separate sphere (the first working to make societies, or at least pockets within them, more Islamic; the second working for political goals consistent with Islamic teachings). Thus a more typical example than

---

6. For an optimistic treatment of the record of integration of Islamist parties—though one that, like the one offered in this book, places considerable explanatory weight on regime structure and political context—see Julie Chernov Hwang, *Peaceful Islamist Mobilization in the Muslim World: What Went Right* (New York: Palgrave Macmillan, 2009).

7. Charles Kurzman and Ijlal Naqvi, "Do Muslims Vote Islamic?" *Journal of Democracy* 21, no. 2 (2010), 57 and 52.

Turkey may be Indonesia, where a variety of Islamist parties have participated.[8] The actors closest to the Muslim Brotherhood model—a Jemaah Tarbiyah movement and the Prosperous Justice Party (PKS)—have had some success in both the social and the political realm. And the autonomous party has shown some ability to make the organizational and ideological commitments we might expect, but it has also discovered that its electoral success may have limits; the best it has been able to do is garner a larger share of what is still a definite minority of the electorate willing to support religious parties. Trapped in an electoral ghetto, movement leaders today are faced with a hard choice: do they set the party free to play the electoral game as fully as possible, knowing that the results may be meager and slow? Or do they pull back on some of their investment in the political process and emphasize other movement goals? There is some indication of discussion within the movement in precisely these terms.

Thus the experiences of broadly focused Islamist movements based on a model similar to that of the Muslim Brotherhood are heavily conditioned in their organizational and ideological commitments, as well as their general political behavior, by the contours of the political system in which they operate. In other words, the sort of analysis we undertook for movements in semiauthoritarian systems is likely to pay off, but the results are likely to be different since the political context is different.

Other Kinds of Movements

What of Islamist movements without the same broad focus? The analysis in this book suggests they will not be subject to the same temptations, quandaries, and tensions. This can be clearly seen in the case of movements that have little use for politics, most notably salafi movements in many countries. Salafi movements, stressing correct practice and careful explication of texts, regularly express disdain for Islamist movements based on the Muslim Brotherhood model for being too political; their wide agenda is, in the salafis' eyes, the road to weakness, compromise, and opportunism. Often loosely organized in a formal sense, gathered not on the basis of bylaws and cells but instead around the learning and teaching of particular specialists, most such movements show a lack of interest in the political process (with some inclined instead to jihadist approaches). In a semiauthoritarian environment, when such movements take this kind of apolitical, even quietist form, they pose little problem for the regime. And Islamist movements

---

8. Saiful Mujani and R. William Liddle, "Muslim Indonesia's Secular Democracy," *Asian Survey* 49, no. 4 (2009), 575–590.

based on the Brotherhood model—in Egypt and Jordan, for instance—regularly charge the regime with favoring their salafi rivals for precisely this reason. A group of rigid purists eschewing politics does not bother rulers. Allowed to pursue study, exegesis, and correct practice, such movements are content to build their networks and feel little pressure to create parties or recast their ideologies in order to function more effectively.

But it is interesting to note that although salafi movements indeed avoid the temptations and pressures of politics on most occasions, there have been some that have succumbed. Most notably in Kuwait (and more recently in Bahrain and Egypt), salafi groups have entered electoral politics. And having done so, they have found themselves beginning to feel the same kinds of pressures as those felt by movements based on the Brotherhood model.

In Kuwait, salafis edged into politics in the 1980s. Since campaigning, even in a small country with tiny electoral districts, required political sophistication, the salafi preference for loose organization was subject to some pressures. Salafis inclined toward politics began to draw on the informal networks built for study, practice, and charitable activity in their campaigns. Over the past decade, they have experimented with even more formal attempts to build a political party. A leading proponent of this approach in Kuwait, Khalid Sultan, speaks openly of his feeling that the Kuwaiti Brotherhood cares more about politics than religion—but in the first decade of the 2000s, his own efforts began to follow his rivals' path. A wealthy businessman, Sultan found himself in a position of being able to lead a salafi political effort, and he soon began to build a proto-party. The relationship between the party (based as it was on the leadership of those more politically inclined) and the broader salafi movement (oriented around religious teaching and learning) showed some signs of stress, especially when the salafis found that their presence in parliament confronted them with ideological and religious dilemmas. When offered seats in a cabinet (by a ruling family that works to co-opt a wide variety of forces), they found the opportunity to have an impact on policy too tempting to avoid. But presence in the parliament also meant dealing with women ministers and deputies who would not cover their hair (in direct contradiction of salafi understandings of religious requirements for women's dress). Would salafi deputies deal with such women in a businesslike fashion, ignore them, or confront them? Would they participate in a cabinet that included them? Such dilemmas became an almost permanent part of salafi politics and were especially acute during election campaigns, when rivals would seek to embarrass them. When Sultan's company (which he owned with his brothers, who did not share his religious inclinations) was found to own shops in Lebanon that sold alcohol, a family argument over whether to stop doing so became a religious and political scandal.

At this point, the movement was too deeply invested in the political process to withdraw easily, but neither was it able or willing to tailor its stances in accordance with short-term political exigencies. Its rivals began to find that salafi politicians would sometimes engage in the same retreat into generalities and ambiguities that characterize the Brotherhood-type movements viewed by salafis as overly political. In short, the more salafis involve themselves in semiauthoritarian politics, the more they respond like Brotherhood-type movements. They can maintain purity only by eschewing politics, which explains why many of them choose to do exactly that.

There are also Islamist movements that do the precise opposite: rather than avoid politics (like the salafis) or combine politics and other activities (like Brotherhood-type movements), some Islamists follow an exclusively political path. Focused largely on politics, these organizations do not find a need to build the broad social movement characteristic of the Brotherhood. Egypt's and Jordan's Hizb al-Wasat follow this path. Both are rare splinter groups from the Brotherhood; the two parties formed on the argument that politics should be prioritized and that it was possible to build an Islamist party that goes beyond generalities and ambiguous ideological statements to a full commitment to operating in accordance with liberal and democratic principles. It was, after all, Egypt's Hizb al-Wasat that began to refer to itself as "a civil party with an Islamic reference" long before its estranged mother movement experimented with similar formulations.

Thus these parties also feel few of the tensions and temptations experienced by movements based more faithfully on the Brotherhood model. They do not hesitate to commit fully to the party form, and their ideological statements are clear and specific. Their problems are different: they have found that semiauthoritarian politics offers few rewards. In Egypt, the party was simply denied legal recognition; without it the movement had nothing else to do except file suit after suit to obtain such recognition. Egypt's Hizb al-Wasat attracted plenty of attention and a healthy dose of intellectual respect—but not a single vote until after the semiauthoritarian regime collapsed in 2011. So its founders occupied their energies for a decade and a half with one legal challenge after another. In Jordan, the party is in danger of becoming irrelevant: it is devoid of any significant constituency and unable to mobilize many Jordanians because of the general futility of the electoral process. A purely political path in a system that is still ultimately closed in most ways to challengers has little to offer.

This consideration of movements that are not broadly based uncovers an interesting (and ultimately paradoxical) feature of broadly focused movements based on the Brotherhood model: Brotherhood-type movements are ideally suited to take advantage of the opportunities presented by semiauthoritarian politics. They are sufficiently interested in politics to participate, sufficiently active in other realms to have organized constituencies, sufficiently supple in organization and ideology to react to ever shifting rules, and sufficiently disciplined to pursue opportunities in a coherent and strategic manner.

This feature is paradoxical because it is the very ability of such movements to take advantage of semiauthoritarian politics that renders them so bothersome and even threatening to semiauthoritarian regimes—and that augments the already existing tendency of semiauthoritarian politics to cycle between liberalization and repression. Movements that disavow politics as well as those that focus only on politics pose far less of a challenge: the former leave the semiauthoritarian regime alone in the political realm; the latter can be safely bottled up. The more expertly the broad-based movements play by the rules of semiauthoritarian politics, the more they suggest the possibility of ultimately breaking the cardinal rule that the opposition can never win. The political process can continue as a cat-and-mouse game so long as the cat allows the mouse to live and the mouse remains a mouse. And that is precisely what semiauthoritarian politics encourages.

A half century ago, an emerging Islamist movement in Kuwait agitated successfully for the banning of alcohol in the country. In 2008, I met one of the leaders of that effort, Jasim al-Mihalhal, now an elder statesman of the movement. I asked him how he had managed the successful campaign against alcohol. He explained that he and his friends gathered at the parliament and then prayed for a favorable result. Islamists still gather and pray, but no longer is their political repertoire so restricted. The Kuwaiti movement has run sophisticated campaigns, developed full political programs, hired a political communications consulting firm, run focus groups, staffed telephone banks, conducted polls, and organized nationwide networks of activists.

Yet for all the growth in sophistication, Islamist movements remain movements first and parties second. Ideological movements entering elections often face a conflict, as Kenneth F. Greene notes:

> Office-seekers are still committed to party goals associated with political change, but they prefer to work from the top down through the bully pulpit. Their refrain is "you cannot change policy unless you first win elections." Others prioritize expressive benefits and prefer to operate behind the scenes by crafting the party's message and expanding its base one heart and mind at a time. The refrain of these message-seekers

is "winning is only valuable if it reflects social transformation from the bottom up."[9]

Islamist movements have developed considerably and have been deeply affected by their participation in semiauthoritarian politics. But the "message-seekers," to use Greene's phrase, still predominate. The movements have learned a lot, but they do not commit themselves fully to prioritizing elections as long as semiauthoritarianism prevails. The problem lies not in their learning abilities (which are impressive). The problem is the lessons they are taught.

---

9. Kenneth F. Greene, "Creating Competition: Patronage Politics and the PRI's Demise," Kellogg Institute Working Paper 345, December 2007, University of Notre Dame. I am grateful to Miriam Kunkler for bringing this passage to my attention.

Bibliography

'Abd al-Fattah, Nabil. *Al-mashaf wa-l-sayf.* Cairo: Maktabat Madbuli, 1984.

Abdel-Latif, Omayma. *In the Shadow of the Brothers: The Women of the Egyptian Muslim Brotherhood.* Carnegie Papers, Carnegie Endowment for International Peace, October 2008.

Abdo, Geneive. *No God but God: Egypt and the Triumph of Islam.* Oxford: Oxford University Press, 2000.

Abu al-Futuh, 'Abd al-Mun'im. *Mujaddidun la mubaddidun.* Cairo: Tatwir li-l-nashr wa-tawzi', 2005.

Abu 'Amr, 'Adnan. "Al-khitab al-siyasi li-hukumat 'hamas' wa-l-mujtama' al-duwali: al-ta'thirat wa-l-masalih al-mutabadila." *Al-tasamuh* 12, no. 7 (2006).

Abu-Amr, Ziad. *Islamic Fundamentalism in the West Bank and Gaza: Muslim Brotherhood and Islamic Jihad.* Bloomington: Indiana University Press, 1994.

Abu Faris, Muhammad 'Abd al-Qadir. *Safahat min al-tarikh al-siyasi li-l-ikhwan al-muslimin fi al-urdun.* Amman: Dar al-Qur'an, 2000.

Abu Rumman, Husayn (editor). *Al-harakat wa-l-tanzimat al-islamiyya fi al-urdun.* Amman: Dar Sindbad li-l-nashr, 1997.

Abu Rumman, Muhammad. *Al-siyasa al-urduniyya wa tahaddi hamas.* Amman: Friedrich Ebert Stiftung, 2009.

Adams, James, Michael Clark, Lawrence Ezrow, and Garrett Glasgow. "Are Niche Parties Fundamentally Different from Mainstream Parties? The Causes and the Electoral Consequences of Western European Parties' Policy Shifts, 1976–1998." *American Journal of Political Science* 50, no. 3 (2006), 513–529.

'Amush, Bassam al-. *Mahattat fi tarikh: jama'at al-ikhwan al-muslimin fi al-urdun.* Amman: Dar Zahran, 2008.

'Anani, Khalil al-. *Al-ikhwan al-muslimun fi misr: shaykhukha tusari' al-zaman.* Cairo: Maktabat al-Shuruq al-Duwaliyya, 2007.

'Anazi, Humud 'Aqaluh al-. *Al-haraka al-tulabiyya al-kuwaytiyya.* Kuwait: Ittihad al-watani li-talabat al-kuwayt, 1999.

Anderson, Margaret Lavinia. *Practicing Democracy: Elections and Political Culture in Imperial Germany.* Princeton, N.J.: Princeton University Press, 2000.

Atacan, Fulya. "Explaining Religious Politics at the Crossroad: AKP-SP." *Turkish Studies* 6, no. 2 (2005), 187–199.

'Awa, Muhammad Salim al-. *Al-islam wa-l-'asr, hiwar: Muhammad Barakat.* Cairo: Maktabat al-Shuruq al Duwaliyya, 2007.

Awadi, Hesham al-. *In Pursuit of Legitimacy: The Muslim Brothers and Mubarak, 1982–2000.* London: Tauris Academic Studies, 2004.

'Awda, 'Abd al-Qadir. *Al-Islam wa-awda'na al-qanuniyya.* Beirut: Mu'assasat al-risala, 1985.

Baker, Raymond William. *Islam without Fear: Egypt and the New Islamists.* Cambridge, Mass.: Harvard University Press, 2003.

Bayat, Asef. *Making Islam Democratic: Social Movements and the Post-Islamist Turn.* Stanford, Calif.: Stanford University Press, 2007.

Berman, Shari. *The Primacy of Politics: Social Democracy and the Making of Europe's Twentieth Century.* Cambridge: Cambridge University Press, 2006.

Bermeo, Nancy. *Ordinary People in Extraordinary Times: The Citizenry and the Breakdown of Democracy.* Princeton, N.J.: Princeton University Press, 2003.

Bermeo, Nancy, and Philip Nord. *Civil Society before Democracy: Lessons from Nineteenth-Century Europe.* Lanham, Md.: Rowman and Littlefield, 2000.

Bishri, Tariq al-. *Al-wad' al-qanuni bayna al-shari'a al-islamiyya wa-l-qanun al-wad'i.* Cairo: Dar al-Shuruq, 1996.

Blaydes, Lisa. *Elections and Distributive Politics in Mubarak's Egypt.* Cambridge: Cambridge University Press, 2010.

Boix, Carles. "The Emergence of Parties and Party Systems." In *The Oxford Handbook of Comparative Politics,* edited by Carles Boix and Susan Stokes. Oxford: Oxford University Press, 2009.

Boix, Carles, and Milan Svolik. "Non-tyrannical Autocracies." Unpublished paper, 2007. Available at http://www.sscnet.ucla.edu/polisci/cpworkshop/papers/Boix.pdf.

Boulby, Marioun. *The Muslim Brotherhood and the Kings of Jordan.* Atlanta: Scholars Press, 1999.

Brown, Nathan J. *Constitutions in a Nonconstitutional World: Arab Basic Laws and the Prospects for Accountable Government.* Albany: State University of New York Press, 2001.

——. "Debating the Islamic Shari'a in the 21st Century: Consensus and Cacophony." In *Shari'a Politics: Islamic Law and Society in the Muslim World,* edited by Robert Hefner. Bloomington: Indiana University Press, 2011.

——. "Dictatorship and Democracy through the Prism of Arab Elections." In *The Dynamics of Democratization: Dictatorship, Development, and Diffusion,* edited by Nathan J. Brown. Baltimore: Johns Hopkins University Press, 2011.

——. "Islamic Constitutionalism in Theory and in Practice." In *Democracy, the Rule of Law and Islam,* edited by Eugene Cotran and Adel Omar Sherif. The Hague: Kluwer Law International, 1999.

——. "The Peace Process Has No Clothes." Carnegie Web Commentary, 15 June 2007. Available at http://www.carnegieendowment.org/files/BrownCommentary june072.pdf.

——. "Shari'a and State in the Modern Muslim Middle East." *International Journal of Middle East Studies* 29, no. 3 (1997), 359–376.

——. "What Can Abu Mazin Do?" Carnegie Web Commentary, 15 June 2007. Available at http://www.carnegieendowment.org/files/abumazinupdatejune 1507.pdf.

Brown, Nathan, Michele Dunne, and Amr Hamzawy. "Egypt's Controversial Constitutional Amendments." Carnegie Web Commentary, 23 March 2007. Available at http://www.carnegieendowment.org/files/egypt_constitution_ webcommentary01.pdf.

Brown, Nathan, and Amr Hamzawy. "The Draft Party Platform of the Egyptian Muslim Brotherhood: Foray into Political Integration or Retreat into Old Positions?" Carnegie Paper 89, Carnegie Endowment for International Peace, January 2008.

Brown, Nathan, and Clark Lombardi. "Do Constitutions Requiring Adherence to Shari'a Threaten Human Rights? How Egypt's Constitutional Court Reconciles Islamic Law with the Liberal Rule of Law." *American University International Law Review* 21, no. 2 (2006), 379–435.

Brown, Nathan, Marina Ottaway, and Amr Hamzawy. "Islamist Movements and the Democratic Process in the Arab World: Exploring the Gray Zones." Carnegie Paper 67, Carnegie Endowment for International Peace, March 2006.

Brown, Nathan, and Adel Omar Sharif. "Inscribing the Islamic Shari`a in Arab Constitutional Law." In *Islamic Law and the Challenges of Modernity*, edited by Barbara Stowasser and Yvonne Haddad. Lanham, Md.: Rowman and Littlefield, 2004.

Calvert, John. *Sayyid Qutb and the Origins of Radical Islamism*. New York: Columbia University Press, 2010.

Capoccia, Giovanni. "Anti-system Parties: A Conceptual Reassessment." *Journal of Theoretical Politics* 14, no. 1 (2002), 9–35.

——. *Defending Democracy: Reactions to Extremism in Interwar Europe*. Baltimore: Johns Hopkins University Press, 2005.

Caride, Paola. *Hamas: From Resistance to Government*. Jerusalem: PASSIA, 2010.

Cavatorta, Francesco. "Neither Participation nor Revolution: The Strategy of the Moroccan *Jamiat al Adl wal-Ihsan*." *Mediterranean Politics* 12, no. 3 (2007), 381–397.

Cavdar, Gamze. "Islamist *New Thinking* in Turkey: A Model for Political Learning." *Political Science Quarterly* 121, no. 3 (2006), 477–497.

Chehab, Zaki. *Inside Hamas: The Untold Story of the Militant Islamic Movement*. New York: Nation Books, 2007.

Chhibber, Padeep. "Who Voted for the Bharatiya Janata Party?" *British Journal of Political Science* 27, no. 4 (1997), 631–639.

Clark, Janine A. "The Conditions of Islamist Moderation: Unpacking Cross-Ideological Cooperation in Jordan." *International Journal of Middle East Studies* 38 (2006), 539–560.

——. *Islam, Charity, and Activism: Middle-Class Networks and Social Welfare in Egypt, Jordan, and Yemen*. Bloomington: Indiana University Press, 2004.

——. "Threats, Goals, and Resources: Islamist Coalition-Building in Jordan." Paper presented at the Annual Meeting of the American Political Science Association, Boston, August 2008.

Clark, Janine A., and Jillian Schwedler. "Who Opened the Window? Women's Activism in Islamic Parties." *Comparative Politics* 25, no. 3 (2003), 293–312.

Clark, Janine A., and Amy E. Young. "Islamist and Family Law Reform in Morocco and Jordan." *Mediterranean Politics* 13, no. 3 (2008), 333–352.

Cohen, Amnon. *Political Parties on the West Bank under the Jordanian Regime, 1949–1967*. Ithaca: Cornell University Press, 1982.

Crystal, Jill. *Oil and Politics in the Gulf: Rulers and Merchants in Kuwait and Qatar*. Cambridge: Cambridge University Press, 1995.

D'Alimonte, Roberto. "Party Behavior in a Polarized System: The Italian Communist Party and the Historic Compromise." In *Policy, Office, or Votes? How Political Parties in Western Europe Make Hard Decisions*, edited by Wolfgang C. Muller and Kaare Strom. Cambridge: Cambridge University Press, 1999.

Diamond, Larry, and Robert Gunter. *Political Parties and Democracy*. Baltimore: Johns Hopkins University Press, 2001.

Einaudi, Mario, and Francois Goguci. *Christian Democracy in Italy and France*. Notre Dame, Ind.: University of Notre Dame Press, 1952.

Esping-Andersen, Gøsta. *Politics against Markets: The Social Democratic Road to Power*. Princeton, N.J.: Princeton University Press, 1985.

Fahmy, Ninette S. "The Performance of the Muslim Brotherhood in the Egyptian Syndicates: An Alternative Formula for Reform?" *Middle East Journal* 52, no. 4 (1998), 551–562.

Fogarty, Michael P. *Christian Democracy in Western Europe, 1820–1953.* Notre Dame, Ind.: University of Notre Dame Press, 1957.

Gaess, Roger. "Interview: Ismail Abu Shanab." *Middle East Policy* 6, no. 1 (1998), 16–20.

——. "Interview with Mousa Abu Marzook." *Middle East Policy* 5, no. 2 (1997), 113–128.

Gaffney, Patrick D. *The Prophet's Pulpit: Islamic Preaching in Contemporary Egypt.* Berkeley: University of California Press, 1994.

Gandhi, Jennifer. *Political Institutions under Dictatorship.* Cambridge: Cambridge University Press, 2008.

Gandhi, Jennifer, and Ellen Lust-Okar. "Elections under Authoritarianism." *Annual Review of Political Science* 12 (2009), 403–422.

Gandhi, Jennifer, and Adam Przeworski. "Authoritarian Institutions and the Survival of Autocrats." *Comparative Political Studies* 40, no. 11 (2007), 1279–1301.

Ghobashy, Mona El-. "The Metamorphosis of the Egyptian Muslim Brothers." *International Journal of Middle East Studies* 37, no. 3 (2005).

Ghurayba, Ibrahim. *Jama'at al-ikhwan al-muslimin fi al-urdun.* Amman: Al-Urdun Al-Jadid Research Center, 1997.

Gordon, Joel. *Nasser's Blessed Movement: Egypt's Free Officers and the July Revolution.* Oxford: Oxford University Press, 1992.

Greene, Kenneth F. "Creating Competition: Patronage Politics and the PRI's Demise." Kellogg Institute Working Paper 345, University of Notre Dame, December 2007. Available at http://citeseerx.ist.psu.edu/viewdoc/download?doi=10.1.1.126.5276&rep=rep1&type=pdf.

——. *Why Dominant Parties Lose: Mexico's Democratization in Comparative Perspective.* New York: Cambridge University Press, 2007.

Gunning, Jeroen. *Hamas in Politics: Democracy, Religion, Violence.* New York: Columbia University Press, 2008.

Hadenius, Axel, and Jan Teorell. "Pathways from Authoritarianism." *Journal of Democracy* 18, no. 1 (2007), 143–157.

Hale, William. "Christian Democracy and the AKP: Parallels and Contrasts." *Turkish Studies* 6, no. 2 (2005), 293–310.

Hamad, Jawad al-, and Iyad al-Barghuti. *Dirasa al-fikr al-siyasi li-harakat al-muqawama al-islamiya, 1987–1996.* Amman: Middle East Publishing Center, 1997.

Hamzawy, Amr, and Nathan J. Brown. "The Egyptian Muslim Brotherhood: Islamist Participation in a Closing Political Environment." Carnegie Middle East Center Paper 19. Carnegie Endowment for International Peace, March 2010.

Hamzawy, Amr, Marina Ottaway, and Nathan J. Brown. "What Islamists Need to Be Clear About: The Case of the Egyptian Muslim Brotherhood." Policy Outlook, Carnegie Endowment for International Peace, February 2007.

Hanley, David. *Christian Democracy in Europe: A Comparative Perspective.* London: Pinter, 1994.

Al-haraka al-islamiyya fi isra'il. Dubai: Markaz al-Misbar, 2009.

Harnisch, Chris, and Quinn Mecham. "Democratic Ideology in Islamist Opposition? The Muslim Brotherhood's 'Civil State.'" *Middle Eastern Studies* 45, no. 2 (2009), 189–205.

Hefner, Robert W. *Civil Islam: Muslims and Democratization in Indonesia.* Princeton, N.J.: Princeton University Press, 2000.

Herb, Michael. *All in the Family: Absolutism, Revolution, and Democracy in the Middle Eastern Monarchies.* Albany: State University of New York Press, 1999.

Hizb jabhat al-'amal al-islami. Guide to Party Life in Jordan, 1. Amman: Al-Urdun al Jadid Research Center, 1993.

Holmes, Stephen. "Precommitment and the Paradox of Democracy." In *Constitutionalism and Democracy,* edited by Jon Elster and Rune Slagstad. Cambridge: Cambridge University Press, 1993.

Hroub, Khaled. *Hamas: A Beginner's Guide.* London: Pluto Press, 2006.

———. "Hamas after Shaykh Yasin and Rantisi." *Journal of Palestine Studies* 33, no. 4 (2004), 21–38.

———. *Hamas: Political Thought and Practice.* Washington, D.C.: Institute for Palestine Studies, 1999.

Hudaybi, Hasan al-. *Dusturuna.* Cairo: Dar al-Ansar, 1978.

Hwang, Julie Chernov. *Peaceful Islamist Mobilization in the Muslim World: What Went Right.* New York: Palgrave Macmillan, 2009.

Ibrahim, Hasanayn Tawfiq, and Huda Raghib 'Awad. *Al-dawr al-siyasi li-l-jama'at al-ikhwan al-muslimin fi zill al-ta'adduduiyya al-siyasiyya al-muqayyada fi misr.* Cairo: Al-Mahrusa, 1996.

Al-ikhwan al-muslimun fi suriya. Dubai: Markaz al-Misbar, 2009.

International Crisis Group. "Ruling Palestine I: Gaza under Hamas." *Middle East Report* 73 (March 2008).

Ismail, Salwa. *Rethinking Islamist Politics: Culture, the State and Islamism.* London: I. B. Tauris, 2006.

'Itani, Maryam, and Muhsin Muhammad Salih. *Sira' al-iradat: al-suluk al-amni li-fatah wa-hamas wa-l-atraf al-ma'niya, 2006–2007.* Beirut: Markaz al-Zaytuna li-l-Dirasat wa-l-Istisaharat, 2008.

———. *Sira' al-salahiyyat bayna fatah wa-hamas fi idarat al-sulta al-filastiniyya, 2006–2007.* Beirut: Markaz al-Zaytuna li-l-Dirasat wa-l-Istisaharat, 2008.

Jarbawi, Ali. "The Position of Palestinian Islamists on the Palestine-Israel Accord." *The Muslim World* 84, nos. 1–2 (1994), 127–154.

Kalyvas, Stathis N. "Commitment Problems in Emerging Democracies: The Case of Religious Parties." *Comparative Politics* 32, no. 4 (2000), 379–399.

———. *The Rise of Christian Democracy in Europe.* Ithaca: Cornell University Press, 1996.

———. "Unsecular Politics and Religious Mobilization: Beyond Christian Democracy." In *European Christian Democracy: Historical Legacies and Comparative Perspectives,* edited by Thomas Kselman and Joseph A. Buttigieg. Notre Dame, Ind.: University of Notre Dame Press, 2003.

Kalyvas, Stathis N., and Kees van Kersbergen. "Christian Democracy." *Annual Review of Political Science* 13 (2010), 183–209.

Kaplan, Sam. *The Pedagogical State: Education and the Politics of National Culture in Post-1980 Turkey.* Stanford, Calif.: Stanford University Press, 2006.

Khalidi, Sami Nasir al-. *Al-ahzab al-siyasiyya al-islamiyya fi al-kuwayt.* Kuwait: Dar al-naba' li-l-nashr wa-l-tawzi', 1999.

Kilani, Musa Zayd al-. *Al-harakat al-islamiyya fi al-urdun wa filastin, dirasa wa taqyim.* Amman: Dar al-Bashir, 1995.

Kirchheimer, Otto. "The Transformation of the Western European Party Systems." In *Political Parties and Political Development,* edited by Joseph LaPalombara and Myron Weiner. Princeton, N.J.: Princeton University Press, 1966.

Kitschelt, Herbert. *The Transformation of European Social Democracy.* Cambridge: Cambridge University Press, 1994.

Klein, Menachem. "Against the Consensus: Oppositionist Voices in Hamas." *Middle Eastern Studies* 45, no. 6 (2009), 881–892.

——. "Hamas in Power." *Middle East Journal* 61, no. 3 (2007), 442–459.

Kselman, Thomas, and Joseph A. Buttigieg (editors). *European Christian Democracy: Historical Legacies and Comparative Perspectives.* Notre Dame, Ind.: University of Notre Dame Press, 2003.

Krämer, Gudrun. *Hasan al-Banna.* Oxford: Oneworld, 2010.

Kurzman, Charles, and Ijlal Naqvi. "Do Muslims Vote Islamic?" *Journal of Democracy* 21, no. 2 (2010).

Lamberts, Emiel. "Christian Democracy and the Constitutional State in Western Europe, 1945–1995." In *European Christian Democracy: Historical Legacies and Comparative Perspectives,* edited by Thomas Kselman and Joseph A. Buttigieg. Notre Dame, Ind.: University of Notre Dame Press, 2003.

LeBas, Adrienne. "Polarization as Craft: Party Formation and State Violence in Zimbabwe." *Comparative Politics* 38, no. 4 (2006), 419–438.

Levitsky, Steven, and Lucan A. Way. "Linkage and Leverage: How Do International Factors Change Domestic Balances of Power?" In *Electoral Authoritarianism: The Dynamics of Unfree Competition,* edited by Andreas Schedler. Boulder, Colo.: Lynne Rienner, 2006.

——. "The Rise of Competitive Authoritarianism." *Journal of Democracy* 13, no. 2 (2002), 51–65.

Lia, Brynjar. *The Society of the Muslim Brothers in Egypt: The Rise of an Islamic Mass Movement, 1928–1942.* Reading, U.K.: Ithaca Press, 1998.

Lindberg, Staffan I. *Democratization by Elections: A New Mode of Transition.* Baltimore: Johns Hopkins University Press, 2009.

——. "Tragic Protest: Why Do Opposition Parties Boycott Elections?" In *Electoral Authoritarianism: The Dynamics of Unfree Competition,* edited by Andreas Schedler. Boulder, Colo.: Lynne Rienner, 2006.

Longley, April. "The High Water Mark of Islamist Politics? The Case of Yemen." *Middle East Journal* 61, no. 2 (2007), 240–260.

Lust-Okar, Ellen. "Elections under Authoritarianism: Preliminary Lessons from Jordan." *Democratization* 13, no. 3 (2006).

——. *Structuring Conflict in the Arab World: Incumbents, Opponents, and Institutions.* Cambridge: Cambridge University Press, 2005.

Lybarger, Loren D. *Identity and Religion in Palestine: The Struggle between Islamism and Secularism in the Occupied Territories.* Princeton, N.J.: Princeton University Press, 2007.

Lynch, Marc. "The Brotherhood's Dilemma." Middle East Brief 25. Crown Center for Middle East Studies, Brandeis University, January 2008.

——. "Islam Divided between Salafi-jihad and the Ikhwan." *Studies in Conflict and Terrorism* 33, no. 6 (2010), 467–487.

Magaloni, Beatriz. *Voting for Autocracy: Hegemonic Party Survival and Its Demise in Mexico.* Cambridge: Cambridge University Press, 2006.

Mahmood, Saba. *The Politics of Piety: The Islamic Revival and the Feminist Subject.* Princeton, N.J.: Princeton University Press, 2005.

Maier, Hans. *Revolution and Church: The Early History of Christian Democracy, 1789–1901.* Notre Dame, Ind.: University of Notre Dame Press, 1965.

Mainwaring, Scott, and Timothy Scully (editors). *Christian Democracy in Latin America: Electoral Competition and Regime Conflicts.* Stanford, Calif.: Stanford University Press, 2003.

Majmuʿat Rasaʾil al-Imam al-Shahid Hasan al-Banna. Beirut: Muʾassasat al-Risala, 1970.

Markaz al-umma li-l-dirasat wa-l-abhath. *Al-intikhabat al-urduniyya li-ʿam 2007 bayn riwayatayn.* Amman, n.d.

Masoud, Tarek El-Miselhy. "Why Islam Wins: Electoral Ecologies and Economies of Political Islam in Contemporary Egypt." PhD diss., Yale University, 2008.

McFaul, Michael. "Transitions from Postcommunism." *Journal of Democracy* 16, no. 3 (2005), 5–19.

McGeough, Paul. *Kill Khalid: The Failed Mossad Assassination of Khalid Mishal and the Rise of Hamas.* New York: New Press, 2009.

Meguid, Bonnie M. "Competition between Unequals: The Role of Mainstream Party Strategy in Niche Party Success." *American Political Science Review* 99, no. 3 (2005), 347–359.

Meijer, Roel. *Global Salafism: Islam's New Religious Movement.* New York: Columbia University Press, 2009.

Milton-Edwards, Beverley. *Islamic Politics in Palestine.* London: I. B. Tauris, 1996.

Milton-Edwards, Beverley, and Stephen Farrell. *Hamas.* Cambridge: Polity Press, 2010.

Mishal, Shaul, and Avraham Sela. *The Palestinian Hamas: Vision, Violence, and Coexistence.* New York: Columbia University Press, 2006.

——. "Participation without Presence: Hamas, the Palestinian Authority and the Politics of Negotiated Coexistence." *Middle Eastern Studies* 38, no. 3 (2002), 1–26.

Misri, Mushir ʿUmar al-. *Al-hayah al-siyasiyya fi zill anzibat al-hukm al-muʿasira.* Mansura, Egypt: Dar al-Kalima, 2006.

Mitchell, Richard. *The Society of the Muslim Brothers.* Oxford: Oxford University Press, 1993.

Monroe, Steve. "Salafis in Parliament: Party Politics and Democratic Attitudes in the Gulf." B.A. honors thesis, Stanford University, 2010.

Moore, Pete W., and Bassel F. Salloukh. "Struggles under Authoritarianism: Regimes, States, and Professional Associations in the Arab World." *International Journal of Middle East Studies* 39, no. 1 (2007), 53–76.

al-Mudayris, Falah ʿAbd Allah. *Jamaʿat al-ikhwan al-muslimin fi al-kuwayt.* Kuwait: Dar Qirtas li-l-nashr wa-l-tawziʿ, 1994.

Mujani, Saiful, and R. William Liddle. "Muslim Indonesia's Secular Democracy." *Asian Survey* 49, no. 4 (2009), 575–590.

Munson, Ziad. "Islamic Mobilization: Social Movement Theory and the Egyptian Muslim Brotherhood." *Sociological Quarterly* 42, no. 4 (2001), 487–510.

Najjar, Baqir Salman al-. *Al-harakat al-diniyya fi al-khalij al-ʿarabi.* Beirut: Dar al-Saqi, 2007.

Neumann, Peter R. "'The Bullet' and the Ballot Box: The Case of the IRA." *Journal of Strategic Studies* 28, no. 6 (2005), 941–975.

Nusse, Andrea. *Muslim Palestine: The Ideology of Hamas.* Amsterdam: Harwood, 1998.

O'Donnell, Guillermo, Philippe C. Schmitter, and Laurence Whitehead. *Transitions from Authoritarian Rule: Tentative Conclusions about Uncertain Democracies.* Baltimore: Johns Hopkins University Press, 1986.

Ottaway, Marina. *Democracy Challenged: The Rise of Semiauthoritarianism.* Washington, D.C.: Carnegie Endowment for International Peace, 2003.

Oweidat, Marina, Cheryl Benard, Dale Stahl, Walid Kildani, Edward O'Connell, and Audra K. Grant. *The Kefaya Movement: A Case Study of a Grassroots Reform Initiative.* Santa Monica, Calif.: Rand Corporation, 2008.

Pargeter, Alison. *The Muslim Brotherhood: The Burden of Tradition.* London: Saqi Books, 2010.

Pearlman, Wendy. *Violence, Nonviolence, and the Palestinian National Movement.* New York: Cambridge University Press, 2011.

Przeworski, Adam. *Democracy and the Market.* Cambridge: Cambridge University Press, 1991.

——. "Democracy as a Contingent Outcome of Conflicts." In *Constitutionalism and Democracy,* edited by Jon Elster and Rune Slagstad. Cambridge: Cambridge University Press, 1988.

Przeworski, Adam, and John Sprague. *Paper Stones: A History of Electoral Socialism.* Chicago: University of Chicago Press, 1986.

Qaradwi, Yusuf al-. *Dirasa fi fiqh maqasid al-shari'a.* Cairo: Dar al-Shuruq, 2006.

Al-Quds Center for Political Studies. "Jordanian Parliamentary Monitor." April 2009.

Roald, Anne Sofie. *Tarbiya: Education and Politics in Islamic Movements in Jordan and Malaysia.* Stockholm: Almqvist & Wiksell, 1994.

Robinson, Glenn E. "Hamas as a Social Movement." In *Islamic Activism: A Social Movement Theory Approach,* edited by Quintan Wiktorowicz. Bloomington: Indiana University Press, 2003.

Roy, Sara. *Failing Peace: Gaza and the Palestinian-Israeli Conflict.* London: Pluto Press, 2006.

Ruparelia, Sanjay. "Rethinking Institutional Theories of Political Moderation: The Case of Hindu Nationalism in India, 1996–2004." *Comparative Politics* 38, no. 3 (2006), 317–336.

Rutherford, Bruce. "What Do Egypt's Islamists Want? Moderate Islam and the Rise of Islamic Constitutionalism." *Middle East Journal* 60, no. 4 (2006), 707–731.

Rydgren, Jens. "Is Extreme Right-Wing Populism Contagious? Explaining the Emergence of a New Party Family." *European Journal of Political Research* 44 (2005), 413–437.

Salah, Tariq, and Munir Adib. "The Brotherhood Delays Announcing the 'Amended' Platform Fearing Fissures." *Al-masri al-yawm,* 27 June 2009.

Salih, Muhsin Muhammad (editor). *Qira'at naqdiyya fi tajribat hamas wa-hukumatiha, 2006–2007.* Beirut: Markaz al-zaytuna li-l-dirasat wa-l-istisharat, 2007.

Sartori, Giovanni. *Parties and Party Systems.* Cambridge: Cambridge University Press, 1976.

Sayigh, Yezid. "Hamas Rule in Gaza: Three Years On." Middle East Brief 41. Crown Center for Middle East Studies, Brandeis University, March 2010.

Schedler, Andreas. "Elections without Democracy: The Menu of Manipulation." *Journal of Democracy* 13, no. 2 (2002).

——(editor). *Electoral Authoritarianism: The Dynamics of Unfree Competition.* Boulder, Colo.: Lynne Rienner, 2006.

——. "The Nested Game of Democratization by Elections." *International Political Science Review* 23, no. 1 (2002).

Schwedler, Jillian. *Faith in Moderation: Islamist Parties in Jordan and Yemen.* Cambridge: Cambridge University Press, 2006.

Schwedler, Jillian, and Janine Clark. "Islamist-Leftist Cooperation in the Arab World." *ISIM Review* 18 (Autumn 2006), 10–11.

Sha'ir, Nasir al-Din al-. *'Amaliyyat al-salam al-filastiniya-al-isra'iliyya: wijhat nazar Islamiyya.* Nabulus: Markaz al-Buhuth wa-al-Dirasat al-Filastiniyah, 1999.

Shapiro, Ian. *The State of Democratic Theory.* Princeton, N.J.: Princeton University Press, 2003.

Sharkey, Heather J. *American Evangelicals in Egypt: Missionary Encounters in an Age of Empire.* Princeton, N.J.: Princeton University Press, 2008.

Shehata, Samer, and Joshua Stacher. "The Brotherhood Goes to Parliament." *Middle East Report* 240 (Fall 2006), 32–40.

Shubaki, 'Amr al-(editor). *Islamiyyun wa dimuqratiyyun.* Cairo: Al-Ahram Center for Political and Strategic Studies, 2004.

Smith, Kristin Andrea. "From Petrodollars to Islamic Dollars: The Strategic Construction of Islamic Banking in the Arab Gulf." PhD diss., Harvard University, 2006.

Stilt, Kristen. "How Is Islam the Solution? Constitutional Visions of Contemporary Islamists." *Texas Journal of International Law* 46 (2010), 73–108.

Sulayman, Khalid. "Al-mumarisa al-dimuqratiyya dakhil hizb jabhat al-'amal al-islami." *Al-mustaqbal al-'arabi,* no. 296 (October 2003), 52–81.

Taggart, Paul. "New Populist Parties in Western Europe." *West European Politics* 18, no. 1 (1995), 34–51.

Tamam, Husam. *Tahawwulat al-ikwhwan al-muslimin.* Cairo: Maktabat Madbuli, 2006.

——. *Tasalluf al-ikhwan: ta'akkul al-atruha al-ikhwaniyya wa-su'ud al-salafiyya fi jama'at al-ikhwan al-muslimin.* Alexandria: Biblioteca Alexandrina, 2010.

Tamimi, Azzam. *Hamas: A History from Within.* Northampton, Mass.: Olive Branch Press, 2007.

Teitelbaum, Joshua. "The Muslim Brotherhood and the 'Struggle for Syria,' 1947–1958 between Accommodation and Ideology." *Middle Eastern Studies* 40, no. 3 (2004), 134–158.

Tepe, Sultan. "Religious Parties and Democracy: A Comparative Assessment of Israel and Turkey." *Democratization* 12, no. 3 (2005), 283–307.

Tétreault, Mary Ann. *Stories of Democracy: Politics and Society in Contemporary Kuwait.* New York: Columbia University Press, 2000.

Tezcür, Güne Murat. "The Moderation Theory Revisited: The Case of Islamic Political Actors." *Party Politics* 16, no. 1 (2010), 69–88.

Tucker, Joshua A. "Enough! Electoral Fraud, Collective Action Problems, and Post-Communist Colored Revolutions." *Perspectives on Politics* 5, no. 3 (2007), 535–551.

Turam, Berna. *Between Islam and the State: The Politics of Engagement.* Stanford, Calif.: Stanford University Press, 2007.

'Umrayn, Khalid Nimr al-. *Hamas: harakat al-muqawima al-islamiyya; juzuruha-nasha'tuha-fikruha al-siyasi.* Cairo: Markaz al-hadara al-'arabiyya, 2001.

'Umush, Bassam 'Ali al-. *Mahattat fi ta'rikh jama'at al-ikhwan al-muslimin fi al-urdun.* Amman: Academic for Publishing and Distribution, 2008.

Utvik, Bjorn Olav. *Islamist Economics in Egypt: The Pious Road to Development.* Boulder, Colo.: Lynne Rienner, 2006.

Wa'i, Tawfiq Yusif al-. *Al-fikr al-siyasi al-mu'asir 'and al-ikhwan al-muslimin.* Kuwait: Maktabat al-Masar al-Islamiyya, 2001.

Warner, Carolyn M. *Confessions of an Interest Group: The Catholic Church and Political Parties in Europe.* Princeton, N.J.: Princeton University Press, 2000.

Webster, Richard. *Christian Democracy in Italy, 1860–1960.* London: Hollis and Carter, 1961.

Wedeen, Lisa. *Peripheral Visions: Publics, Power, and Performance in Yemen.* Chicago: University of Chicago Press, 2008.

White, Jenny B. *Islamist Mobilization in Turkey: A Study in Vernacular Politics.* Seattle: University of Washington Press, 2002.

Wickham, Carrie Rosefsky. *Mobilizing Islam: Religion, Activism, and Political Change in Egypt.* New York: Columbia University Press, 2002.

——. "The Path to Moderation: Strategy and Learning in the Formation of Egypt's *Wasat* Party." *Comparative Politics* 36, no. 2 (2004), 205–227.

Wiktorowicz, Quintan. *The Management of Islamic Activism: Salafis, the Muslim Brotherhood, and State Power in Jordan.* Albany: State University of New York Press, 2001.

Willis, Michael J. "Morocco's Islamists and the Legislative Elections of 2002: The Strange Case of the Party That Did Not Want to Win." *Mediterranean Politics* 9, no. 1 (2004), 53–81.

Yadav, Stacey Philbrick. "Understanding 'What Islamists Want': Public Debate and Contestation in Lebanon and Yemen." *Middle East Journal* 64, no. 2 (2010).

Yousef, Mossab Hassan. *Son of Hamas.* Carol Stream, Ill.: Tyndale House, 2010.

Ziyada, Radwan. *Al-islam al-siyasi fi suriya.* Abu Dhabi: Emirate Center for Strategic Studies and Research, 2008.

Zollner, Barbara. *The Muslim Brotherhood: Hasan al-Hudaybi and Ideology.* Abington, U.K.: Routledge, 2009.

Zumai, Ali Fahed Al-. "The Intellectual and Historical Development of the Islamic Movement in Kuwait, 1950–1981." PhD diss., University of Exeter, 1988.

Index

'Abbas, Mahmud, 199, 200
Abu al-Futuh, 'Abd al-Mun'im, 92, 140, 141, 185
Abu Faris, Muhammad, 82, 146, 192
Abu Qura, 'Abd al-Latif, 95
al-'Adl wa-l-Ihsan (Morocco), 81
'Akif, Muhammad Mahdi, 67, 78, 92, 158, 165
AKP (Justice and Development Party)
      (Turkey), 48–49, 171n, 222, 236
Algeria, 19, 20, 21–22, 211, 234
Amman Declaration, 192–93
analogy mongering, 4, 34–37
anti-system parties, 44–51
Arab nationalism, 96, 189
Arab Socialist Union (Egypt), 88
armed wings. *See* violence
authoritarianism
      and democracy as nondomination, 225
      and ideology, 176–77
      international Islamist comparisons, 234–35
      and loyalty vs. opposition, 202
      and Muslim Brotherhood (Jordan), 97, 155,
          234, 235
      and Muslim Brotherhood (Kuwait), 103–4,
          108, 234, 235
      Palestinians, 200, 234, 235
      and semiauthoritarian instability, 28–29
      vs. semiauthoritarianism, 15–16, 18
'Awda, 'Abd al-Qadir, 172, 173

Badi', Muhammad, 93, 141
Bahrain, 20, 22, 238
Bani Arshid, Zaki, 144, 207
al-Banna, Hasan
      on alternatives to Muslim Brotherhood
          model, 81
      and Boy Scouts, 61
      and Cairo location, 63
      death of, 65
      and electoral participation, 6
      and Islam in Islamist ideology, 171
      and Muslim Brotherhood as model, 10
      and Muslim Brotherhood (Jordan), 95
      and Muslim Brotherhood (Kuwait), 104–5
      and organization, 67
      and Palestinians, 116
      and party slogans, 59, 62

on unity, 176
      See also Muslim Brotherhood
Bayat, Asef, 220
Bharatiya Janata Party (BJP) (India), 49–51
BJP (Bharatiya Janata Party) (India), 49–51
Boy Scouts, 61, 63
boycott strategy, 23, 137, 160
      Hamas, 121, 160
      Muslim Brotherhood (Egypt), 93, 141, 160
      Muslim Brotherhood (Jordan), 27–28, 30,
          101, 103, 160
Bush, George W., 4

cabinet membership, 154–55
      Hamas, 123, 161, 163
      international comparisons, 41, 50
      and limited commitment, 163
      Muslim Brotherhood (Egypt), 65, 161, 163
      Muslim Brotherhood (Jordan), 96, 99,
          154–55, 161, 163, 189
      Muslim Brotherhood (Kuwait), 110, 111,
          112–13, 161, 163, 193, 194–95
      and regime strategies, 22
      See also loyalty vs. opposition
Capoccia, Giovanni, 44, 52
Center Parties, 80
Christian Democratic model, 34–40
      and ideology, 53, 171n
      and international actors, 34–35
      and social movements, 36–38, 39
coalitions. *See* cross-ideological alliances
Communist parties, 42, 47
constituent outreach, 24, 54–55, 219
cross-ideological alliances, 146–51
      and democracy as discussion, 221
      Hamas, 197, 198
      and limited commitment, 163
      Muslim Brotherhood (Kuwait), 110, 111–12,
          147–51, 161, 163
      and 2011 upheavals, 207

debates over politicization. *See* internal debates
      over politicization
democracy
      as discussion, 218–23
      European interwar collapse of, 39–40, 45, 46

253